INTERNATIONAL POLITICAL ECONOMY SERIES

General Editor: Timothy M. Shaw, Professor of Political Science and International Development Studies, and Director of the Centre for Foreign Policy Studies, Dalhousie University, Nova Scotia, Canada

Recent titles include:

Manuel R. Agosin and Diana Tussie (*editors*)
TRADE AND GROWTH: NEW DILEMMAS IN TRADE POLICY

Mahvash Alerassool
FREEZING ASSETS: THE USA AND THE MOST EFFECTIVE
  ECONOMIC SANCTION

Inga Brandell (*editor*)
WORKERS IN THIRD-WORLD INDUSTRIALIZATION

Richard P. C. Brown
PUBLIC DEBT AND PRIVATE WEALTH

Bonnie K. Campbell (*editor*)
POLITICAL DIMENSIONS OF THE INTERNATIONAL DEBT CRISIS

Bonnie K. Campbell and John Loxley (*editors*)
STRUCTURAL ADJUSTMENT IN AFRICA

Jerker Carlsson, Gunnar Köhlin and Anders Ekbom
THE POLITICAL ECONOMY OF EVALUATION

Steen Folke, Niels Fold and Thyge Enevoldsen
SOUTH–SOUTH TRADE AND DEVELOPMENT

David P. Forsythe (*editor*)
HUMAN RIGHTS AND DEVELOPMENT
THE UNITED NATIONS IN THE WORLD POLITICAL ECONOMY

David Glover and Ken Kusterer
SMALL FARMERS, BIG BUSINESS

William D. Graf (*editor*)
THE INTERNATIONALIZATION OF THE GERMAN POLITICAL
  ECONOMY

Betty J. Harris
THE POLITICAL ECONOMY OF THE SOUTHERN AFRICAN PERIPHERY

Jacques Hersh
THE USA AND THE RISE OF EAST ASIA SINCE 1945

Bahgat Korany, Paul Noble and Rex Brynen (*editors*)
THE MANY FACES OF NATIONAL SECURITY IN THE ARAB WORLD

Howard P. Lehman
INDEBTED DEVELOPMENT

Matthew Martin
THE CRUMBLING FAÇADE OF AFRICAN DEBT NEGOTIATIONS

James H. Mittelman
OUT FROM UNDERDEVELOPMENT

Paul Mosley (*editor*)
DEVELOPMENT FINANCE AND POLICY REFORM

Dennis C. Pirages and Christine Sylvester (*editors*)
TRANSFORMATIONS IN THE GLOBAL POLITICAL ECONOMY

Stephen P. Riley (*editor*)
THE POLITICS OF GLOBAL DEBT

Garry Rodan
THE POLITICAL ECONOMY OF SINGAPORE'S INDUSTRIALIZATION

Jorge Rodríguez Beruff, J. Peter Figueroa and J. Edward Greene (*editors*)
CONFLICT, PEACE AND DEVELOPMENT IN THE CARIBBEAN

Patricia Ruffin
CAPITALISM AND SOCIALISM IN CUBA

Frederick Stapenhurst
POLITICAL RISK ANALYSIS AROUND THE NORTH ATLANTIC

Arno Tausch (with Fred Prager)
TOWARDS A SOCIO-LIBERAL THEORY OF WORLD DEVELOPMENT

Nancy Thede and Pierre Beaudet (*editors*)
A POST-APARTHEID SOUTHERN AFRICA?

Peter Utting
ECONOMIC REFORM AND THIRD-WORLD SOCIALISM

David Wurfel and Bruce Burton (*editors*)
THE POLITICAL ECONOMY OF FOREIGN POLICY IN SOUTHEAST ASIA

States, Markets and Regimes in Global Finance

Tony Porter

Assistant Professor of Political Science
McMaster University, Hamilton

St. Martin's Press

First published in Great Britain 1993 by
THE MACMILLAN PRESS LTD
Houndmills, Basingstoke, Hampshire RG21 2XS
and London
Companies and representatives
throughout the world

A catalogue record for this book is available
from the British Library.

ISBN 0–333–58884–3

Printed in Great Britain by
Antony Rowe Ltd
Chippenham, Wiltshire

First published in the United States of America 1993 by
Scholarly and Reference Division,
ST. MARTIN'S PRESS, INC.,
175 Fifth Avenue,
New York, N.Y. 10010

ISBN 0–312–09982–7

Library of Congress Cataloging-in-Publication Data
Porter, Tony, 1953–
States, markets and regimes in global finance / Tony Porter.
p. cm. — (International political economy series)
Includes bibliographical references and index.
ISBN 0–312–09982–7
1. International finance.   2. Financial institutions,
International.   I. Title.   II. Series.
HG3881.P654   1993
332'.042—dc20   93–18911
                                         CIP

For Emily, Neal and Marion

Contents

List of Tables

List of Figures

Acknowledgements

There are several people to whom I wish to express my thanks for their contributions to this project in its various phases. I am grateful to Professors Maureen Molot, Lynn Mytelka and Lorraine Eden for their instructive, challenging and helpful comments. Paul Guy and Jean-Pierre Cristel of the International Organization of Securities Commissions and Michael Howell, formerly of Salomon Brothers, assisted me with very useful information. I also owe a debt to many unnamed people who played an important role in facilitating my research, including librarians who tracked down information and regulators who provided me with insights. McMaster University provided funds for the index. A deep thanks goes to Emily Brown for her many roles in this and other projects during these past years.

TONY PORTER

The author and publishers are grateful to Salomon Brothers International Limited for permission to use their data in Tables 4.2, 4.3 and Figure 4.3.

1 Introduction: Theory, International Institutions and Global Finance

What holds our increasingly globalized world together? International competition and conflict are intense. The world is divided into mutually distrustful sovereign states. Instead of fragmentation and chaos, however, there is a surprising degree of regularity and order. This book seeks better to understand how such regularity and order comes about in global financial markets. These markets are often seen as uncontrollable and plagued by recurring instability. As we shall see, this image is misleading. There are strong sets of social institutions which organize these markets and which themselves display identifiable patterns as they evolve. Understanding these institutions and patterns helps us better understand both global finance and the sources of international order more generally. This book will focus not only on the two most important interstate institutions for regulating international financial firms, the Basle Committee on Banking Supervision, and the International Organization of Securities Commissions, but also on the private international institutions that play a central role in organizing international financial markets.

A NEW WAVE OF INTERNATIONAL RELATIONS THEORIZING

The discovery and analysis of such international institutions in the pages that follow draws upon and contributes to the exciting new wave of theorizing that has rejuvenated the study of international relations over the past two decades. This new theorizing has transformed our understanding of the sources of international governance.

Historically there have been a great number of explanations and schemes devised for understanding and promoting regularity and order in international relations. In the period between the First and Second World Wars state leaders and students of international relations placed a great deal of hope in elaborate legal structures that would be built

1

above, and would constrain, individual nation-states. The failure of the League of Nations to prevent aggression and war led to widespread disillusionment with the idea of strong supranational institutions.

Since the Second World War theorists have made many attempts to explain the cohesiveness of the international system while avoiding the idealism that plagued the interwar period. Initially these attempts took two sharply divergent tacks. Some theorists argued that order and security were fleeting and would have to come from relying on the individual nation-state. Others acknowledged that the building of international institutions was a far more painstaking process than earlier theorists had realized but argued that such institutions would slowly and inexorably emerge from the ground up, one region at a time, out of the interactions of individual citizens.

In the past two decades, however, many theorists have seen these initial responses to the discrediting of elaborate supra-national structures as flawed for a variety of reasons. In response to such dissatisfaction there has been a wave of far-reaching theoretical innovation that has revitalized the study of international relations while challenging the philosophical foundations of the field. Theorists began to devote much more attention to the relationship between global markets and state actions, giving birth to the rapidly expanding subfield of international political economy. Some began to ask whether the infatuation of postwar theorists with statistical analysis and other techniques imported from the natural sciences had led them to overlook important features of the international system that were not quantifiable. As in other fields there was increasing questioning of the assumption that rational utility-maximizing actors, whether individual citizens or states, are the unchanging bedrock of human societies and a reawakening of interest in the way in which social institutions constitute such rational actors. Unlike the interwar period, which emphasized formal institutions such as codified laws and constitutions, this new institutionalism began to stress the importance of informal social institutions such as unwritten diplomatic practices. Each of these theoretical innovations is invaluable in the search for the sources of order in global finance upon which this book embarks.

As the new wave of theorizing has opened up new vistas it has also given us hints of sets of relationships hitherto overlooked and ignored. One of these sets of relationships is particularly important. Despite the wealth of new insights into how the structure of various industries has changed, which has been made possible by the emergence of international political economy as a field, and the wealth of new insights into patterns of cooperative behaviour between states, which has been made possible by new developments in the study of international institutions, these two burgeoning research programs remain remarkably discrete and disconnected. Identifying and exploring the relationship between the changing structure of international industries and the interstate institutions that seek to regulate these industries is a central goal of this book.

TWO KEY INTERSTATE INSTITUTIONS

As noted above, there are two interstate institutions that have played a leading role in regulating international financial firms. The first, for banking regulation, is the Basle Committee on Banking Supervision. The second, for securities regulation, is the International Organization of Securities Commissions (IOSCO) in Montreal.[1] Although both institutions were established in 1974 they differ in their strength.[2] In this book I argue that this difference is related to differences in the two industries that they seek to regulate.

The Basle Supervisors' Committee includes bank supervisors from the Group of Ten countries plus Luxembourg.[3] Since the formation of the Committee in 1974 it has produced several agreements that have been central to the emerging regime for the coordination of international banking regulation.[4] One set of agreements, the 1975 Basle Concordat and its modifications in 1983, 1990 and 1992, aimed to enhance cooperation between regulators of multinational banks, in particular by specifying a division of labour between home and host regulators.

An equally important agreement is a set of capital adequacy standards approved in 1988. These capital standards seek to limit the growth of assets, such as loans, by specifying minimum capital/asset ratios. Previously banks were pursing strategies of rapid growth of assets funded by deposits. Because capital is more expensive than deposits, and because it can be used to stave off bankruptcy, capital/asset ratios are an effective tool for restraining bank growth and ensuring bank soundness (Chessen, 1987; Dale, 1984:57; for a contrary view see "Capital Adequacy," 1990, October 13:88). As Chapter 3 will show, the Basle Committee's work on capital/asset standards reversed a historical tendency for these standards to decline and strengthened the power of state regulators relative to international banks.

Coordination of international securities regulation is much less developed than is the situation in banking. In contrast to the multilateral efforts of the Basle Supervisors' Committee, international securities regulation rests more heavily on bilateral agreements. IOSCO does, however, represent an important multilateral forum for international securities regulation, dealing with standards for the issuing and trading of securities, the prevention of fraud, the capital adequacy of securities firms and the promotion of securities markets in the developing world. It currently has ninety-one member agencies.[5]

IOSCO's most concrete achievements are in the related areas of enforcement and information sharing. IOSCO's Resolution on Reciprocal Assistance (the "Rio Resolution"), adopted in 1986 and signed by 40 agencies from 35 countries, is the ancestor to the increasing number of bilateral and multilateral agreements that have been the most concrete evidence of international enforcement of securities regulations. This was supplemented by a 1989 Resolution on Cooperation, currently signed by 18 agencies from 16 countries, urging modification of domestic rules as needed to implement the Rio Declaration.[6] In other areas IOSCO's main accomplishments involve the publication of studies clarifying the problems involved in international securities regulation, and ongoing negotiations over new standards. The most important current negotiations are over capital standards for securities firms. IOSCO has not therefore produced as detailed, concrete agreements as has the Basle Supervisors' Committee, although it is incorrect to characterize it, as Spero does, as "primarily a talk shop for regulators" (Spero, 1988/9:124).

Expanding our knowledge of these two international institutions is useful because they have received little attention in the international relations literature. Although financial flows are now 50 times as large as trade flows (Spero, 1988/9) less has been written about international financial regimes than about international trade regimes. Although there have been a number of studies of the politics of international banking and of the international monetary regime (Aronson, 1977; Cohen, 1983, 1986; Frieden, 1987; Gowa, 1983; Keohane, 1984; Odell, 1982; Pauly, 1988; Strange, 1986, inter alia), these have generally focused on balance of payments financing and exchange rate determination, and only indirectly on the regulation of multinational financial firms. Where such regulation has been discussed it has tended to focus on the relationship between individual states and multinational banks, ignoring the role of international institutions such as the Basle

Supervisors' Committee and IOSCO.[7] This alone would be a reason to study these examples of emerging international cooperation in international finance.

INTERNATIONAL RELATIONS THEORY AND INTERNATIONAL INSTITUTIONS IN GLOBAL FINANCE

Just as important, however, is the opportunity that an examination of these institutions offers for understanding the relationship between industry structures and interstate regulatory institutions. The new wave of theorizing about international relations makes three positive contributions and and has two shortcomings with respect to this task.

One major contribution of the new wave of theorizing is to recognize the influence of informal interstate institutions that do not satisfy such conventional criteria of strength as a high degree of centralization, a formalized constitution, and the possession of tangible resources and mechanisms to force states to comply with rules. A wide variety of recent approaches, including regime analysis (Krasner, 1983), post-modernism (Der Derian and Shapiro, 1989), structuration theory (Wendt, 1987), Gramscian analysis of hegemony (Cox, 1983) and the analysis of "governance without government" (Rosenau and Czempiel, 1992) stress the influence of informal principles, norms, rules, decision-making procedures, discourses, texts, practices and ideologies on international actors. In contrast to an earlier liberal emphasis on the international influence of free-floating ideas, from which coherent preconstituted actors learned, these new approaches see informal institutions such as practices as embodying and reproducing ideas in social structures that have the capacity to not only offer coherent actors new sets of insights from which to choose, but also to constitute these actors, creating their very identities.

Judged by conventional criteria the institutions upon which the present book focuses would not merit attention. Neither the Basle Committee on Banking Supervision nor the International Organization of Securities Commissions have the type of supranational organizational strength for which international relations theorists used to search. The non-state international institutions that I will examine are even less formalized than are these two interstate institutions. However, these institutions play a key role in organizing markets despite their lack of formalization. Indeed the Basle Committee, which is less formalized than IOSCO, is more effective.

A second major contribution of the new wave of theorizing is to emphasize the relationship between economic processes and state actions. International political economy as a field of study has moved far beyond the traditional obsession with the "high" politics of war and related diplomacy. By emphasizing such features of the international system as the power of multinational corporations, the influence of changes in markets such as the 1973 oil price shock, and the importance of economic power as evident in the case of Japan, international political economy has shown that state actions are not just responses to the actions of other states. It would not be possible to study global finance in any meaningful way without taking economic processes seriously. A regulator in the Basle Committee or IOSCO responds at least as much to the economic actions of non-state actors as to the actions of regulators and other state actors.

A third contribution of the new wave of theorizing is to expand the sources and definitions of legitimate knowledge upon which we base our understanding of international relations (Lapid, 1989). The postwar enthusiasm for quantitative methods drawn from the natural sciences led to the neglect of whole areas of study because they did not proffer a sufficient number of cases upon which to base techniques such as regression analysis.[8] Furthermore the careful interpretative work that is needed to understand the meanings of components of institutions such as norms is not compatible with quantitative measurement techniques (Kratochwil and Ruggie, 1986). Reliance on quantitative methods for studying an issue area such as the regulation of international financial firms, in which just two interstate institutions play leading roles, and in which shared understandings are subject to deliberate secrecy and other measurement problems, would be impossible. The new proliferation of epistemologies, while disconcerting to some theorists, offers many possible solutions to problems such as these. In this book I use careful historical comparison of controlled cases in a manner that has been employed effectively by institutionalist scholars working on the border between comparative politics and international relations (Evans, Rueschemeyer and Skocpol, 1985:348). The banking and securities industries are similar enough in terms of geographical location and historical evolution that contextual fluctuations can be treated as controlled. Despite these similarities the strength of the interstate institutions that regulate the two industries differs sufficiently to be treated as an independent variable needing explanation.

Despite the alternatives for analyzing global finance that are provided by the new theorizing in international relations there are two serious shortcomings of this theorizing that need to be addressed. The first of these is that the insights that have been developed into informal international social institutions have not generally been applied to economic actors. International relations theorists have assumed that the relevance of international social institutions such as regimes is their effect on states. The economic features of the system are treated either as resources that are manipulated by states or as natural forces not subject to the influence of social institutions. Given that economic actors such as multinational corporations are as highly organized and capable of intention as states, this analytical exclusion of economic actors from the types of effects that social institutions have on states is unwarranted.

Economists have devoted a great deal of attention to institutions in recent years. Works such as Williamson's 1975 *Markets and Hierarchies* emphasize the role of internal corporate organizational structure in coping with problems of information and transactions costs ignored by earlier neoclassical economists who assumed that information was perfect and transactions costs were zero. This new institutional economics has been applied very effectively to understanding the multinational corporation by economists such as Dunning (1988) and Rugman (1981, 1986). While insights from this literature will be further discussed and applied in Chapter 2, the literature remains inadequate for understanding the impact of international social institutions on economic actors because it too sharply differentiates between market and hierarchy. Markets are treated as external to the firm and as free of organization while hierarchies are treated as internal unproblematic authority structures. As some critics have noted, such an approach ignores the role of informal social institutions, which can operate within the firm to reproduce authority structures and outside the firm to organize interactions between firms. It is this third type of interaction, which has been termed "clans" by Ouchi (1980), to which the concept of international social institutions can be applied.

If the new wave of theorizing underestimates the impact of international social institutions on economic actors it also underestimates the impact of economic actors on interstate interactions. State interactions are seen as driven either by the intentionality of rational unified states wielding firms and markets as resources or by non-economic social institutions such as interstate regimes. The possibility that there is a dynamic interaction between international economic social institutions and interstate institutions is precluded. This is particularly ironic because much recent theorizing about regimes has been inspired by approaches from the new institutional economics such as transactions cost analysis (Keohane, 1984). Considering that transactions costs analysis was developed for explaining how private hierarchical institutions can carry out many of the functions traditionally associated with the state (such as the protection of property rights and the enforcement of contracts) this neglect of private international institutions by theorists who draw on transactions costs approaches is surprising.

HOW THIS BOOK IS ORGANIZED

The first task of this book is to use the new theorizing in international relations as a jumping off point to address the relationship between the organization of industries and international institutions at a general level and with respect to the two international financial industries upon which I am focusing: banking and securities. Chapter 2 is devoted to this task. In Chapter 2 I first assemble a set of usable theoretical components from a variety of existing literatures. These literatures develop many of the points concerning informal social institutions to which I have referred above. They support the view that markets are neither natural forces nor objects wielded by states but are rather complex social institutions. I then move beyond these literatures to suggest that interstate regimes and non-state "private" regimes potentially carry out many of the same functions in the organization of international markets. This suggests two alternative hypotheses about the relationship between international industries and regimes.

The first hypothesis is that private and interstate regimes are substitutes – that interstate regimes emerge when private regimes are absent or in decay. Private regimes would be likely to exist in oligopolistic industries. As a few powerful firms are weakened by increasing competitive pressures and other sources of loss of control over markets, states are likely to be able and willing to step in and construct interstate regimes.

The second, alternate, hypothesis is that private and interstate regimes complement each other – that highly organized private actors have the power to act through states and to contribute to the setting up of interstate regimes. Such a relationship would be likely to occur in oligopolistic industries dominated by a few powerful corporations. This would be the type of relationship at an international level that has been identified domestically by theorists who argue that regulatory agencies are captured by the industries they regulate. These hypotheses are both plausible but are mutually exclusive. Interstate regimes are either associated with oligopoly and private regimes or they are associated with intense competition and no private regime. The remainder of Chapter 2 is devoted to developing a method for assessing which of the two hypotheses is supported by empirical analysis. As the remaining chapters of this book will show there is strong support for the first hypothesis.

Chapter 3 provides the first test of the hypotheses by analyzing international banking as an industry. The evolution of the interstate regime for regulating banking organized around the Basle Committee on Banking Supervision is discussed further in order to assess its strength. On a number of different measures there is clear evidence that the interstate banking regime has dramatically increased in strength since 1974 when the Basle Committee was set up. The international banking industry is then examined. A variety of empirical evidence indicates that competitive pressures were increasing over this time period and that there was no effective private regime. This chapter therefore supports the first of the two hypotheses discussed above.

Chapter 4 analyzes the international securities regime and compares it with the international banking regime. This provides two more tests of the hypotheses. The first test is to analyze the relationship between the strength of the securities regime and the securities industry. Like the banking regime organized around the Basle Committee, the securities regime organized around the International Organization of Securities Commissions has increased substantially in strength since its creation in 1974. As in the banking industry this strengthening of the interstate regime was accompanied by increasingly intense competition at the industry level and a weakening of private forms of regulation. Thus the first hypothesis is again confirmed. The second test discussed in Chapter 4 is to compare the securities industry with the banking industry. I find that the interstate securities regime is weaker than the interstate banking regime while the banking industry is experiencing more intense competitive pressures and displays less evidence of a private regime. I therefore have a third confirmation of the first hypothesis.

The findings of Chapters 3 and 4 begin to fill in our understanding of the relationship between interstate regimes and the structure of industries. In Chapter 5, the concluding chapter, I return to focus on theory to help determine whether the relationships discussed in the empirical analysis are simply correlations or involve causation. Addressing this question involves difficult philosophical disputes that are ongoing in international relations as a field of study. In this chapter I develop a model of causation based on structuration theory and argue that changes in industry structure do cause changes in interstate regimes. The chapter concludes by addressing the relevance of the findings for banking and securities industries for other international industries and international theory more generally.

2 Rethinking Regimes: Industry and Institutions

Our goal in this book is better to understand international regulatory institutions in general, and institutions for regulating global finance in particular, by analyzing the relationship between such institutions and the structures of the industries they seek to regulate. In this chapter I develop a theoretical framework for analyzing this relationship. This task involves three steps. The first step is to scan a variety of existing literatures for relevant insights. The second step is to draw on these insights to construct a hypothesis that specifies a relationship between industry structures and the strength of international regulatory institutions. The third step is to develop a method for testing this hypothesis that takes into account the grave doubts that are current in the study of international relations regarding the usefulness of scientific testing.

INSIGHTS FROM EXISTING LITERATURES

While literature that directly addresses the relationship between international regulatory institutions and industry structures is scanty there are a wide variety of literatures that provide a good starting point for analysis. In this section I look at these literatures. Three key points emerge. The first is that a great variety of institutions play a key role in organizing markets, notwithstanding the image that is sometimes presented of markets as natural and as capable of operating free of human institutional contrivances such as state regulations. The second point is that private institutions play an important role in regulating domestic markets and that understanding the relationship between these institutions and state regulatory institutions is important in understanding regulation in general. The third point is that the relationship between industry structures and state regulatory agencies has been a key focus of economic studies of domestic regulation. Surprisingly, while these points are well developed in the study of domestic regulation, they have hardly been considered in the study of regulation at an international level.

Each of the six literatures that I will examine here has its own distinct focus. The first literature draws on concepts developed in the study of international relations to explain the emergence of international institutions. The second draws on economic theory and focuses on domestic regulation. The third analyzes corporatism and looks at the relation between private and state regulation. The fourth, the new institutional economics, revises neoclassical economic theory in order to explain institutions. The fifth focuses on domestic financial markets and helps clarify the role of institutions in those markets. The sixth has been labelled "neo-institutionalism" and focuses on the relationship between domestic socio-economic structures and state capacity. As my purpose here is to find insights relevant to understanding the relationship between international regulatory institutions and industry structures, and because none of these literatures claims to address this relationship, there is no need for extensive review. Instead I will simply highlight key insights and omissions of each literature.

The International Relations Literature

As discussed in Chapter 1, the new wave of international relations theorizing has greatly enhanced our understanding of international institutions and how to study them. The role of economic factors, including production processes, from the growing field of international political economy; the role of non-formal institutions in shaping state actions from regime analysis; and the dangers of relying too heavily on narrow empirical methods modelled on the natural sciences are all contributions of this new wave of theorizing.

International Political Economy

In the present book the principal contribution of international political economy is to draw our attention to the importance of underlying economic structures. This approach alerts us to such relevant features of the international system as the way in which states compete economically as well as militarily, the way in which control over production processes are an important source of political power, and the way in which the actions of individual states are affected by markets. However, with the exception of those theorists who have focused on international regimes, when it comes to institutions the international political economy literature has tended to focus on individual states and highly organized international institutions such as the International Monetary Fund and the World Bank while underestimating the importance of informal institutions. An exception is Robert Cox who has drawn on the Gramscian concept of hegemony to argue that international ideological structures can be profoundly important. For instance, the "internationalizing of the state" involves "interstate consensus formation regarding the needs or requirements of a world economy that takes place within a common ideological framework." Cox sees this hierarchically structured consensus as powerful enough that participants internalize it and states modify their structures in response to it (Cox, 1987:254). These ideological structures are not random and free-floating but reflect a corresponding internationalization of production.

While Cox's discussion of ideology is useful in highlighting one type of informal international institution it has an important limitation with respect to the present effort to analyze institutions for regulating financial firms. Cox is discussing very large-scale institutions that emerge across the globe in a single historical period. A more specific type of analysis is needed to understand institutions in particular industries.

Regime Analysis

A number of international relations theorists have agreed on a widely cited definition of regimes as "principles, norms, rules, and decision-making procedures around which actor expectations converge in a given issue area" (Krasner, 1983:1). Regimes can include formal highly organized features such as written constitutions and explicit voting procedures as well as informal features such as tacit understandings, unwritten conventions, and implicit power relations. In contrast to the large-scale global institutions such as those discussed by Cox, which are sometimes labelled "orders" (Young, 1989) regimes exist within particular issue areas. Issue areas can be broad, such as "international trade" or narrower, such as "shipping." Regimes are thought to modify state actions and bring about greater international cooperation, and are therefore seen as important in explaining the reproduction of international regularity and order.

Although regime analysis has been criticized for imprecision, theoretical weakness and faddishness (Strange, 1983), it offers several insights that are useful for analyzing the regulation of global finance. The ambitiousness of the goals of regime analysis, which includes developing a single organizing concept for disparate issue areas, addressing implicit normative features not easily measured and explaining cooperation while retaining the self-interested state as a central analytical unit, have contributed to the problems to which the critics have pointed. Despite the problems experienced by regime analysis in pursuing them, these ambitious goals have opened up new angles for inquiry.

Regime analysis has avoided both the unrealistic emphasis on formalized supra-national institutions of the interwar period as well as the unrealistic dismissal of international institutions common in the postwar period. By moving beyond formalized supranational institutions regime analysis has been better able to account for the problems encountered by such institutions due to hidden relations of power and unresolved normative conflicts. The focus on international issue areas avoids some of the problems of postwar liberal research program, which focused on micro and regional interactions and which was abandoned when confronted with persistent evidence of close linkages between regions and uneven rates of integration within regions. It has also avoided the problems of the realist dismissal of institutions by discovering new types of institutionalized cooperation that explain why there is regularity rather than chaos in the international system while acknowledging the persistence of state power and the ineffectiveness of formal supranational institutions.

Regime analysis makes three main contributions to the specific task that is the subject of this book. First, it suggests that an issue area such as global finance may have its own set of international institutions with a variety of specific life-histories. The possibility that these institutions are being organized into a coherent global whole and are following parallel integrative trajectories is to be regarded with skepticism and investigated rather than assumed, as was the case in some earlier liberal approaches. Second, regime analysis suggests that the absence of a strong hierarchical regulatory body for finance that controls states and firms from above does not mean that there are no significant institutions for regulating global finance. It means rather that we must take informal arrangements into account in searching for such institutions. Third, regime analysis acknowledges that the practice of power politics is important in shaping international institutions but does not preclude cooperation. In the chapters that follow it will become clear that this insight is relevant to understanding the roles of the most powerful states in global finance, the US, the UK and Japan.

Despite these contributions regime analysis makes little attempt to relate the changes at an industry level, such as those identified by international political economists, to the evolution of regimes. I now turn to another literature for which this relationship is central.

Lessons from the Domestic Regulation of Industries

Considering that international economic regimes generally have an important regulatory function, it is surprising that more effort has not been made by regime analysts to draw on the literature on the domestic regulation of industry. Unlike the international relations literature, the literature on domestic regulation has consistently stressed the relationship between industry structure and the nature of regulatory regimes. In this section the "public interest" approach and the "private interest" approach to domestic regulation will be examined.[1]

Traditionally the analysis of regulation assumed that regulators were carrying out social goals. These goals have included the control of monopoly power, the prevention of "excess profits" from economic rents, compensation for spillovers and offsetting inadequate information (Breyer, 1982). As Moran (1986) has pointed out, not only the traditional formalistic study of regulation, but also more recent Marxist approaches which stress the function that the autonomous state plays in ensuring the reproduction of capitalism against the short-run interests of individual firms, are consistent with the public interest view of regulation.

More recently a sustained attack on the public interest view has been carried out by skeptics, especially by economists applying rational choice models to regulatory agencies. These skeptics have argued that these agencies serve private interests. Capture theory, which argues that regulators are coopted by regulatees, is an older and milder example of a private interest approach. In capture theory regulation is intended to be in the public interest, but is perverted. In contrast, Jordan (1972:153) argues that regulation is *designed* to protect producers:

> the actual effect of regulation is to increase or sustain the economic power of an industry. Such a situation could result if regulation converted a formerly competitive or oligopolistic industry into a cartel, if it increased the effectiveness of an existing cartel, or if it maintained an existing monopoly (or cartel) where rival firms would otherwise enter to provide competition in response to the growth of markets or the development of technology.

Similarly, Stigler (1975:114) argues that "as a rule, regulation is acquired by the industry and is designed and operated primarily for its benefit." Stigler identifies four functions of regulation that benefit regulatees: subsidies, control over new entrants, control over substitute products, and price fixing. Stigler uses the example of US railways, which turned to the state when threatened by the emergence of an intercity trucking industry.

An increasing number of the social goals given as the reasons for regulation have been attacked by some economists as inappropriate or as not being served by existing regulatory arrangements. For instance the market is seen as capable of developing mechanisms for providing information, such as ratings agencies, and oligopolists are seen as held in check by the threat of new entry, thus making disclosure and anti-trust regulations unnecessary. For Brozen (1982:xxi) the impact of this new wave of pro-market theorizing is profound enough to be called a "revolution."

In both the public and private interest approaches the structure of the industry is seen as closely related to the regulatory regime. For the public interest approach a central conceptual tool has been the structure–conduct–performance paradigm, which ties high levels of concentration in an industry to negative performance indicators such as supranormal profits. This paradigm has provided a guide for deciding which industries should be regulated. For the private interest approach the structure–performance correlation remains relevant, but the causal link runs from the state to the industry rather than from the industry to the state, as in the public interest approach. Much of the new wave of pro-market theorizing rejects the structure–conduct–performance paradigm, arguing for instance that high profits may stem from the superior performance of large firms rather than from their control of markets. At the same time, the importance attributed to market structure in analyzing regulatory regimes has not diminished.

Transferring the insights of this domestic literature to the international level presents challenges but is worthwhile. The first challenge is that there is no state at the international level and thus the task of tracing the connections between industry structure and regulatory institutions is more complex. Second, as discussed above, the lack of consensus in the literature means that there is no readily available model that can be unproblematically employed. However the contention that there is a relationship between industry structure and regulatory regimes is supported strongly enough by each of the approaches within this literature, despite their disagreement on the nature of this relationship, that it is worth searching for such a relationship for global finance.

Corporatism

While the public and private interest approaches to regulation have developed out of the study of regulatory agencies, the literature on corporatism has developed out of more general studies of the state. Dating from the mid-1970s, the modern study of corporatism addresses the apparent displacement by organized private interests of important functions of the state, including electoral democracy and industry regulation. Developed partly in reaction to pluralist analysis of the state, this literature has treated the organized group as intermediating between the state and group members, with the group having an organizational dynamic of its own rather than simply representing interests. The title of Streeck and Schmitter's 1985 book, *Private Interest Government: Beyond Market and State*, captures this theme.[2]

The literature on corporatism is useful because it explicitly focuses on the relationship between state regulation and private interest groups while taking more seriously sociological insights into institutions than do economists pursuing the private interest approach to regulation. For instance organized groups are seen as defining and creating and not simply transmitting interests. The organizational factors involved in self-regulatory agencies, including symbiotic relationships with the state, are stressed, rather than attributing these organizational functions to the spontaneous working of the market.

In contrast with the literature on international regimes, the corporatism literature treats state agencies and organized private interests as alternative regulatory arrangements. According to its advocates (Streeck and Schmitter, 1985), private interest government can solve many of the collective action problems that the market cannot, while being less costly, more effective at enforcement and more legitimate than are some state agencies.

Also relevant to the regimes literature, with its emphasis on issue areas, is the increasing tendency of the corporatist literature to emphasize industrial sectors rather than specific firms or national economies as a whole. Cawson (1985:11) has called this "meso-corporatism" to distinguish it from the "'system steering' concerns of macro-corporatism" and the relationships between states and individual firms of microcorporatism. Cross-national comparisons using national aggregates may conceal sharp performance differences between sectors (Kitschelt, 1991), and may obscure the role of organized interest groups at the sectoral level (Cawson, 1985). Hollingsworth and Lindberg (1985) have initiated an interesting cross-sectoral analysis of the US economy attempting to explain the mode of sectoral governance with reference to characteristics of the sector such as resource scarcity and information complexity. They distinguish two modes of governance in addition to the more familiar categories of markets and hierarchies: community[3] and associations.

In short, the literature on corporatism addresses at a domestic level many issues relevant to regime creation and strength by relating these to differences in the structure of industries in different sectors. Given the increasing globalization of industries it is likely that an international focus such as that pursued in the present book may be useful for the literature on corporatism that has not yet moved beyond cross-national comparison.[4]

The New Institutional Economics

The New Institutional Economics (NIE) has argued that two assumptions underpinning much of the liberal neo-classical approach to economics – that the flow of information and the enforcement of contracts are relatively costless processes – are not tenable empirically and preclude important theoretical insights. Oliver Williamson (1975, 1985, 1986, 1988, 1990), in particular, has focused on the impact of transaction costs on the way in which economic activity is organized. According to Williamson,

> transaction cost economies are realized by assigning transactions (which differ in their attributes) to governance structures (which are the organizational frameworks within which the integrity of a contractual relationship is decided) in a discriminating way (1986:41).

Three factors are particularly important in understanding this process: bounded rationality, opportunism and asset specificity. For example, prior to purchasing an idiosyncratic machine, the purchaser has difficulty identifying the costs and benefits of its future operation (bounded rationality). The seller has an incentive to conceal information (opportunism). Purchasing the machine may leave the purchaser at the mercy of the supplier for future transactions such as parts (asset specificity). Thus it may be more efficient for the purchaser to bring the production of the machine into its own governance structure. The NIE has therefore rediscovered the importance of institutions in making certain transactions possible. The institutions discovered include voluntary contracts, corporate hierarchies, trade associations (Aoki, Gustafsson and Williamson, 1990), joint ventures (Dunning, 1988, Chapter 6) and alternative systems of property rights established by states (for example North, 1981; North and Thomas, 1973). There has been some use of this type of analysis for understanding the role of institutions in international markets. Rugman (1981), for instance, explains the multinational corporation by arguing that intrafirm transactions conducted through hierarchical corporate structures substitute for arms-length trade conducted through markets when there are high transactions costs.

Two points are especially relevant for understanding global finance. First, private institutions, such as those involved in hierarchically organized multinational corporations, play an important role in organizing international interactions. Second, the emergence of these institutions is associated with a specific set of transactions for which the arm's-length interactions characteristic of markets are not appropriate.

While the NIE has been important in emphasizing the importance of institutions in non-market economic transactions, it tends to inadequately consider the institutional nature of market transactions. The market is often regarded as natural, non-institutional, and ontologically prior to non-market transactions. This view is captured in the use of the term "market failure" to refer to non-market transactions. This view coexists uneasily with the corresponding notion that market failure involves inadequate specification of property rights, a function that is generally carried out not by markets, but by states.[5]

The view that the market is natural and non-institutional is tenable neither empirically nor theoretically. As Polanyi (1944:44) has argued, history knows of "no economy prior to our own, even approximately controlled and regulated by markets." Furthermore, the creation of a market economy was carried out and enforced by the state (Polanyi, 1944:139) through actions such as enclosures, new Poor Laws, laws to enforce property rights and new sets of regulations. It is not just social institutions created by the state that are essential for the functioning of markets. Hodgson (1988:178) notes the importance of habit and routine in such vital functions as establishing patterns of consumption, forming prices and communicating information about products.

In addition to inadequately considering the institutional nature of markets, the new institutional economics has made little attempt to sketch out the relationship between transactions costs and international regulatory institutions. While some regime theorists have borrowed concepts from the new institutional economics, they have restricted their analysis to the transactions costs of *states* and have ignored the role of transactions costs of *private actors*. They have also ignored the role of non-state institutions in reducing transactions costs. This neglect is peculiar given the centrality of such issues for the transactions costs tradition (for an example of such neglect see Keohane, 1984:86).

In short, the new institutional economics contributes to our understanding of international financial regulation by pointing to the variety of institutional arrangements that are involved in economic transactions. Therefore there is likely to be a link between transactions at an industry level and regulatory regimes and this link is likely to be affected by the types of transactional problems identified by the NIE. Furthermore the NIE pushes us to consider the role of private institutional arrangements as alternatives to interstate regimes.

Analysis of Financial Markets

A variety of institutional mechanisms for making market transactions possible have been discussed in the above literatures. Are such institutional mechanisms necessary in financial markets? Popular images of international financial markets as virtually unregulated and of stock exchanges as paradigmatic cases of free markets seem to suggest that financial transactions may differ from real exchanges and may therefore be better able to function "naturally" and without institutions. There is, however, a growing literature on finance that indicates that financial transactions also heavily rely on institutions. I will illustrate this with four brief examples: money, bank intermediation, corporate finance and the stock exchange.

Money

One scholar has noted, "Money does not exist in a vacuum. It is not a mere lifeless object, but a social institution" (Einzig, 1949:25, cited in Shearer, Chant and Bond, 1984:16). Even in primitive societies the way in which money emerged depends crucially on the particular customs, values and social institutions of a particular society (Einzig, 1949:26).

In modern societies money has become further removed from any natural or real object, and has become increasingly socially constructed. All modern societies have shifted from commodity money, which has an intrinsic value, to fiat money, the value of which is backed up only by the state's guarantee that it can be redeemed for goods and services. As Frankel (1977) has persuasively argued, money cannot exist without trust. When the social institutions that sustain this trust decay, money deteriorates.

Current developments further highlight the socially constructed nature of money. As Poster has noted,

> The word "money" now refers to a configuration of oxides on a tape stored in the computer department of a bank. The connection between the oxides and the function of exchange medium is arbitrary, revealing its social constituted character, and the representational aspect of "money" is sustained through language, through configurations of language, its referent being remote and difficult to discern (Poster, 1990:13).

At an international level the value of currencies is shaped by social–psychological factors to an important degree. In the mid-1960s, as financial markets were more closely linked, exchange rates became increasingly determined by expectations rather than by real factors (Mussa, 1981:3–5). The demise of the Bretton Woods system, symbolized by the Nixon measures of 15 August 1971, and the severing of the last remaining connection between the international monetary system and gold, further enhanced the role of social–psychological factors in the determination of the value of money (Group of Ten, 1986:247).[6]

Bank Intermediation

The institutional quality of bank intermediation has been analyzed by theorists using the NIE (Diamond, 1984; Stephan Williamson, 1986; for applications to international banking see Rugman, 1981; Rugman and Kamath, 1986; Cho, 1985; Millar, 1990). The hierarchical structure of a bank allows it to intermediate between creditors and borrowers in situations where the requisite conditions for market transactions do not exist. Assessing the creditworthiness of borrowers may require detailed assessment and close monitoring, which would be impossible for dispersed investors whose only relation with the borrower is through a market.[7]

Furthermore, as Gerschenkron (1966) pointed out, bank intermediation rests on a prior development of certain social institutions related to standards of business practice. In countries where these had not developed the state needed to step in, as in nineteenth century Russia:

> the standards of honesty in business were so disastrously low, the general distrust of the public so great, that no bank could have hoped to attract even such small capital funds as were available, and no bank could have successfully engaged in long-term credit policies in an economy were fraudulent bankruptcy had been almost elevated to the rank of a general business practice (1966:19–20).

Corporate Finance

The study of corporate finance has displayed a similar trajectory to that of other social sciences, with institutions initially seen as irrelevant in the postwar period, but attracting increasing attention more recently. In a 1958 article Modigliani and Miller argued that, based on certain assumptions including competitive markets, costless information and an absence of transaction costs, the degree to which firms rely on debt finance as opposed to equity finance is irrelevant to firm value.[8]

More recently, however, this model has been seen as inadequate for explaining the great variety of financial contracts on which corporations rely (Barnea, Haugen and Senbet, 1985:4) and the great variation in debt/equity ratios between countries (Mayer, 1990). New models have been developed that focus on the way in which social institutions, such as debt contracts and corporate governance structures, address problems such as information assymmetry, contract unenforceability and agency problems (Diamond, 1984; Hubbard, 1990; Barnea, Haugen and Senbet, 1985; Masulis, 1988; Jensen and Meckling, 1976; Bhattacharya and Constantinides, 1989; Williamson, 1988a).[9]

Stock Markets

Stock markets have been seen as epitomizing capitalist free markets. Until recently the institutional structure of the stock market, including the impact of its physical organization, informal social norms and formal rules, was seen as irrelevant to its financial functioning. More recently, however, a number of theorists have challenged this view (Adler and Adler, 1984; Cohen *et al.*, 1986; Schwartz, 1988). Based on this new approach one can argue that stock markets require sustaining social institutions, which can include *inter alia* insider trading laws, disclosure regulations, generally accepted accounting principles, a developed financial press, self regulatory organizations and trading regulations such as detailed obligations of brokers to execute trades in a specified order, to post prices and to honour their posted prices.

These four examples, money, bank intermediation, corporate finance and stock markets, each dealing with a different aspect of the financial system, all indicate that the social institutions that underly financial transactions are essential for these transactions to be able to take place. Thus even in financial markets, which are sometimes seen as symbolizing free and unregulated transactions,[10] social institutions are important. These examples from financial markets echo the points made about markets in general above.

Neo-institutionalism

The neoinstitutionalist trend in comparative politics, which has also been labelled comparative political economy (Evans and Stephens, 1988), offers a way to understand the impact of non-state social institutions on the conduct of state actors (Evans, Rueschemeyer and Skocpol, 1985; Evans and Stephens, 1988; Hall, 1986; Ikenberry, 1988; Krasner, 1988; Skocpol, 1976, 1979, 1980; Thomas, Meyer, Ramirez and Boli, 1987).[11] While neoinstitutionalism in comparative politics is most closely identified with the effort to "bring the state back in" as an autonomous self-interested actor that can shape society, equally important is the insight that institutional structure can severely constrain the choices of state actors. This is evident in the focus on state capacity in relation to the challenges it faces in the world system, but also in the careful analysis of the way in which existing domestic institutions influence the formulation of policy.

Skocpol (1976, 1979), for instance, in her analysis of revolutions in France, China and Russia, argues that agrarian bureaucracy, an institutional structure in which the state is tied to a landed upper class embedded in local authority relations, poses a severe constraint to state leaders faced with pressures from the world system:

> Governmental leaders' realm of autonomous action tended to be severely limited, because few fiscal or economic reforms could be undertaken which did not encroach upon the advantages of the traditional landed upper classes which constituted the major social

base of support for the authority and functions of the state in agrarian bureaucracies (1976:180).

Other theorists have placed a similar stress on the constraining effect of institutions. For instance Hall (1986) explains the differences between state economic intervention in Britain and France with reference to "the structural constraints implicit in the socioeconomic organization of each nation" (1986:231). A collection of articles edited by Ikenberry, Lake and Mastanduno (1988) focuses on the impact of the organizational structure of the American state on US foreign economic policy. Evans and Rueschemeyer and Skocpol (1985) have analyzed the constraints imposed by state capacity on the ability of Third World states to contribute to economic transformation.[12] Gerschenkron (1966) and Zysman (1983) are examples of institutionalist analyses of this type that are applied to financial systems. Gerschenkron argues that state leaders of late industrializers, constrained by existing social institutions but faced with competitive pressures, are forced to innovate institutionally. Zysman argues that the way in which the state conducts industrial policy is fundamentally constrained by the structure of its financial system.

These examples from comparative politics are cases where the impact of domestic or industry-level social institutions on state action has been very important. While regime analysts have sought to trace the impact of international social institutions on state action, the narrow focus on interstate institutions, without linking these institutions to either domestic or industry-level institutions, has limited the approach's ability to demonstrate the relevance of institutions as effectively as have comparativists. On the other hand, comparativists, while recognizing the importance of competitive pressures imposed by the world system on the state, have not analyzed the institutional character of these pressures with the same diligence as they have domestic institutions.

INSTITUTIONS AND INDUSTRIES: THE STARTING POINT SUMMARIZED

The above brief summaries of five literatures have given us useful insights from which to construct a more coherent understanding of the relationship between industry structure and regime formation. Six points stand out:

1. Markets require social institutions in order to function. The image of natural, institution-free, market forces is misleading. Problems such as the need to enforce contracts, transmit information, and prevent opportunism require institutional solutions. This is the case even for financial markets, often considered the most unregulated.

2. Such social institutions exist at a variety of levels: they can be intrinsic to markets, such as shared understandings about prices; they can function within corporate hierarchies to facilitate intracorporate transactions; and they can be imposed on the market by the state, as in property laws.

3. Market, corporate and state institutions can perform many of the same functions. As the NIE points out, corporate hierarchies can facilitate transactions when markets fail to transmit information or states fail to specify or enforce property rights. As the literature on corporatism points out, private interest associations, through self-regulation, are carrying out many functions previously carried out by the state, perhaps even more effectively.

4. Whether institutions are intrinsic to markets, embedded in intracorporate hierarchies or provided by states, is likely to be determined to some degree by factors, labelled "transactions costs" by the NIE, such as the difficulty of acquiring information and organizing enforcement.

5. State actions can be shaped by what Hall calls "the structural constraints implicit in the socioeconomic organization of each nation" (1986:231). As Gerschenkron pointed out, the state may have to step in more strongly in countries where market institutions are weaker. As the literature on domestic regulation points out, the emergence of state regulation may be related in some way to the degree of oligopoly within regulated industries. As the international political economy literature has pointed out, domestic economic structures can shape foreign policy as well as domestic.

6. State actions can also be shaped by international interstate institutions in which many key features may not be formalized in such instruments as constitutions and written rules, and in which specific issue areas may have their own evolutionary histories. As the regime literature has stressed, the absence of strong global hierarchical organizations that sit above and control states does not mean that international institutions do not play an important part in shaping state actions.

These six points strongly suggest that there may be some connection between the institutional structure of industries, state actions and regime formation. The nature of this connection remains unclear however. Sharp disagreements exist on the relationship between domestic industry structures and state regulation. None of the literatures examined attempts to analyze the relationship between industry structures and the formation of international regimes. At a domestic level private institutions can substitute for institutions created by the state. Is this so internationally? If states are influenced by domestic socio-economic institutions and informal interstate institutions, can they be influenced by private international regimes? If state regulation, corporate hierarchies and market institutions can be substitutes for each other, can interstate regimes and international private regimes also be substitutes? In order to understand further the relationship between industry structures and interstate regimes we need to go beyond these existing literatures.

INDUSTRY STRUCTURE AND REGIME FORMATION: TOWARDS A NEW APPROACH

In order to develop our understanding of the impact on regime formation of industry structures three steps are necessary: (1) to clarify the nature of the entities involved; (2) to develop a plausible relationship between these entities; and (3) to devise a method for testing the hypothesized relationship. In this section I will address these in turn.

The Entities Involved: Regimes and Industry Structures

Interstate Regimes

I have already discussed the advantages of the regime concept over the more formalistic approaches to international institutions. Krasner's oft-cited definition of regimes as "sets of principles, norms, rules, and decision-making procedures around which actor expectations converge" is a useful starting point in specifying the nature of the relevant international regulatory institutions. As with any definition, behind Krasner's statement stand a whole set of assumptions about the way in which the world works. As discussed in previous sections, a key advantage of the regime approach is its ability to take informal issue-specific institutions seriously. This aspect of the regime approach is worth preserving.

In the issue area of international finance, the Basle Committee on Banking Supervision and the International Organization of Securities Commissions are the only interstate institutions that directly seek to regulate international banking and securities markets respectively. Although the participants in these institutions are central bankers and other financial regulators, and therefore do not fit the conventional image of statesmen, they do come from state agencies. These institutions can therefore be considered *interstate* institutions. While other interstate institutions, such as the International Monetary Fund and the European Community, do address international financial regulation to some degree, their roles and mandates, which are either not directly focused on regulation or are regional rather than global, prevent them from challenging the leading roles of the Basle Committee and IOSCO. I will discuss the roles of the Basle Committee and IOSCO and their relationship to other interstate institutions in much greater detail in Chapters 3 and 4.

There is even more reason to use the regime concept when analyzing the Basle Committee and IOSCO than when analyzing other international institutions such as the IMF because the formal features of the former are much less developed than the latter. By highlighting the informal features of institutions regime analysis allows us to explain the effectiveness of institutions such as the Basle Committee and IOSCO. The traditional focus on organizations that have a legal identity, material resources, a fixed central location, and constitutions and other sets of rules that are formalized and written, is not well-suited to the analysis of the leading interstate institutions in global finance. The Basle Committee is surprisingly free of the features of formal organizations. While IOSCO possesses more of these features they only superficially reflect the significance of the institution.

Since the term "regime" refers to much more than the formal features of organizations it is more accurate to refer to an interstate regime for regulating banking regime centred on the Basle Committee and an interstate regime centred on IOSCO than to call the Basle Committee and IOSCO regimes themselves. The terminology in subsequent chapters will therefore reflect this distinction.

Industry Structure

What are the features of industries that are likely to be most relevant to understanding the relationship between changes at the industry level and the emergence of interstate regimes? One feature of industries is a variety of *actions*, such as the launching of a new product by a particular corporation. For present purposes, however, the *structure* of industries is more likely to be relevant because of the role of structures in social reproduction.

Giddens' (1984:17) reference to structure as "the properties which make it possible for discernibly different social practices to exist across varying spans of time and space and which lend them 'systemic' form" captures a general meaning attached to the term. Theorists treat these properties in vastly different ways however. Giddens (1984:xxxi) himself stresses both rules (including "normative elements and codes of signification") and resources (involving control of human agents and material objects). Similarly, for Waltz (1979:100–1) structures are defined by ordering principles, the functions of differentiated units and the distribution of capabilities of the units. For other theorists, such as Gilpin (1987:81), structures are more simply defined as those parts of a system that remain stable. Metatheoretical differences regarding the types of knowledge and entities that are considered legitimate and real contribute to the varying ways in which structure is used. For instance, positivists, with their reliance on empirically observable data, would ignore such entities as underlying principles and might focus on easily measured capabilities. A major divide is between theorists who treat structures as attributes of the system's units (such as the distribution of capabilities) and those who treat structures as holistic entities which constitute units (Wendt, 1987).

In the study of domestic regulation analysis of the structure of industries has generally involved a focus on measures such as concentration ratios. Concentration ratios are obtained by calculating the share of a certain small number of firms of total activity in a market. For instance, an industry in which three firms control 80 per cent of production has a highly concentrated structure. Analysis of the role of social institutions in the structure of markets, such as shared norms and tacit agreements, is much less developed. In part this is due to the difficulty of such analysis: norms are less tangible and tacit agreements are often deliberately concealed. It is also due to the metatheoretical inclinations of the economists involved in this field of study, including the view that analysis of social institutions is less scientific than research based on hard numbers, and the view that the attributes of units are more real than hidden structures.

While the debate over the nature of structure is very important it can be safely put aside in the present chapter by adopting a broad notion of structure. Participants in the debate all agree that structures shape the actions of individual units. We can avoid the question of whether attributes of units or hidden social institutions are more important by treating them as alternative measures of a single phenomenon. Thus we can treat markets with high concentration ratios and strong sets of shared cultural norms as highly organized in comparison with markets where these features are absent. Those theorists who prefer attributes of units as indicators of structure would not disagree that normative structures are likely to play a role since there must be some mechanism to connect the distribution of resources with the modified actions of the firms involved. While they would see this role as derivative of the distribution of resources in contrast with theorists who place more stress on hidden structures, the most relevant point here is that there would be no disagreement that structures measured by analyzing norms and structures measured by analyzing attributes of units are closely associated if not the same.

Even though I am treating the distribution of resources and normative structures as two aspects of a single phenomenon it is necessary to distinguish them and further clarify their meaning, both to facilitate applying them to global finance and to understand better the relationship between them. In order to do this I will treat the distribution of resources as a continuum running from intense atomistic competition to oligopoly. I will develop the notion of a "private regime" to refer to the normative structures of an industry. I will now look more closely at these two aspects of the structure of markets.

Oligopoly and the intensity of competition As noted above the most common measure of market structure in the study of domestic regulation is the concentration ratio. This ratio measures the degree to which the top few firms dominate markets. Although there are a great number of ways to calculate such ratios they all seek to provide quantitative measures that vary from pure competition, in which each firm has an equal market share, to monopoly, in which one firm controls the entire market. As I will discuss further below, it is possible to construct concentration ratios for international banking and securities markets. There are two problems with relying on concentration ratios however.

The first problem is the difficulty of obtaining comparable data across industries and across time. Luckily there is widespread agreement among economists that concentration ratios and the profitability of industries are correlated. Although there are sharply differing explanations for this correlation the relationship is well enough established to treat profitability as an alternative measure of the degree of competition in an industry. I will discuss the relationship between profitability and concentration ratios, and how to apply these to global finance, in the section on testing below.

The second problem of concentration ratios is that they say nothing about the variations in the intensity of competition that may occur at any given concentration ratio. One can easily imagine two markets in which the top four firms control 80 per cent of sales but in which the ferocity of competition sharply differs. In part such differences could be related to the strength of normative structures, and I will address these when discussing private regimes below. An additional important factor, however, is the nature of technology. Briefly put, products can vary from simple commodities that can be produced by many firms and whose single most important feature for buyers is price, to more complex products with a variety of specialized features requiring a high degree of technological sophistication to produce.

There are a number of reasons that markets involving simple commodities are likely to be more intensely competitive. It is likely to be easier for new firms to enter the market, for consumers to abandon traditional suppliers and for substitute products to be found than is the case with technologically sophisticated products. Many analysts have argued that entire industries go through life cycles, with products becoming increasingly like commodities as familiarity with the technology involved grows. When comparing across industries it is therefore possible to distinguish differences in the nature of technology depending on the stages of the life cycles that the respective industries are at. An assessment of the nature of technology in an industry can therefore be an important additional way to measure the intensity of competition.

Private regimes   The concept of a private regime is a useful way to address the normative and cultural aspects of industry structure. The use of the term "regime" in this context suggests, echoing the literatures reviewed above, that non-state institutions can carry out many of the functions carried out by states, and that the informal features of these arrangements are likely to be as important as the formal organizational features.

Treating the normative and cultural aspects of industry structures in this way differs from two possible alternatives. The first alternative is to attempt to assess the degree of industry influence in regimes in general without distinguishing between interstate and private regimes. The second alternative is to use the term "cartel" instead of "regime". I shall address these alternatives in turn.

The first alternative, which involves expanding the existing meaning of the regime label to include private arrangements, appears useful because it addresses the inevitable interpenetration of private and interstate institutional arrangements. The state can operate through, or even create, private associations. Conversely, private actors may wield such control that state policies, while vital, are very constrained. In these cases it may be very difficult to distinguish two separate regimes, one private and one organized by states. The problem with not trying to distinguish between private and interstate regimes, however, is that such an alternative does not easily permit analysis of private arrangements as part of relatively autonomous industry-level processes and makes it difficult to problematize the relationship between interstate and private regimes. The problem of the interpenetration of the two types of regimes, while significant, is similar in the analysis of domestic politics and has not been insurmountable. For instance, the inconclusiveness of the debate between "society-centric" and "state-centric" approaches (Nordlinger, 1986) has not forced us to abandon the distinction between state and civil society domestically, but rather to be sensitive to the complexity of the relationship. Similarly, at the international level it is worth distinguishing between private and interstate regimes as long as we do not reify these concepts.

The second alternative is inadequate because of the limited meaning of the term "cartel." The concept of a cartel explicitly includes coordination of action but in conventional definitions such coordination is restricted to marketing arrangements. For instance, Hexner (1946:24) defines a cartel as "a voluntary, potentially impermanent, business relationship among a number of independent, private entrepreneurs, which through coordinated marketing significantly affects the market of a commodity." In contrast, private regime, as with the corporatist notion of private interest government, can include a much greater variety of social institutions involved in making markets possible than is captured by the term "cartel." In addition to collusive marketing arrangements, the establishment of principles and rules of business conduct and control over entry may be carried out by private regimes. Domestically private interest governments have the potential to restructure industries in response to crisis by shifting resources to more competitive products (Dyson, 1983:55), and it is possible that similar functions could be carried out by international private regimes.

A difference between a cartel and a private regime is the degree to which the institution is involved in regulation of its own members. Although cartels may devote some effort to disciplining their members, the main focus is outwards, towards potential competitors and consumers. In contrast, a private regime provides the social institutions that shape the conduct of its participants, that make it possible for a market to exist. Cartels and private regimes are not mutually exclusive categories, but rather alternative theoretical constructs that may describe different functions carried out by the same set of social institutions. The distinction between a cartel and a private regime is therefore similar to the distinction between an alliance and an interstate regime.

As with interstate regimes there is no assumption that private regimes will or will not promote global collective welfare. This is similar to the notion of private government that can involve an illegitimate abuse of power on the one hand or a contribution to public policy goals on the other (Streeck and Schmitter, 1985:17).

Due to the lack of attention devoted to international private interest associations[13] there is no defined body of literature that provides a listing of institutions that could qualify as private regimes. In the 1940s, when international cartels were a pressing policy issue that related to the power struggle of which the Second World War was a part, there were a number of studies of international cartels[14] that would be an important starting point for any historical analysis. More recently organizations such as the International Air Transport Association and the International Federation of Stock Exchanges, and more informal arrangements such as strategic partnerships (Mytelka, 1991), are obvious candidates, but case studies are needed to pull together any meaningful comprehensive set of examples, a task that is beyond the scope of the present book. In order to preserve the distinctiveness of the private regime concept, individual multinational corporations, while sharing many characteristics with private regimes, would be excluded as would more general associations involving important private actors such as the Trilateral Commission.

It is useful to add a formal definition to the above limning of the private-regime concept. Krasner's definition of regimes, which was cited above, can serve as a definition of a private regime since it refers to "actors" and not "states." However in order to emphasize the self-regulatory function of private regimes the following definition is more useful: a private regime refers to a set of social institutions that organize the activity of firms within a particular issue area.

What are private regimes likely to look like in global finance? In subsequent chapters I will look at a number of aspects of these regimes. As with interstate regimes there are certain organizations that play an important role in these regimes. The International Securities Markets Association, the Group of Thirty, the International Federation of Stock Exchanges and the International Council of Securities Associations are examples to which I will return in subsequent chapters. Equally important, however, are more informal ongoing practices such as syndication techniques. Most international bank loans and bonds are too large for an individual financial firm to handle. Firms therefore cooperate in highly organized syndicates complete with a hierarchical division of labour and strong sets of injunctions constraining the conduct of firms. Although each individual syndicate only lasts as long as the bank loan or bond for which it is designed, the practices involved in these cooperative activities persist and develop over time. In addition the close cooperation of top firms may lead to other types of shared cultural norms that can be a source of governance.

The Relationship between Industry Structure and Interstate Regimes

Having now more clearly described the relevant features of industry structures and interstate regimes I can now further address the relationship between the two. If there is a relationship it is likely to be one of two alternatives. The first alternative is that a strong interstate regime is likely to emerge when industries are highly competitive and lack private regimes. The second alternative is that a strong interstate regime is likely to emerge where industries are highly organized with oligopolies and strong private regimes.

As will become clear in ensuing chapters it is the first of these two alternatives that is supported by the data. In this section I will first indicate theoretically why this might be so. Yet the second alternative is also plausible and the theoretical literature reviewed above suggests several reasons why we might expect the data to support it, an important consideration in ensuring that the first alternative is falsifiable. I will review these reasons in this section as well.

There are eight interconnected reasons for thinking that strong interstate regimes will emerge when markets are characterized by intense atomistic competition and when private regimes are absent or in decay. I will review these in turn.

1. Oligopoly, technological innovation and control   Rapid technological innovation can be a weapon with which oligopolistic firms retain control of markets. By retaining the specialized ability to produce these innovations within a firm hierarchy or within a strategic partnership with a few other firms (Mytelka, 1991) an important tool exists with which to preserve a private regime. The ability of oligopolists to prevent dissemination of their technological advantage is likely to be an important factor in the degree to which private regimes can restrain competitive pressures. It is not likely that state regulators will be able to develop formalized regulations to cope with such firms, nor is it likely that such firms will desire or need state regulation.

2. The role of the state can be informal with a private regime   It seems likely that the preeminence of a few corporate hierarchies in an industry would be associated with an informal form of state involvement since close contact between corporate officers and state managers would be possible. This informal regulation could be based on tacit understandings and face-to-face meetings that could be modified on an ad hoc basis. Studies of policy networks and corporatism seem to lend support to this (Banting, 1986; Coleman, 1988; Lowi, 1979). In short, where private hierarchies are strong, the state's regulatory practices may be ad hoc and informal and an interstate regime would be very weak or non-existent.

3. Where markets are oligopolistic the smallness of the number of firms facilitates communication and control   Collective goods theory supports this view. A small number of like-minded participants are likely to be able to negotiate informal agreements (Eden and Hampson, 1990). In contrast, with a large number of competing participants, some form of enforcement is likely to be required if collective goods are to be provided. Thus governance by a private regime is likely to be supplanted by state involvement with its enforcement capabilities as competition increases.

4. Trends in industrial concentration are not unidirectional   If it were true that markets are constantly becoming more concentrated then it would be unlikely that strong interstate regimes and atomistic competition would be associated since there are many examples of interstate regimes that have emerged in markets that have existed for a long time. However, many analysts of the multinational corporation have indicated that corporate hierarchies and oligopoly can decay over time. For instance Magee (1977), drawing on Vernon's product-cycle model, argues that there is an industry-technology cycle of three phases: invention, innovation and standardization. An industry is least competitive at the innovation stage as firms are unlikely to make heavy investments in R&D without hope of appropriating technological rents, something that is enhanced with a monopolistic or oligopolistic structure. As technology matures it is increasingly difficult for firms to prevent competition emerging.[15] Similarly, Dunning (1988:73–4,86,98,100,102,107) notes that around the turn of the nineteenth century innovations in tropical agricultural industries and new resource industries were accompanied by the creation of hierarchies, but that subsequently there has been a shift to more market-based transactions.[16]

5. *If international markets characterized by atomistic competition develop out of oligopolistic markets, then it is likely that the transition will involve a decay of a private regime and the introduction of a formalized interstate regime due to the need for a formalized definition and enforcement of property rights.* The new institutional economics associates competitive markets with clearly specified property rights, a function that is usually carried out by states. In competitive markets, which involve large numbers of similar transactions, such property rights cannot be renegotiated on an ad hoc basis with each transaction, but must be codified in bodies of law. In contrast, internalizing transactions within a corporate hierarchy or in alliances between firms allows a more informal and less codified set of rights and obligations to govern these transactions.

6. *Oligopolists in maturing industries will press for state assistance* In an industry that is becoming more competitive, it is not only likely that more formal state-sponsored rules governing transactions will be required for these markets to function, but it is also likely that the former oligopolists will press for rules to restrict new entrants in an attempt to preserve their hold over the industry. Analyses of state responses to the problems of surplus capacity (Strange and Tooze, 1981) address this phenomenon to some extent. This would indicate that state regulations are deployed when private regimes are in decay. It also corresponds to aspects of a corporatist approach that stress the degree to which private interests attempt to forestall state intervention

by organizing self-regulatory associations. This suggests that private interests prefer self-regulation to state regulation, and that the latter only occurs in response to weaknesses on the part of private interests.

7. The instability of competitive markets can be an incentive and justification for the state to step in with a formalized regulatory regime Although "destructive competition" has increasingly come under attack as a justification for regulation it has been advanced historically by state regulators and their supporters for many cases of US regulation. The state's interest in stability and order is likely to lead to increased incentives to intervene in volatile competitive markets.

8. From a Weberian perspective modernism involves a parallel growth of markets and of bureaucracy In this view, which has been further developed by theorists of late modernity such as Foucault (1984), both markets and the growth of state bureaucracy are manifestations of a modern process of rationalization. One would therefore expect to find the growth of formalized interstate regimes accompanying the expansion of competitive international markets.

In short, there are a number of reasons to suppose that the formation and strengthening of formalized regulatory regimes is associated with competitive markets, rather than with the predominance of private "regimes." There are, however, alternative reasons for supposing that private regimes and interstate regimes would be positively associated, and it is to three of these that I now turn.

Why the Strength of Private and Interstate Regimes may be Associated

1. Strong private interests are likely to be able to control the state and to create interstate regimes in their own interest This view corresponds to some private interest approaches to domestic regulation in which regulations are created to further strengthen already powerful producer interests. It corresponds to Marxist approaches that see international institutions as controlled by a powerful and well organized capitalist class. It corresponds as well to aspects of the corporatist approach which sees a symbiotic relationship between states and organized private interests. Furthermore one can envisage a feedback process where an oligopoly is powerful enough to use the regime to enhance its power, leading to further "capture" of the regime.

2. *Threatened oligopolies might be able to forestall competitive pressures by turning to the state for protection* This view corresponds to other private interest approaches in which it is *threatened* oligopolies that turn to state regulators for protection. This possibility was also cited in the previous section as a reason for the contrary view that competition and interstate regimes may be associated. The difference in this scenario is that the oligopolies are successful in retaining their hold over the market by manipulating the state, while in the contrary scenario they fail and the interstate regime is associated with increasingly intense competitive pressures.

3. *Deregulation and competition* There is much current conventional wisdom that associates a weakening of formal state regimes with an expansion of competitive markets. For instance, Franklin Edwards, former regulator and Director of the Study of Futures Markets at Columbia University notes:

> The structure of the US financial system is undergoing tremendous change. Although this change is in its early stages, its direction seems clear: the elimination of geographic and product constraints that in the past have prevented open and unfettered competition among all financial institutions (1988:113).

In this view, even though the regulations to which Edwards refers were enacted in order to encourage an atomized competitive financial system their effect was perverse and their removal will be associated with an expansion of competitive forces.

Devising a Method for Testing the Hypothesized Relationship

We now have, as discussed in the previous section, two plausible but contradictory relationships between industry structure and the emergence of interstate regimes. In the present section my goal is to develop a way of assessing which of these alternatives is supported by the data for global finance. There are two distinct tasks involved in this. The first is to return to the concepts of industry structure, private regimes, and interstate regimes in order to develop ways to measure their emergence and change. The second is to address the meaning of "testing," taking into account the profound criticisms of the notion of empirical testing that have been developed by the new wave of theorizing in international relations.

Interstate regimes

How can we treat interstate regimes as variables that can be measured across time and across industries? To treat regime as a dichotomous variable that is either present or absent is problematic because of the difficulty of sharply differentiating between these two states in some cases, and because of the importance of being able to distinguish a greater amount of variation among regimes that do exist. In contrast, analyzing regime *strength* allows us to construct a continuous variable that avoids these problems.

The most frequent approach to measuring regime strength is to assess compliance with regime injunctions, especially when such compliance is costly (Haggard and Simmons, 1987:496). This measure is particularly attractive because it taps most directly the effect of regimes – their ability to modify the actions of self-interested states – which makes them theoretically interesting. It corresponds closely to the Weberian notion of power as the ability of an actor (the regime) to accomplish its goals despite resistance on the part of another actor (the state).

Compliance alone is an inadequate measure of regime strength however. As Smith (1989) has pointed out, this is an inherently static concept. Since the world is constantly changing, a strong organization may be one that can rapidly alter regime injunctions in response to change. Furthermore, measuring compliance inevitably involves interpretative questions regarding the meaning of state actions, making objective measurement difficult.

The concept of institutionalization is an additional way to measure regime strength, which is useful. This theoretical construct is based on the assumption that there are certain features of all organizations that accompany and contribute to their effectiveness in coping with challenges. If these features are present then it is likely that the organization will be able to produce compliance in the future even if there are presently no operative injunctions. These features also provide alternative indicators that do not necessitate interpretation of compliance when such interpretations are contested.[17]

In addition the concept of institutionalization addresses more directly the metatheoretical assumption of regime analysis that social institutions are important than does a measure of state behaviour. The various features of institutionalized organizations are important because they are indications that such social institutions are present. If, for instance, we are investigating the possibility that interstate regimes and private regimes are substitutes, then it is useful to be able to determine the degree to which interstate regimes have the institutional capacity to carry out market-organizing functions.[18]

While a variety of indicators of institutionalization have been proposed (Huntington, 1968:12; Keohane, 1989; Smith, 1989),[19] three are particularly important: specificity, learning and autonomy. These can be ranked in this order based on the relevance of each for the ability of the institution to produce compliance. These will be discussed in turn, drawing on Huntington (1968:12), Keohane (1989), Smith (1989) and Haas (1990). The first three of these authors develop institutionalization as a central analytical concept while Haas treats it as one aspect of a larger complex of features of organizations that are successful at coping with change.

Specificity is defined by Keohane as the degree to which expectations are clearly specified in the form of rules. As the Weberian tradition has stressed, such codification appears to be a common feature of modern rationalized bureaucracies. Making commitments explicit makes monitoring and enforcement of compliance more likely. Vague wording in agreements or unresolved underlying conflicts are often associated with organizational weaknesses. This can be assessed by looking at the agreements arrived at in the regimes.

Learning is a central concept for Haas (1990:23), who defines it as "the process by which consensual knowledge is used to specify causal relationships in new ways so that the result affects the content of public policy." This definition does not capture the way in which Haas uses the concept to specify features of organizations that deal proactively with change, incorporating new problems into integrated conceptual frameworks that build on previous work, rather than an ad hoc pattern of dropping unresolved items off agendas as new problems emerge. Haas (1990:33) explicitly contrasts his concept of learning with the neo-Darwinian concept of adaption in which an organism's stability is a key and valued factor in its ability to cope with environmental challenges. Such a view of adaption was central to Huntington's analysis of institutionalization and has been a source of much criticism. The concept of learning allows us to assess the ability of an institution to cope with change while avoiding the problems attached to the concept of adaption. Learning can be assessed by examining the sequence of issues with which a regime deals and determining whether new issues are integrated into a coherent practical trajectory, or added in an ad hoc fashion to an existing eclectic set of issues.

Autonomy is defined by Keohane as the extent to which the institution can alter its own rules rather than relying on outside agents to do so. In his definition of autonomy Huntington stresses the ability of an organization to resist outside pressure. The existence of leadership socialization and recruitment mechanisms that reduce rapid turnover at the core of the system are an indications of autonomy. While autonomy is not as important as the above measures, since an organization can be both autonomous and irrelevant, both Keohane's and Huntington's indicators are a useful supplement since dependence on outside forces can be an important sign of weakness. Autonomy can be assessed by examining the degree to which the regime relies on actions taken outside its multilateral framework, as with unilateral or bilateral actions.

In sum, the degree to which a regime has been formed, and its strength, can be assessed by measuring the degree to which it is institutionalized. The following four measures will be used: (1) compliance with regime injunctions; (2) specificity; (3) ability to learn; and (4) autonomy. These are ranked in order of importance, based on the degree to which they relate to the ability of the regime to modify the actions of those actors subject to its injunctions.[20] Each of these indicators describes features that are likely to be present in a process of regime institutionalization and strengthening. They are therefore interrelated. For instance, specificity increases the difficulty of complying with regime injunctions. Since they are not quantitative these indicators will not be aggregated. They will, however, be treated as a composite indicator in the sense that similar indications of regime strength on each indicator will strengthen the claim that regime strength has been meaningfully assessed. If the indicators are contradictory then the theoretical justification for using institutionalization as a concept will be challenged.

Industry Structures

As discussed above, I am examining two aspects of industry structure: the attributes of units as measured by such indicators as concentration ratios, and normative structures as evident in the degree to which a strong private regime exists. As also indicated previously concentration ratios can be supplemented with other indicators of the intensity of competition such as profitability and the nature of technology in the industry. This section will further specify how I will develop these various indicators. I will do this by drawing on three approaches to studying industry concentration and competition: the structure–conduct–performance hypothesis; Michael Porter's model; and analyses of technological development.

The structure–conduct–performance hypothesis The most traditional method of analyzing industry structure is to measure indicators of market structure and firm performance that have been shown to be correlated in numerous studies across many industries. This correlation has come to be called the "structure–conduct–performance hypothesis," which holds that the degree of concentration in a market influences the conduct of firms and the price and profit performance of the market (Green, 1990). Rhoades, a senior economist with the Federal Reserve, comments that this hypothesis

> is probably one of the most intensively investigated hypotheses in economics.... It is notable that almost all of these studies support the hypothesis.... As a result, research findings in this area have been widely accepted and applied by the courts as well as the antitrust authorities (Rhoades, 1977:1).

Although the study of concentration in the financial sector is less developed than in other industries, Rhoades' review of pre-1977 studies of the banking industry indicates that the correlation appears to hold for banking.[21]

Although there is room for further testing and refinement of the structure–conduct–performance hypothesis itself, in the present study it will be taken as an established relationship, allowing the use of both structure and performance indicators to measure the intensity of competition in markets. These indicators are the degree of concentration, spreads and profitability.

In recent years two strong challengers to the structure–conduct–performance hypothesis have emerged (Green, 1990, Chapter 3). The first of these reverses the direction of causation so that it runs from performance to structure. There are two tendencies within this set of challengers. The first argues that superior performance is responsible for oligopoly and high profits (Green, 1990:55). The second argues that strategic behaviour is able to deliberately create oligopoly and supranormal profits by erecting barriers to entry (Jacquemin, 1987). Neither of these presents a problem for the use of the structure–

conduct–performance hypothesis here, since it is the correlation of concentration and profits and not the direction of causation which is important in using them together as a composite measure of market structure. The second set of challengers are those who deny the relevance and likelihood of oligopoly by stressing the importance of the threat of new entry, which can make even a single-firm industry operate as if it is competitive. This is a more serious caveat for the use of the structure–conduct–performance hypothesis and will be addressed through the use of Michael Porter's model below.

Four formulas have been most frequently used to measure the degree of concentration of an industry. The simplest formula is the concentration ratio, which measures the domination of a market by a specific number of top firms. For instance, the US Justice Department, in enforcing the anti-trust provisions of the Sherman Act in the securities industry, has been tough on horizontal mergers when the top four firms have accounted for more than 75 per cent of the market (Hayes, Spence and Marks, 1983:172). The measures of market share have varied; for instance for banks, both assets and revenues have been used. The second and third formulae are the Herfindahl indexes and Gini coefficients. Both measure the inequality of market shares between all firms in a market, not just the inequality between a top group and the rest of the industry. The Herfindahl index, in addition, varies with the number of firms in the market.[22] A fourth formula is the constancy ratio, the ratio of a given number of top firms that reappear in subsequent years. As Jacquemin (1987) points out, the criterion for choosing one measure over another can only be based on the theoretical purposes for which the measure will be used.

For my purpose here concentration ratios and constancy ratios are more useful than Herfindahl indexes and Gini coefficients. The intra-industry cooperation that I am seeking to measure is likely to be organized by a small number of dominant firms, because these firms can sustain a private "regime" through their own close interaction and domination of the rest of the industry. The inequality between the smaller firms in the industry, and the number of smaller firms, is less relevant. Subject to certain limitations, data is available to calculate these ratios for both international industries. Concentration ratios are more easily compared over time than are constancy ratios[23] and they will therefore be used.

Although structure–conduct–performance studies have traditionally focused on the concentration of firms, concentration by territory and nationality are also relevant for international industries. If firm concentration were held constant, one would expect concentration by territory and nationality to be factors in reducing competitive pressures because oligopolistic private "regimes" are more likely to develop between firms with shared cultural traditions. Furthermore, the social institutions that make such cooperation possible are strengthened if they are embedded in shared locations and regulatory systems. Therefore measures of concentration by territory and nationality will be examined in Chapter 4 as well.

In the securities and banking industries, the spread is the difference between the price at which the financial firm receives the funds and the price at which the funds are provided by the firm to borrowers. Large spreads can indicate the ability of the major firms to dictate prices to their "suppliers" and "buyers," and are therefore a useful measure of the intensity of competition. Caution must be exercised, however, since spreads in financial transactions also reflect risk.

Measures of bank profitability, including return on assets and return on equity, are readily available. The profitability of international securities firms is more difficult to assess. Enough data can be obtained for both industries, however, to make this a useful indicator.

In the case of each of these measures, data sources, limitations, calculations and results are presented in Chapter 4.

Michael Porter's model The quantitative measures of industry structure discussed in the previous section by themselves are inadequate. Michael Porter's (1985) model allows us to address two weaknesses of the indicators discussed in the preceding section. The first weakness is that work on contestable markets (Baumol, Panzar and Willig, 1982) has argued that concentration alone is not an adequate indication of the intensity of competition in a market – it is important to assess the ease with which firms can enter markets. The second weakness is that such quantitative measures do not adequately describe the relationships of power that shape markets.

Porter starts from the assumption that firms can shape their environment, including the structure of the industry within which they operate. There are two key strategic choices facing firms. The first is to choose which industry is likely to be most profitable. The second is to choose a strategy for operating within that industry (Michael Porter, 1985:1). Porter's approach is therefore sharply different from approaches that assume that all markets are perfectly competitive, for in such industries higher than average profits would be competed away by new firms entering or by existing firms adding capacity.

Although Porter's orientation – to help firms devise more profitable strategies – is very different from the orientation of the present study, his treatment of industry structure as socially constructed matches the approach to markets taken here. Furthermore his practical concerns have led him to distinguish five identifiable features of industry structures that provide a useful supplement to the quantitative measures discussed in the previous section.

For Porter the five features that determine the intensity of competition in markets are (1) the bargaining power of suppliers, (2) the bargaining power of buyers, (3) the threat of new entrants, (4) the threat of substitute products or services and (5) rivalry among existing firms. It is the first four of these categories that are particularly important here, since rivalry among existing firms has been addressed in the previous section.

These five features determine who appropriates the value produced by firms. For instance, buyers with strong bargaining power will capture more of the value embodied in a product than buyers with weak bargaining power. Factors influencing buyer power include buyer concentration versus firm concentration, buyer volume, buyer switching costs relative to firm switching costs and the importance of the product's price relative to the buyer's total purchases. Substitutes can place a ceiling on the price that the firm can charge for its product, strong suppliers can appropriate value from firms and new entrants can compete away profits. Porter (1985:9) cites the automobile and heavy truck industries as ones in which firms create tremendous value but are unable to retain much of this value as profits.

Although it may be difficult to distinguish these features under certain conditions (for instance when a buyer becomes a new entrant, or produces substitute products), the framework does help improve our ability to assess the intensity of competition. This framework has only recently begun to be applied to financial services (Ballarin, 1986; Meerschwam, 1991). For financial firms, the "suppliers" are depositors or investors, and "buyers" are borrowers. There is no source of quantitative data that would permit a quantitative analysis of Porter's categories of competition similar to the quantitative analysis of the more traditional measures of market structure carried out above. There is, however, adequate qualitative information available from documents and from the trade press with which to draw conclusions about the competitive pressures arising from each of these four sources. This reliance on qualitative analysis is not necessarily a weakness since some dimensions of market power, such as threats, are not easily quantified.

Analyses of technological development The ability of firms to retain control over the technology they produce is thought by many analysts of the corporation to be related to the institutional structure of an industry. Although the literature is continuing to develop, the likelihood that there is such a relationship is strong enough that assessment of the nature of technological change can be a useful supplement to the above measures of the intensity of atomistic competition in the industry.

Some of the literature relevant to this question has been discussed above. The new institutional economics, for instance, suggests that firms may internalize transactions within hierarchies in order to retain control over knowledge for which property rights are inadequately specified. In this view corporate hierarchy is positively correlated, and competitive markets negatively correlated, with the production of specialized knowledge.[24]

Recent work by Mytelka and others (Mytelka, 1991; Reich, 1991) on strategic partnering and networking suggests that the relationship is more complex than suggested by a simple distinction between markets and hierarchies. Firms are increasingly engaging in knowledge-producing alliances with other firms as an alternative to internalizing transactions within the hierarchy of the single firm.

Both the new institutional economics and the literature on strategic partnering share the view, however, that social institutions that supplant arm's-length market transactions are associated with technological innovation. In both approaches, sets of non-market social institutions are chosen because they are functional for knowledge production.

A somewhat different but compatible view is developed in the literature on monopolistic competition. In this literature innovation may reduce competition by allowing a firm to create a unique product, producing a monopoly in that submarket until competitors can produce comparable products. Ballarin (1986:27) notes that "a lack of product differentiation ... tends to increase expressions of hostility through such non-subtle forms as generalized price reductions. This can have devastating effects on the profitability of the industry." Innovation, therefore, can reduce competitive pressures.

Each of these bodies of literature is compatible with the view that an increasing inability to retain control of new knowledge is associated with increased competitive pressure. Particularly if knowledge production involves high fixed costs, vulnerability and aggressive behaviour can result if firms are unable to offset these costs by higher revenues resulting from competitive advantages derived from innovation.

This statement of the relationship between the ability of firms to retain control over technology and competitive pressures provides a useful way in which to incorporate a technological indicator into the measure of industry structure. As with the structure–conduct–performance indicators, this relationship could itself be the focus of further empirical testing, but is being treated as an assumption in the construction of this variable. As noted in the next section, the use of untested assumptions has been conventional in positivist methodology. More recent approaches have stressed the importance of establishing the plausibility of assumptions because, since Kuhn, it has been recognized that empirical data on relationships of variables is not a sufficient basis upon which to choose theories, since this data can be consistent with more than one theory. The references to the literature on technological change in this section have aimed to establish the plausibility of the assumption that the ability to retain control over technology can be used as a measure of the intensity of atomistic competition and of the likelihood that a private regime exists.

Private regime   The measures of industry structure discussed in the previous sections, while primarily oriented to analyzing structure as a distribution of capabilities of the constituent units, also indirectly addressed the question of how to assess the role of private regimes within an industry. I can more directly address the role of private regimes by seeking to measure their strength and degree of institutionalization just as was proposed for interstate regimes above. Because of the involvement of states which must publicly legitimize their actions there is much more information available on interstate regimes than on private regimes. In analysing private regimes, therefore, it will not be possible to assess as thoroughly the various indicators of strength as I will for interstate regimes. I will, however, be employing a similar method to assessing private regimes for the international banking and securities industries.

Operationalization of the Variables: Summary

We have now specified more clearly how industry structure and interstate regimes can be treated as two measurable variables. Because I am treating the banking and securities industries as two distinct cases, and because I am looking at the evolution of the regimes in the two industries over time, there are two types of comparison with which to assess the relationship between the two variables. The first comparison is within each industry over time. I will be able therefore, to first assess whether measures of the strength of the Basle Committee and IOSCO are negatively or positively correlated with the intensity of atomistic competition in their respective industries over the period since 1974 when they were first formed. The second comparison is across industries. If the degree of atomistic competition and the strength of interstate regimes are positively correlated and I find that the Basle Committee is stronger than IOSCO, then I should find that the banking industry has experienced more intense atomistic competition than has the international securities industry.

Both variables are theoretical constructs involving untested and untestable assumptions. This has been a widespread approach to empirical testing since Milton Friedman's popularization of Karl Popper's epistemology, and it is relatively uncontroversial.[25] There are, however, several more intense controversies regarding the appropriateness of empirical testing to which I now turn.

"Testing": What Constitutes "Proof"?

For much of the 1960s and 1970s the prevailing practice for testing hypotheses was to empirically establish covariance between variables. In the present context this might involve using statistical analysis to assess the degree to which the interstate regimes and industry structures, treated as dependent and independent variables respectively, are correlated. There are two serious problems with this approach, however, both of which have been highlighted in the study of international relations by the new wave of theorizing.

The first problem is that theories are "underdetermined" by facts. Conflicting theories can usually offer plausible alternative explanations for any single set of facts. This is because facts are only meaningful when embedded in theoretical constructs that are not testable empirically. For instance, when making use of international statistics the theorist must make certain assumptions about whether or not the state should be treated as a real entity or whether alternative entities such as individuals, ethnic groups or firms are more real. Thus one's *metatheoretical* assumptions shape one's assessment of the relevance and meaning of facts.

The second problem is that correlations are not explanations. Although there is much dispute about what constitutes an adequate explanation (Dessler, 1991) there is general agreement that correlations need to be integrated with some kind of higher-order theory if they are to be considered explanations. For instance by itself the correlation of a falling barometer with thundershowers does not provide a meaningful explanation of the latter (Dessler, 1991:345). Because there is no consensus on what such a higher order theory looks like or how it can be tested each theorist should strive to be self-conscious and explicit about the relationship of correlations to such theories.

In the social sciences explanations must take into account the role that actors' own intentions play in causing events, although there is no agreement on the relative weight that must be given to these intentions as opposed to structures. Here I adopt a structurationist model that is compatible with the metatheoretical assumptions of the new wave of theorizing discussed at the outset of this chapter. The structuration approach is a metatheory associated with the work of Anthony Giddens (for example 1984), although as Wendt (1987) points out, there are many other theorists whose approach is similar enough to merit a structurationist label. The structuration approach attempts to integrate both structure and agency in its explanations. It emphasizes "the active, reflexive character of human conduct" (Giddens, 1984:xvi). Structure is grounded in routinization – "the repetitiveness of activities which are undertaken in like manner day after day" (p. xxiii). These patterns are generated, not by some deep structural force but by the often unintended consequences of the actions of individual agents. These routines are both *resources* that are drawn upon by actors and the *media* through which action is carried out.

Patterned mutual expectations, or "roles," are a key way in which the identities and power of actors are defined.[26] An actor therefore formulates goals based on these roles, and not simply to maximize wealth or power in the abstract. Choice is also constrained by the existing social institutions through which actors must work if they are to achieve their goals. At the same time, actors do not just mechanically respond to roles and resource constraints, but creatively attempt to solve problems in a practical manner.

In this way, causation is established not by invoking mysterious deep structures, and not by invoking the voluntaristic inclinations of individuals, but by tracing a link between correlated variables through the intentions of actors as limited by the institutional constraints that have developed though prior practices.

How can this abstract model of causation be applied to my cases of global financial regulation? Five types of evidence are required to fully satisfy these criteria. First, the intensity of competition in the industry needs to be correlated with the strength of the interstate regime. As noted above, the variables vary on two dimensions: within an industry over time, and between industries. Second, strengthening of the interstate regime needs to be a practical solution to problems associated with competition. Third, the perceptions of regulators involved in creating the regime need to be compatible both with their roles as regulators and with their roles in bringing about the functional solution. Fourth, the regulatory instruments involved in the regimes need to be shown to be the best available ones given the existing development of social institutions in the industry. Fifth, the relationship revealed between the variables should be one which would not have been predicted by existing theories. Hegemonic stability theory, the transactions cost approach and the epistemic communities approach will serve as the competing explanatory generalizations.

It is important to note that if my explanation of regime strengthening satisfies the above five criteria this does not render all alternative theories obsolete. In the social sciences it has been increasingly recognized that alternative paradigms and explanations can coexist, each addressing a particular aspect of reality. In particular, the approach adopted here, while not placing the realist view of self-interested power-maximizing states at the centre of the analysis, does not deny that such a view has some relevance. The contributions and limitations of realism and other alternative approaches will be discussed when comparing theories in Chapter 5.

As with all research, a number of theoretical linkages that are implicit in this approach will not be investigated in any depth. As noted above, the construction of the two variables draws on a variety of theoretical assumptions. Some of these could be made the subject of future investigation. One example is the causal links between the tendency of technology to dissipate and the intensity of competition in these industries. In addition to such "intra-variable" relationships, the linkages between the variables could be further investigated. For example, the exact steps between the recognition by supervisors of a problem, and their construction of an institution with the features specified as indicators in my independent variable, would be of interest, although it may involve a type of ethnography that is impractical given the regulatory penchant for secrecy.[27]

This epistemology is compatible with the approach that has come to be adopted by comparativists working within a neoinstitutionalist framework. In their concluding chapter to *Bringing the State Back In*,

Evans, Rueschemeyer and Skocpol (1985:348) draw out certain common methodological features of the contributions to the volume. The contributions

> have clearly abstained from elaborating, or invoking, all-encompassing, deductive theoretical frameworks.... They draw research questions, concepts, and causal hypotheses from a variety of existing theoretical debates.... Then they explore such ideas through comparative and historical research. Each investigation springs from concern with certain analytical problems and each provides a testing ground for analytical orientations or causal hypotheses potentially generalizable to other contexts. These studies are therefore highly theoretically engaged, even though they invert the normal priorities of "grand theorizing".... Comparisons across countries and time periods and an emphasis on historical depth, the tracing out of processes over time, are optimal strategies for research on states.

The goal, therefore, is not to prove or disprove grand theories with empirical cases, but rather to more modestly test middle-range theory while preserving a keen sensitivity to world-historical context.

In contrast to many efforts to apply regime analysis, my case studies are well suited to such a method. Young (1989:208–9) points out that it is difficult to meaningfully compare disparate regimes such as ones in trade and money given contextual fluctuations:

> The trick here is to select cases, at least initially, in such a way as to hold as much as possible constant, other than the relevant institutional arrangements themselves. Such a procedure will minimize interpretive ambiguity and make it possible to attribute variance in collective outcomes to the impact of institutional arrangements with some degree of confidence.

My two cases minimize this problem. Since the banking and securities industries are both financial services industries, I may be able to treat many variables as if they are controlled. For instance, the distribution of power among countries is likely to be similar for each industry.

Two cases, however well-chosen, cannot serve as a definitive test of the hypothesized relationships. If the cases do support one of the two hypotheses, then further research is needed in other issue areas to estabish the degree to which it is generalizable. As well, such support will strengthen – but not, of course, prove – my claim that focusing on the relationship between non-state social institutions and regime formation is a useful approach from which further meaningful hypotheses can be generated.

3 The Regime for Bank Regulation

This chapter examines the relationship between the interstate regime for international banking and the structure of the international banking industry. The chapter is divided into four sections. The first section reviews the rapid process of globalization of banking. In the second section I will assess the strength of the Basle Committee on Banking Supervision, the leading international bank regulatory institution, which is at the core of the interstate regime. In the third section I will analyze the structure of the industry. The fourth section concludes the chapter by analyzing the relationship between changes in the interstate regime and changes at the industry level since 1974 when the Basle Committee was founded.

Three important conclusions emerge from this analysis. First, on the four measures discussed in Chapter 2, compliance, specificity, ability to learn and autonomy, the banking regime has displayed increasing strength since the formation of the Basle Committee. Second, both quantitative indicators, such as concentration ratios, and qualitative indicators, such as descriptions of technological change, reveal that international banking was characterized by increasingly intense atomistic competition over the period during which the interstate regime was being constructed. In addition, there are indications that there is no private regime and that previous sets of mutual understandings between top banks were disrupted by the entry of competitors into international banking markets. Thus the third important conclusion of the chapter is that the evidence supports the hypothesis, discussed in Chapter 2, that interstate regimes are associated with an intensification of atomistic competition and a decay of private regimes. I will then turn, in Chapter 4, to an analysis of the securities industry, which will further confirm this relationship.

THE GLOBALIZATION OF BANKING

Defining International Banking

Delineating the banking industry from the securities industry, the subject of Chapter 4, has become increasingly difficult as the barriers that existed in many countries between the two types of firms have been progressively weakened (Meerschwam, 1991). In general, a bank can be defined as an institution which accepts relatively short-term deposits from the general public (Shearer, Chant and Bond, 1984:196). A bank intermediates between depositors and borrowers. In contrast, a securities firm arranges direct financing between lenders and borrowers, as for instance when it sells corporate bonds to investors. If banking activity is cross-border, involves two currencies or takes place outside the bank's country of origin then it can be considered international.

Indicators of Globalization

The process of rapid globalization of banking has been extensively documented elsewhere and is only briefly summarized here as a prelude to the more specific concerns of this chapter. There are a number of indicators of the process of globalization of banking that has occurred since the Second World War.[1]

First, international banking has grown more rapidly than world domestic product and world exports of goods and services. Between 1964 and 1985 international banking, as measured by net international bank credit, grew at a compound rate of 26 per cent per year, while trade grew at 12.5 per cent and output at 10.5 per cent (see Bryant, 1987:20–2, from which these figures are taken).

Second, the degree of globalization can be indicated by the percentage of bank business with some international characteristic. Figure 3.1 displays the increasing percentage of bank assets that have become foreign for various banking markets. "All G10" includes the assets of all bank offices located in the member-states of the Basle Supervisors' Committee. Figures for the three most important banking markets in the Group of Ten, the US, Japan and the UK are displayed separately for comparison. The series labelled "G10 + Offshore" groups the Group of Ten assets together with all offshore centres in developing countries (such as Hong Kong). This series attempts to capture the effect of the migration of Group of Ten banks to these offshore centres. Data are only available from 1975 for this series.

Third, a rapid increase in the number of foreign branches and subsidiaries of banks is an indication of globalization. For instance, between 1960 and 1986 these increased from 37 to 380 for Japanese banks, from 131 to 899 for US banks and from three to 170 for Dutch banks (see Bröker, 1989:147–8 for these and more complete statistics).

Figure 3.1   Share of commercial bank assets that are foreign, various countries, 1960–89

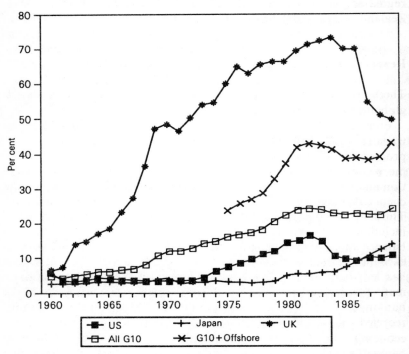

Note: There are many difficulties in accurately measuring the degree of internationalization of banks over time. For instance, the above figure does not include loans to residents in foreign currency. Inclusion of such loans would raise the degree of internationalization. On the other hand, assets of other financial institutions, which tend to be less internationalized, are also not included. Bryant (1987:26–7) was able to construct a more precise measure of internationalization, but only for one year.

Source: IMF, 1990b: various country tables and Table 7xd.

Fourth, in recent years the national regulatory regimes that had kept national banking industries relatively isolated from international competitive forces have undergone far-reaching change in most OECD countries. These changes have been spurred on by multilateral efforts such as those of the European Community, the OECD and

General Agreement on Tariffs and Trade, as well as more unilateral efforts at liberalization in countries that have traditionally been tightly regulated, such as Australia, Canada, Denmark, Finland, New Zealand, Norway, Portugal and Sweden (Bröker, 1989:197).

Reasons for Globalization

There are a number of different reasons that have been given for the globalization of banking.[2]

First, the increasing share of banking transactions in relation to trade in goods and services generally can be attributed to a secular process of financial "deepening" that occurs as economies become more complex (Bröker, 1989:122; International Bank for Reconstruction and Development, 1989:45). Second, banks follow their corporate clients abroad in order to retain important commercial relationships. Third, in the post-Bretton Woods era, private financial institutions, including banks, have increasingly become the mechanism by which balance of payments deficits are financed. Fourth, the instability in exchange rates and interest rates since the demise of Bretton Woods has led to increased demand for international hedging instruments, many of which are provided by banks (Group of Ten, 1986). Fifth, the banking system was the mechanism by which petrodollars were recycled following the oil shock of 1973. Sixth, the reasons given by economists for non-financial firms going abroad may apply as well to banks. The value added by banks may involve idiosyncratic knowledge or knowledge for which property rights are inadequately specified and that cannot be profitably sold on competitive markets, and thus banks may open branch offices as a means of retaining firm-specific advantages in such knowledge production (see the NIE literature on banks cited in Chapter 2). Seventh, rapid technological change has decreased the costs of transmitting financial information and of using computer-based models designed to calculate the risks involved in such products as multi-currency transactions. Eighth, escaping domestic regulatory regimes can be an incentive for banks to engage in international transactions.

Despite these pressures contributing to globalization the process has not been without its challenges and setbacks. There have been several sets of events that have posed particular problems for banks as they have sought to expand their international activities. First is the threat for the system as a whole, and for individual banks, as banks experiment with risky, poorly understood, new products designed to cope with the uncertainty of the global financial system. The second is the danger of problems in a single bank affecting the whole system due to increasing interdependence of banks, encouraged by such innovations as the international interbank market in which banks engage in large volumes of lending to each other. The third challenge is the debt crisis, which threatened the stability and profitability of international banks. The fourth challenge is a process of "securitization," in which products more closely resembling securities replace the bank loans that have traditionally formed the core of bank business. The significance of these challenges will become apparent as I analyze international banking below.

THE REGIME FOR INTERNATIONAL BANKING

In this section I trace the emergence of a regime for regulating international banking organized around the work of the Basle Committee on Banking Supervision, with the goal of assessing the strength of the regime.[3] After a brief description of the main features of the Committee, I will give a more detailed account of its accomplishments, including the major agreements that it has produced, and of its structure and process, including its relationship to the United States and to regulators from outside the Group of Ten. This provides the basis for an analysis of the indicators of regime strength discussed in Chapter 2: compliance, specificity, ability to learn and autonomy. It will become apparent in this discussion that the Basle Committee has displayed a surprising degree of strength given its lack of formal visible organizational structure and the difficulties it has faced in regulating powerful international banks.

Main Features of the Basle Committee

The Basle Committee on Banking Supervision, until 1990 called the Committee on Banking Regulations and Supervisory Practices, was founded by the central bank governors of the Group of Ten countries at the end of 1974 in response to the problems experienced by the Bankhaus Herstatt and other banks in that year. Its initial stated goals were to develop general principles for bank supervision and to improve contacts between bank supervisors (BSC, 1982:2; Bank for International Settlements, 1984:56). The Bank for International Settlements (BIS) provides the Secretariat for the Committee, and it is at the BIS headquarters in Basle that the Committee meets three or four times a year. The countries represented on the Basle Committee include the Group of Ten countries plus Luxembourg. Generally each country on the Basle Committee sends two delegates. The agencies that participate are listed in Table 3.1.

Table 3.1   Institutions represented on the Basle Committee on Banking Supervision

Belgium	Banking Commission National Bank of Belgium
Canada	Office of the Superintendant of Financial Institutions Bank of Canada
France	Banking Control Commission Bank of France
Germany	Federal Banking Supervisory Office Deutsche Bundesbank
Italy	Bank of Italy
Japan	Bank of Japan Ministry of Finance
Luxembourg	The Luxembourg Monetary Institute
Netherlands	The Netherlands Bank
Sweden	Sveriges Riksbank Royal Swedish Banking Inspectorate
Switzerland	Swiss National Bank Swiss Federal Banking Commission
United Kingdom	Bank of England
United States	Federal Reserve Board Federal Reserve Bank of New York Office of the Comptroller of the Currency Federal Deposit Insurance Corporation
Secretariat	Bank for International Settlements

Sources: Cooke, 1984a; Norton, 1989b.

The Accomplishments of the Basle Committee

The Basle Committee's accomplishments can be divided into two main areas. The first involves an international agreement, the Basle Concordat of 1975, which was modified in 1983, 1990 and 1992. Through the Concordat supervisors have attempted to establish several innovations in international bank regulation: an international division of responsibility, common principles, mechanisms for information sharing and a decentralized mechanism to force supervisors to comply with common standards. The second area is the creation of common risk-weighted capital-asset standards, a key tool used by supervisors to ensure the stability of banks. Work began on these standards in the late 1970s resulting in a remarkably specific agreement in July 1988. Since 1988 the Committee has been involved in refining and monitoring the implementation of the agreement. The Basle Committee has also produced a variety of technical papers on other matters but these are less important and will not be discussed here.

The agreements of the Basle Committee, unlike the Banking Directives of the European Economic Community, are not binding on national authorities. Even so, as will be evident in the discussion of the degree of compliance with regime injunctions below, the Concordat and its revisions and the capital accord have gained widespread acceptance not only amongst the members of the Basle Committee, but among bank supervisors world-wide.

The 1975 Concordat

After declaring that "the basic aim of international cooperation in this field should be to ensure that no foreign banking establishment escapes supervision," the 1975 Concordat began to specify a division of responsibilities between supervisors in home and host countries. The Concordat distinguished between three types of ownership structures for foreign banking establishments (branches, subsidiaries and joint ventures) and three features of these establishments that should be supervised (liquidity, solvency and foreign exchange operations).[4] The Concordat specified that for all three types of establishments and for all three aspects of supervision the primary responsibility should rest with the *host* authority with one exception: the solvency of branches should be regulated by home authorities. The Basle Committee felt that host supervisors were better able to regulate offices in their jurisdiction because they were more likely to be familiar with local conditions, and because, for subsidiaries and multinational joint ventures, the owner-ship structure created a relatively autonomous unit in the host country which could be relatively easily monitored. The solvency of branches was treated as an exception because it was impossible to distinguish from the solvency of the parent bank.

The Concordat also called for better transfer of information, greater cooperation on international bank inspections and the modification of bank secrecy laws where they prevented the transfer of information.

Although the 1975 Concordat was a landmark in terms of setting down some initial principles for international cooperation in bank supervision, it contained three serious flaws (see Dale, 1984:173–5). First, ensuring that a bank was supervised in a particular jurisdiction was of limited value since the Concordat made no attempt to establish standards for the quality of such supervision. Second, because the Concordat was not released publicly for five years, and because its language was not adequately precise, there was considerable confusion among supervisors and banks regarding the division of responsibility among supervisors. Third, there was no enforcement mechanism to ensure that supervisory authorities, many of which were not repre-sented on the Basle Committee, would comply with the provisions of the Concordat. The Basle Committee attempted to address these weaknesses with the Revised Concordat of 1983.

The 1983 Revised Concordat

There were several key ways in which the 1983 Concordat differed from the 1975 Concordat. The first and most important was the stress on a principle that was contrary to the earlier Concordat's emphasis on host country responsibility: consolidated supervision. Consolidated super-vision requires the home authority to supervise the global operations of the multinational banks headquartered in its jurisdiction. Since the home offices of most banks were in the member-states of the Basle Committee, the revised Concordat's emphasis on consolidated super-vision gave them an important lever over loosely regulated offshore centres such as the Bahamas or the Cayman Islands. Consolidated supervision also shifted power to the regulators and away from banks since the head office of banks was made responsible for collecting information from foreign branches and subsidiaries. Without consoli-dated supervision foreign subsidiaries were only required to supply information to local authorities. This allowed banks to shift transac-tions to lightly regulated locations and put the onus on states to cooperate in order to get a picture of the overall health of the bank. While banks could still take advantage of the complexity of multinational structures to misreport financial data, such conduct was now fraudulent and therefore likely to take place less frequently. Several other changes were also important. A decentralized enforcement mechanism was specified: if either the home or host supervisor determined that the other's supervision was inadequate then that supervisor should prohibit the home country's banks from opening new offices in the host country. The difficulty of supervising some bank holding companies due to their complex ownership structure was addressed. The 1983 Concordat also denied responsibility for the lender-of-last-resort function, which involves a commitment from central banks to step in and provide financial assistance to troubled banks, thus placing a greater onus on banks to exercise self-discipline and to be prudent, strengthening the hand of bank regulators relative to banks. Finally the 1983 Concordat recognized the need for standards for supervision by establishing the principle that "supervision should be adequate," although nothing was done to spell out such standards.

The 1990 Supplement and 1992 Revisions to the Concordat

Two further sets of modifications were made to the Concordat in 1990 and 1992. In 1990 a supplement was issued. This supplement aimed to improve the information flow between supervisors by spelling out the types of information that should be shared, by affirming the Committee's commitment to the removal of secrecy constraints, and by highlighting external audits as a mechanism of control.

In 1992 further revisions were made in a document entitled "Strengthening International Cooperation Between Banking Supervisory Authorities," issued in response to the problems revealed by the BCCI scandal. Although the degree of complexity of the BCCI's corporate structure made it exceptionally difficult to supervise,[5] it is clear that the crisis would not have become as severe if the Concordat had been more effective. For instance important information was available to auditors but was not distributed to supervisors. More importantly the criteria for judging home or host supervision upon which supervisors should have denied access to BCCI offices were inadequately spelled out.

The 1992 document stressed four minimum standards to which different supervisory authorities are supposed to hold each other. The first standard was that all banks should be supervised by a home authority with the capacity for consolidated supervision. In contrast to previous agreements the criteria were provided for assessing such capacity: the home authority must (a) receive consolidated information from banks and be able to confirm this information through on-site inspections; (b) be able to restrict bank corporate structures that undermine consolidated supervision; and (c) be able to prevent the bank from opening offices in foreign jurisdictions.

The second standard was that both home and host supervisors should approve the creation of cross-border establishments and should consciously divide up responsibilities for supervision upon such approval. The document therefore calls for a more positive joint action on the part of home and host supervisors than did the 1990 supplement, which stated that "host authorities should as a matter of routine check that the parent authority has no objection before granting a banking licence" (BSC, 1990:37). Both the capital and organizational strength of the bank should be considered in granting approval.

The third standard enjoins home and host supervisors to grant rights for on-site inspections in each other's jurisdictions before consenting to the creation of cross-border banking establishments.

The fourth standard calls for host supervisors to refuse or restrict applications of banks from inadequately supervised home jurisdictions. If such banks are permitted to operate then the host supervisor must take the responsibility for adequate supervision.

In contrast to the 1983 Concordat, which shifted responsibility to the home authorities, the 1992 document stresses and further specifies joint responsibility. In part this was an immediate practical response to the BCCI scandal in which the home jurisdiction, Luxembourg, had failed to adequately supervise the worldwide operations of the bank. More generally, however, it sought to address the need for closer cooperation between supervisors in response to increasingly complex corporate structures.

The Concordat process as a whole indicates that international bank supervision has evolved considerably since 1975. I now turn to the most ambitious accomplishment of the Basle Committee, the 1988 accord on capital adequacy.

The 1988 Agreement on Capital Adequacy

At the end of the 1970s the members of the Basle Committee began to focus on capital adequacy standards as an effective tool for supervision of international banks (BSC, 1982:7). As this section will show, the capital standards developed by the Basle Committee constitute a relatively new tool for bank supervisors but one that offers important advantages for international supervision. Capital standards significantly shift the administrative and financial burden of ensuring that banks are run prudently from supervisory authorities to banks and their shareholders. The standards operate through market forces, which are more effective and less costly for supervisors than older supervisory tools such as detailed individual monitoring of internal bank operations. They are sufficiently general that they can be used to regulate a great variety of financial products in many jurisdictions in contrast to alternative regulatory systems that relied on combinations of tacit understandings and more specific injunctions, neither of which were easily translated or transported into new situations.

Although there are sharp differences over how best to define bank capital it is useful to start with a simplified general discussion of its character and functions. One way of looking at bank capital is to treat it as equal in value to the bank's net worth – subtracting what the bank owes (its liabilities) from what it is owed (its assets). A second way to look at bank capital is to analyze the ownership claims that it involves. Put simply the capital is divided up and owned by shareholders in the form of shares, also called equities. Like shares in other types of companies these ownership claims come with specific rights and obligations. As owners shareholders generally have the right to exercise control over the management of the bank. Unlike bondholders, who generally have a right to a fixed stream of payments, shareholders' returns are related to the net worth of the firm, which in turn relates to the firm's performance. While shareholders do well if a firm performs well they can lose money if the firm does not perform well and the value of its capital declines.

There are several implications of these features of capital that are relevant for regulators. Capital can act as a cushion for firms that safeguards them in difficult times. A firm is considered bankrupt if its liabilities exceed its assets – in other words if its capital is exhausted. If the bank actually does go bankrupt all other claims upon the bank, including those of depositors and bondholders, are honoured before the claims of shareholders. Thus a large amount of capital reduces the possibility of bankruptcy and reduces the negative effect of bankruptcy upon depositors and holders of bank debt. For a variety of reasons, including the effect of bank problems on the economy as a whole, a responsibility of bank supervisors has been to minimize such negative effects. Therefore an additional positive effect of requiring banks to hold adequate levels of capital, from the point of view of regulators, is to shift the costs of protecting banks from deposit insurance funds and other sources of bank bailouts funded by the state to the shareholders of banks. Since their capital is at risk, and since they have the right to exercise control over bank management, an effect of high capital standards is to increase the incentive for shareholders to monitor the management of the bank to make sure it is run prudently (on bank capital see Kareken, 1984; Norton, 1989b:1302; Orgler and Wolkowitz, 1976).

While the above description of the characteristics of capital captures its most significant features at a general level there are in practice a great number of difficulties and controversies involved in defining capital. For instance, *long-term subordinated debt*, which is like equity because it cannot be quickly withdrawn and because the claims of its holders are subordinate to claims of depositors and other creditors, could be counted as capital. Because countries differ in the degree to which they rely on subordinated debt this issue was a contentious one in the negotiations over the capital accord of 1988.

Because capital is more expensive than deposits as a source of funds for banks, competitive banking markets produce a downward pressure on bank capital in relation to total bank assets. As an industry average this figure dropped from 60 per cent at the beginning of the nineteenth century, to 20 per cent at the turn of the twentieth century, to less than 10 per cent since the early 1950s (Orgler and Wolkowitz, 1976:3). By the early 1980s the ratio for many banks had fallen below 5 per cent. The average for the 17 largest federally chartered banks in the United States was 4.63 per cent (Kareken, 1984:45).

Not only was the ratio of capital to total bank assets falling, but also a growing proportion of the business of international banks was "off balance sheet" and therefore was not included in the figure for total assets. This off-balance sheet business included contingent commitments, as in note issuance facilities, which involve a commitment on the part of the bank to support the issuer of notes if they were not purchased in the market. Thus the declining ratio understated the risks that capital was expected to cushion against. In part this was another aspect of an overall process of securitization, as described earlier in this chapter. In part it was an effort by banks to get around the constraints imposed by the capital requirements that supervisors had imposed. While these commitments were an important source of fees for the banks, they added a risk to their portfolio that was not reflected in the assets included in their balance sheet and in existing capital to assets ratios.

The Basle Committee's work on capital adequacy, while most evident in the July 1988 agreement, represents a long process of cooperation that started at the end of the 1970s. The German and Swiss systems had focused on capital adequacy well before the Basle process, and national supervisors were beginning to reexamine their approach to bank capital by the late 1970s. Discussion of the need to address the erosion of capital also began in the Basle Committee at this time. By the beginning of the 1980s the Basle Committee was systematically monitoring capital ratios of leading banks (Cooke, 1990:314). Supervisors were unilaterally trying to strengthen capital adequacy in an increasing number of countries by 1982 (IMF, 1983:14).[6] This work resulted in a report calling for convergence of capital standards, endorsed by the Group of Ten central bank governors in 1982. By 1983 the concept of "tiers" to distinguish between types of capital had been developed by the Committee (Cooke, 1990:318). By the end of 1986 the Committee had developed a complex definition of capital with six tiers, and had developed risk-weights for six categories of assets, which included off-balance sheet items (Cooke, 1990; Norton, 1989b:1341).

The document issued in July 1988 was remarkably detailed and technical for an international agreement. It specified standards for assessing the adequacy of a bank's capital in relation to the varying degrees of risk associated with the different types of assets that it possessed. National supervisors were expected to make the necessary modifications in their national regulations by the end of 1992. There were three main elements to that agreement.

First, the Committee settled upon a definition of capital that consisted of two tiers. The first tier, core capital, included equity and published reserves from post-tax retained earnings. In the second tier, supplementary capital, a variety of capital-like elements, including general loan loss reserves and subordinated term debt, were permitted subject to certain restrictions and at the discretion of national supervisory authorities.

Second, a set of five risk-weighted categories was established and different types of assets and off-balance sheet items were allocated to each of these categories. For instance a claim on an OECD central government was given a zero per cent risk weight, while a loan to a corporation has a 100 per cent risk weight. Thus in calculating the assets against which capital needs to be held, riskless assets such as a claim on an OECD central government would not be counted, while a risky asset such as a corporate loan would be counted in full. A set of conversion factors to make off-balance-sheet items equivalent to other assets was established. Third, a target standard ratio of capital to risk-weighted assets was established. This was set at 8 per cent. Tier-one capital is required to be at least half of this. The deadline for this standard to be met is the end of 1992. Each country was called upon to implement the guidelines at a national level, including introducing legislation if needed.

Since July 1988 the Committee has engaged in ongoing work related to its capital adequacy agreement, including monitoring compliance, integrating new innovations into the framework as they are generated by the market, and extending the agreement to cover additional types of risk (BSC, 1990:60). Particularly important is discussion with securities regulators to determine whether differences in the international regulation of the two industries can be reduced. A major concern of banks with the July 1988 agreement was that securities firms would not be subject to the requirements, and would therefore enjoy a competitive advantage over banks in the increasing number of activities in which both engage. The Committee held joint meetings with Group of Ten securities regulators beginning in 1988, and throughout 1992 intense negotiations were carried out in joint meetings of the Basle Committee and the Technical Committee of the International Organization of Securities Commissions (Waters, 1992a, 1992b; BSC 1992).

This review of the content of the major agreements that the Basle Committee has produced provides a starting point for assessing the strength of the regime. More information about the structure and process involved in the work of the Committee is also important, however, and will be provided before proceeding to the indicators of strength.

Structure and Process of the Regime

On first examining the Basle Committee it appears to be quite unstructured. For instance it does not have a published organization chart with spelled out hierarchical relationships of authority. Its four chairs (George Blunden from the Bank of England from its inception until 1977, Peter Cooke from the Bank of England between 1977 and October 1988, Huib J. Muller from De Nederlandsche Bank NV from October 1988 to 1991, and Gerald Corrigan, chief of the New York

Federal Reserve Bank from 1991) do not exercise formal authority over the other members of the Committee.

To take this unstructured appearance at face value, however, would be a mistake, partly because the Committee's penchant for secrecy conceals its structure, and partly because its tight consensus-based process makes it remarkably efficient in exercising leadership relative to other groupings. These groupings, while not formally part of the Basle Committee, can be seen as in a subordinate position in relation to the Committee, and this relationship is therefore an important part of the structure of the regime as a whole. I will discuss each of these characteristics of the Committee in turn.

The secrecy with which the Basle Committee operates is evident in the comments of Huib J. Muller (1988), then Chairman-designate of the Committee, in his address to the 5th Annual International Conference of Banking Supervisors:

> I think we are already and are becoming ever more, in a phrase we coined yesterday, a corpus, perhaps even a sect. We don't like publicity. We prefer, I might say, our hidden secret world of the supervisory continent.

The secrecy of the Basle Committee was remarked upon by the authors of a 1986 General Accounting Office study on the work of the Committee. Despite their mandate from Congress to conduct the study, the authors were denied access to a significant number of Committee documents (US General Accounting Office, 1986:42).

Secrecy in leadership deliberations is an important source of power in relationships of authority. Secrecy, which is deliberately exercised and prevents the flow of information out from leadership bodies, should be distinguished from isolation, which indicates a breakdown in flows of information into leadership bodies, and is a sign of weakness. Secrecy allows deliberation free of political pressures from subordinates and makes it more difficult for those at whom policy initiatives are aimed to resist. Secrecy indicates a high degree of institutional control over the individual members of a leadership body.[7]

Given this degree of control of information over its operations, it is not surprising that the Basle Committee has not explicitly spelled out its internal organizational structure. Reference to such structures in Committee documents are limited to vague comments. For example, to respond to innovative capital instruments, the Committee "set up a mechanism" (BSC, 1990:12).

Despite this secrecy we do know that the Committee operates by consensus (US General Accounting Office, 1986:42) and is therefore less hierarchical than are many organizations. This consensual process can be regarded as having both strengths and weaknesses in relation to the Committee's effectiveness.

A consensual process, if it requires unanimity, can result from the unwillingness of member states to cede sovereignty to a supranational organization since each state has a veto over decisions. This is an indication of weakness (Haas, 1990). On the other hand, consensus can indicate the development of an esprit de corp and commitment to the process, with participants being willing to forgo legalistic objections and formal procedures for the sake of achieving common goals. For instance, the United Nations Security Council shifted to increasing use of consensus to restore its preeminent role after a period of disillusionment with the Council's effectiveness during the 1950s (Bennett, 1991:65). These apparently contradictory implications of consensus can only be resolved through analysis of particular institutions to determine whether procedures such as majority voting are being used to speed decision-making for the sake of the institution's goals, or to ensure that participants are able to engage in logrolling and other tactics to protect their individual interests at the expense of the institution's effectiveness.

The General Accounting Office saw the Basle Committee's consensual process as a weakness: "the Committee operates by consensus, and once its members reach agreement it has no power to assure that the agreement is adopted by member countries ... it would be unrealistic to expect nations to cede their national sovereignty" (US General Accounting Office, 1986:42). This view, however, underestimates the contrary impact of consensus on Committee functioning. Comments by Peter Hayward, Secretary to the Basle Committee, are revealing of the role of consensus in the capital standards negotiating process. This process was considerably more difficult than previous discussions in the Committee due to the weightiness of the obligations to which members were committing themselves:

Although not legally enforceable as a treaty, and although the Commmittee is not a formally constituted international organization, nonetheless the agreement is considered to be binding on the members and the agreement itself states that the Committee will continually monitor its application.

Some feared that this process could change the character of the Committee ... to some extent this fear has been borne out, and the negotiations on the capital agreement were extremely tough. But in other discussions members have been just as frank, in part at least because members of the Committee have a good deal of personal confidence in each other. In part, the process is helped because much of the consensus building takes place in informal working groups where the process of mutual education is allowed full rein (Hayward, 1990:790–1).

Thus it appears that the Committee's consensual process has contributed to the Committee's effectiveness. Yet the tough negotiations leading up to the capital agreement clearly strained the consensual process. The breakdown of consensus is also evident in the temporary defection of the US and the UK from the multilateral process, as discussed below. The defection itself was a violation of the spirit of the Committee, especially as it involved secret coordination of positions between the US, the UK and Japan before a September 1987 Committee meeting (Tobin, 1991:243–4). The bitter response of some Committee members (Norton, 1989a, 1989b: 1345; Tobin, 1991:222) to this defection is also an indication of the strain that developed. Tobin (1991:222) notes of the US/UK actions that "one Cooke committee member described it as a 'bombshell.' It seemed to break away from every norm that had developed in the previous decade of international supervisory cooperation." In short, while the Committee's structure and process is generally very effective this incident revealed its limits.

The United States and the Committee

An important element in assessing the strength of international institutions is the degree to which they simply reflect policies developed unilaterally by their most powerful member-states. Some of the strongest critics of the possibility of the autonomy of international institutions are hegemonic stability theorists (see for example Snidal, 1985). Hegemonic stability theory argues that a single state with a preponderance of power plays a crucial role in creating and sustaining regimes. Some analysts have seen evidence of such a role for state power in the Basle Committee's work. For instance Kapstein (1992:265) argues that the reason for converging policies "is found in the power capabilities and shared political purpose of the United States and Britain." Tobin (1991:220) refers to the capital negotiations as "the process by which the US proposal became international." If the US did indeed play such a key role then it would be difficult to see the international banking regime as having much strength.

The key feature of the Basle process, which seems to support the idea that the power of the US state was vital to its success, was the bilateral negotiations between the US and the UK to develop their own common standards on capital adequacy that were initiated in 1986 and resulted in the release of a joint proposal on 8 January 1987. These bilateral negotiations were initiated by the US due to dissatisfaction with the slow speed with which the Basle Committee was progressing. The threat of being left out of negotiations between the two largest financial markets put pressure on other supervisors. US and UK regulators conducted secret negotiations with Japanese regulators and brought the resulting agreement to the Basle Committee (Tobin, 1991). As noted above, this heavy-handed pressure imposed by the United States on the Committee led to resentment on the part of the smaller states.

There is good reason to doubt that the US played such an important role, however. Europeans and not the Americans were the first to advocate a risk-weighted assets approach to capital adequacy. The US was a latecomer to the approach. Indeed US regulators, rather than seeking to provide stability for the system as a whole, were drawing on techniques from other countries in order to improve their control over US banks, were seeking to reduce the competitive challenge from Japan and were willing to desert the multilateral process at a key point.[8]

It is useful to trace the evolution of US policies on capital standards in order to indicate the degree to which they lagged behind the Basle process. The United States had relied on capital adequacy measures in the immediate postwar period. These were quite primitive, however, and were abandoned. During the 1970s there was a shift towards reliance on more informal tools for bank supervision. Even as late as the beginning of 1979, when other countries were already engaged in strengthening capital ratios, as noted above, capital adequacy was not a Federal Reserve Board focus (Holland, 1986:789). It was work in the European Community rather than from the US that the Committee drew on when initiating its own work on capital adequacy ratios in the late 1970s (Cooke, 1990:316).[9] By the early 1980s US supervisors were once more interested in developing a more formalized measure of capital adequacy ("Developments in Banking Law," 1990:55; Gordon, 1991). Problems developed, however, in achieving consensus between the three main regulators of commercial banks (the Federal Reserve, the Office of the Comptroller of the Currency, and the Federal Deposit Insurance Corporation), from the perverse effects of an overly simplistic, non-risk-weighted ratio,[10] and from a legal challenge to the right of regulators to enforce capital standards. It wasn't until the enactment of the International Lending Supervision Act of 1983 that US regulators had a legal basis for enforcing capital standards and a mandate to pursue international agreements concerning capital adequacy (Holland, 1986:793).

The first public proposal involving a risk-based approach by a US regulator, issued by the Federal Reserve Board on 15 January 1986, contained "many of the main elements of the approach followed in Basle" (Cooke, 1990:325) and used as a justification the need to bring US capital adequacy policies into line with other countries which had already adopted risk-based approaches (in Europe) or were moving in that direction (Japan) (Federal Reserve Board, 1987:5119; Holland, 1986:804).[11] The 1987 bilateral accord between the US and the UK drew from UK regulatory experience, itself influenced in key ways by the Basle process (Price, 1987:87), rather than from US-initiated regulatory techniques. In short, the US followed behind and relied upon the Basle Committee's work to an important degree.

Furthermore US actions can be interpreted as attempting to impose an idiosyncratic approach to regulation on its main competitor, Japan. The stability of the Japanese banking system had been ensured by interlinkages between banks and their corporate clients, including cross-holding of equity (Meerschwam, 1991). In the negotiations the Japanese failed to have these "latent reserves" acknowledged (see Federal Reserve regulator Taylor's comments in US House of Representatives, Committee on Banking, Finance and Urban Affairs, 1988:20).

There are several indications that the US was making use of international negotiations to impose standards on its own banks. Cooke (1990:325) notes with respect to the US–UK accord that "the US authorities were anxious to move forward their proposals in the face of opposition on a number of points from their banks." The 1988 accord caused difficulties for US money centre banks, which had several complaints: other financial institutions such as investment banks were not subject to the regulations; the Japanese banks were thought at the time to be able to raise capital easily;[12] US regional banks were better capitalized; the use of loan loss provisions as capital was restricted[13] and US bank stocks were depressed due to LDC loan losses ("Developments in Banking Law," 1989:66). Estimates of the capital required by different countries' banks at the time of the accord indicate the costliness of the accord to US banks (Table 3.2).

Table 3.2   Anticipated Basle-related equity needs, various countries, July 1988

Country	Estimated new capital needed Federal Reserve estimate	ICBA and other estimates
United States	$15 billion	$10 billion
Japan	$26–38 billion	$50 billion
France		$13 billion
West Germany		none
Switzerland		none
United Kingdom		none

Notes: Federal Reserve estimate for Japan includes $6–8 billion already raised. ICBA Banking Analysis estimates are for the US and Japan. France, West Germany, Switzerland and the UK are based on *Wall Street Journal* research.

Source: Norman, 1988:3,17.

The 1988 accord was also used by the US as a basis to impose standards on firms that the accord itself had exempted because they were not primarily international.[14] For instance, the application of capital standards to the thrift industry was met with loud expressions of pain. The Annual Review of Banking Law ("Developments in Banking Law," 1990:61) noted that "some experts predict that as many as two-thirds of the nation's thrifts will ultimately fail due to the risk-based capital requirements, leading one S&L executive to disdain the effective date of the [Office of Thrift Supervision] requirements as the 'Pearl Harbor Day of the industry."

In sum, US regulators used the international negotiations in two ways: to regulate US banks and to alter the rules to the advantage of US banks. These were related: regulators wished to implement capital standards but were reluctant without international agreement because the new standards would otherwise further constrain a banking sector that was already losing market share internationally ("Developments in Banking Law," 1990:55; US House of Representatives, Committee on Banking, Finance and Urban Affairs, 1988:5,9,13). The US role in the negotiations appears to be one of a declining power drawing on international regulatory techniques to deal with the shortcomings of its own system, while doing all it could to slow the decline of its market share.

The Relationship of the Basle Committee to Supervisors not Represented on the Committee

Since the 1975 Concordat the Basle Committee has recognized the importance of having its agreements accepted by countries not represented on the Committee. It has developed three particularly important institutional mechanisms for doing this. First is the creation of organizations of supervisors from outside the Group of Ten. Second is the holding of biennial conferences to which supervisors from around the world are invited. Third is the education and training of supervisors.

The Offshore Group of Banking Supervisors, founded in October 1980 at the initiative of the Basle Committee, is the most important of the groupings from outside the Group of Ten because it includes many small states with a reputation as lightly regulated havens for multi-national banks. The Offshore Group currently has 19 members: Aruba, Bahamas, Bahrain, Barbados, Bermuda, Cayman Islands, Cyprus, Gibraltar, Guernsey, Hong Kong, Isle of Man, Jersey, Lebanon, Malta, Mauritius, Netherlands Antilles, Panama, Singapore and Vanuatu (Powell, 1991). Although the Offshore Group claims to have modified some of the policies and attitudes of the Basle Committee, the overall impact of the Group's creation has been to restrict the regulatory advantages of offshore centres by creating greater acceptance of the Basle Committee's agreements. According to one supervisor, the Offshore Group had no choice but to accept the initiatives of the Committee since recalcitrant offshore centres could have been punished by Group of Ten supervisors by not permitting Group of Ten banks to open offices in those centres.

Other international supervisory groups with which the Basle Committee has close relations include the Contact Group of EC Supervisory Authorities (an informal and autonomous group that first met in 1972), the EC Banking Advisory Committee (formed in 1979 as provided by the First Banking Coordination Directive of 1977); the Banking Supervisory Sub-Committee of the Committee of Governors of the EC central banks established in February 1990, the Commission of Supervisory Authorities of Latin America and the Caribbean (first discussed at the Basle Committee's 1979 International Conference of Bank Supervisors, with the first meeting held in 1981), the Nordic Supervisory Group (whose origins go back to a 1925 meeting), the SEANZA Forum; the Gulf States' GCC Committee of Banking Supervisors (formed in 1981), the Group of Banking Supervision Officials in Arab Countries established 1991 to study Basle

Committee Decisions, the Caribbean Banking Supervisors Group (formed in 1982), and the Group of Banking Supervisors from Central and Eastern European Countries established in 1990 and hosted by the Basle Committee's former chair, Huib Muller.[15] These international supervisory groups vary substantially in the nature of their connection to the Basle Committee, with some (such as the European Community committees) relating as equals, and others (such as the Arab and Eastern European committees) highly dependent on the Basle Committee. Taken as a whole this network of relationships is a powerful mechanism for extending the reach of the Basle Committee's agreements beyond the Group of Ten.

The biennial International Conferences of Bank Supervisors (ICBS), held at the initiative of the Basle Committee, are important fora at which the Committee promotes its supervisory initiatives. Documents produced by the Basle Committee are circulated, discussed and endorsed at these meetings. As well as providing a forum for contact between individual supervisors, the meetings provide an occasion at which meetings of other organizations concerned with bank supervision can occur, either separately or jointly with the Basle Committee. The *Report on International Developments in Banking Supervision* is prepared and distributed by the Basle Committee to coincide with the ICBS meetings. There have been seven meetings to date: London, 1979; Washington, 1981; Rome, 1984; Amsterdam, 1986; Tokyo, 1988; Frankfurt, 1990; and Cannes, 1992.

Training and education take place not only through the dissemination of the Basle Committee's research, but also through more formal programs. For instance, the Committee organized courses to familiarize younger up and coming supervisors, from developed and developing countries, with issues under discussion in the Committee. These have been held in 1987, 1989 and annually beginning in 1991 (BSC 1988b:39, 1990:70, 1992:106).

In sum, the Basle Committee possesses relatively well-developed channels through which it can promote its agreements beyond its own membership.

Assessing the Strength of the Banking Regime

The above discussion of the accomplishments, structure and process of the Basle Committee has suggested that the banking regime has a number of strengths, including an ability to produce relatively detailed international agreements and to promote compliance with these agreements within and beyond the Committee's member-states, the commitment of its members to a set of common principles, norms, rules and decision-making procedures, and reliance of the world's most powerful state upon work initiated by the Committee. It is useful, however, to turn to the four indicators discussed in Chapter 2 – compliance, specificity, learning and autonomy – in order to assess more rigorously the strength of the banking regime.

Compliance

Compliance is an indication of the strength of a regime when there are both a cost in implementing its rules and a general adherence to those rules. Compliance with the injunctions of the Basle Committee will be assessed with respect to the Concordats and to the capital accord of July 1988.

The costs of implementing the Concordats involve the resources needed to modify domestic regulatory systems and to carry out ongoing new supervisory functions, as well as the loss of business for lightly regulated financial centres. Pecchioli's 1983 and 1987 studies of international bank supervision for the OECD summarize a number of indicators of the progress of the Concordat. He concluded in 1983 that despite substantial development in the application of the approach "considerable information gaps remain" (1983:98). Since then further implementation of this aspect of the regime has been accomplished. Table 3.3 summarizes this progress based on information provided in these two studies by Pecchioli. The widespread acceptance of the principles of the 1983 Concordat was indicated by its endorsement by about 90 countries who attended the 1984 International Conference of Banking Supervisory Authorities and who pledged "to ensure that their supervisory systems conformed to the principles set out in the document" (BSC 1985:1–2). They also agreed to participate in a questionnaire drawn up by the Basle Committee on the supervision of bank foreign offices. The information collected would be administered, centralized, held and updated at the Committee's Secretariat in Basle. As has been noted by regime analysts, such monitoring is a key component in ensuring compliance. By 1986 nearly 100 countries had responded to the questionnaire (BSC, 1986:2). The Concordat has also had an effect on the internal operations of multinational banks, influencing them to expand and centralize at the head office their internal reporting systems (Pecchioli, 1983:98). External auditors have come to play a larger role in multinational bank supervision.

Table 3.3   Compliance with the Concordat

Country	Which offices?		Which risks?				% 1987	% 1983
	B	S	S	L	C	E		
Australia	2	2	n.a.	n.a.	n.a.	n.a.	100	100
Austria	2	1	1	1	0	0	42	33
Belgium	2	2	2	1	2	1	83	67
Canada	2	2	2	2	2	2	100	100
Denmark	2	2	2	1	2	1	83	83
Finland	2	2	2	2	2	2	100	58
France	2	2	2	0	2	1	75	67
Germany	2	2	2	0	2	0	67	50
Greece	2	1	2	2	2	n.a.	90	n.a.
Ireland	2	2	2	2	2	0	83	67
Italy	2	2	1	0	0	0	42	42
Japan	2	2	2	2	2	0	83	83
Luxembourg	2	2	2	1	2	1	83	50
Netherlands	2	2	2	0	2	2	83	83
Norway	2	2	n.a.	0	n.a.	n.a.	67	100
Portugal	2	0	0	0	0	0	17	17
Spain	2	2	1	1	1	1	67	50
Sweden	0	2	2	0	2	0	50	25
Switzerland	2	2	2	0	2	0	67	50
Turkey	1	n.a.	n.a.	n.a.	n.a.	n.a.	50	n.a.
UK	2	2	2	1	2	1	83	75
US	2	2	2	2	2	2	100	100
% 1987	93	90	87	45	82	39		
% 1983	93	73	78	42	53	33		

Notes: Table 3.3 assesses the degree to which consolidated supervision has been adopted as of 1987. Offices include branches and subsidiaries. Risks include solvency, liquidity, concentration, and exchange rates. Cells were assigned a score of two if consolidated supervision exists for that type of office or risk. A score of one indicates that consolidated supervision is only proposed, or is weakened by exceptions. Zero indicates that no consolidated supervision exists. An aggregate indicator was then constructed for each row and column, indicating the percentage that the total score for that row or column is of the total possible score given available information. Similar aggregate figures from 1983 are presented for comparison. The average score for all columns increased from 62 per cent to 73 per cent from 1983 to 1987. The chart therefore indicates that consolidated supervision was adopted more widely over this four-year period. This method of assessing compliance inevitably involves a degree of subjectivity and inaccuracy and is therefore only a very rough guide.

Sources: Based on Pecchioli, 1983:97, 105 and 1987:Annex II.

Although the capital accord has involved more costs than has the Concordat, compliance with the accord is strong. As noted previously, supervisors began tightening their supervision of capital levels from the beginning of the 1980s. Figure 3.2 indicates the resulting reversal of the decline in capital standards. Of these countries, France, Switzerland, the US and the UK show the most dramatic increase in capital–asset ratios. Although German banks appear to have lower levels of capital in comparison with other countries in Figure 3.2, in fact a larger proportion of German bank capital consists of equity than in other countries, and therefore is better quality capital from the point of view of regulators. Because of this German banks have been traditionally

Figure 3.2   Capital/asset ratios, selected countries, 1974–89

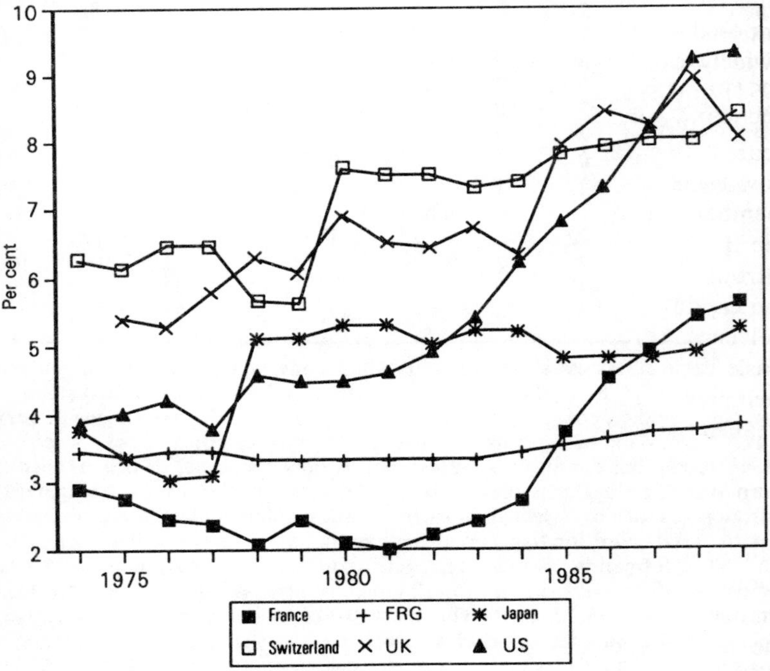

Sources: IMF, *International Capital Markets: Developments and Prospects*, various issues.

considered to have high capital standards, and it is therefore not surprising that the German ratios would rise more slowly than other countries' in the 1980s. The declining Japanese ratios from 1980 to 1985 reflect the Japanese bank strategy of rapidly expanding assets – the expansion that US regulators sought to constrict through the capital accord. The slowness with which Japanese ratios have risen since 1987 reflects the unexpected difficulties of Japanese banks in raising new equity due to the stockmarket crash in October of that year. Despite the German and Japanese exceptions, it is clear that a general strengthening of capital standards occurred throughout the 1980s.

In the aftermath of the capital accord, there is evidence that adherence to the rules has occurred, and that this has involved substantial costs. At the time that the accord was issued the Basle Committee (BSC, 1988a:4) noted that it would "require substantial changes in national regulations." Costs include those for supervisors to alter regulations, those related to the collection of new data and those imposed on the banks under their control. By 1990 the accord had been "widely carried through into national systems" (Price Waterhouse, 1991) and was in force in most of the main financial centres (BSC, 1990; Price Waterhouse, 1991). In September 1992, as the deadline neared, the Basle Committee noted that "the capital agreement has now been fully incorporated within the supervisory framework of all member countries.... Virtually all countries outside the membership of the Basle Committee with international banks of significant size have introduced, or are in the process of introducing, arrangements based on the capital agreement" (BSC, 1992:20–1). The EC's Own Funds and Solvency Directives are particularly important since they build the Basle capital standards into a legally binding framework for all EC members. Although differences in implementation persist these do not weaken the accord because they are relatively insignificant and because in some cases they involve more stringent application of the standards than was called for by the accord.

Implementation of the accord involved substantial costs for the banks. An extensive survey by Price Waterhouse (1991) found that about half of banks surveyed needed to raise new capital or make changes to their asset portfolio. Costs were higher than expected due to the deteriorating economic climate (Alexander, 1990:18).

One indication of the strength of the capital accord is the degree to which it has modified the social institutions within the market. Measuring the strength of banks based on their capital adequacy rather than the size of their assets is becoming increasingly the norm.

Banks "generally have been spurred to make important modifications to their internal control and management information systems in order to monitor their businesses more effectively from the point of view of risk management and efficient allocation of capital" (Price Waterhouse, 1991:4) and the long-run impact on bank management and organizational structure is likely to be profound (see for instance articles in *The Bankers Magazine*, including Jewett, Shelton, Lelogeais and Wee, 1989:10; Humphrey and Humphrey, 1988). The *Banker's* annual listing of the world's top banks used capital rather than assets as the criterion beginning with their July 1989 report. Banks themselves are increasingly publishing their risk-based capital ratios (Price Waterhouse, 1991:11). Rating agencies have begun using capital adequacy in assessing the strength of banks (Cooper, n.d.). The overall impact of these changes is to alter the notion that banks should stress asset growth rather than profits (IMF, 1991b:37–8).

An indication of the strength of the capital accord is continued compliance with it, despite its perceived contribution to what has been termed the "global capital crunch" (on the "crunch" see "On the World Agenda," 1991:15; and Bank of England, 1991:259). The impact on Japanese banks, which had been the central mechanism by which Japanese excess savings had been exported abroad, is particularly important. In such circumstances pressures to defect from the capital agreement increase. While regulators have considered weakening their application of the capital accord in response to these pressures (for example "Thoroughly Modern," 1991:95–6), these moves have not yet involved a violation of the agreement itself, nor do the regulators appear to be inclined to violate the accord. Indeed according to the IMF (1991b:11) the overall trend among regulators has been to strengthen rather than weaken supervision in response to the capital crunch.

In sum, there is evidence of substantial compliance with the major agreements of the Basle Committee – the Concordats and the capital accord of July 1988 – despite the increased costs attached to compliance with the regime as each agreement came into effect. I now turn to an assessment of the indicators of institutionalization to supplement this analysis of strength based on compliance.

Specificity

Specificity refers to the degree to which actor expectations are clearly specified in the form of rules. The specificity of agreements is related to compliance as an indicator since it is generally more difficult to comply with more specific agreements. The major agreements of the Committee, the Concordat with its modifications and the capital agreement, represent a progressively increasing degree of specificity. The 1983 revision of the Concordat clarified the responsibilities of home and host supervisors, strengthened the language of the injunctions, introduced some enforcement measures and specified guidelines for holding companies for the first time. The 1990 and 1992 modifications further spelled out what was expected of bank supervisors. The 1988 capital agreement is far more detailed than either of the previous two major agreements. Very specific guidelines concerning the measurement of capital, the weighting of risks, the treatment of off-balance sheet items and the implementation of the agreement were all included. Since the 1988 accord further work has clarified ambiguity concerning loan loss reserves (BSC, 1992:19) and has begun to address areas not previously covered under the accord such as interest rate risk.

Despite this increasing degree of specificity, the capital agreement remained quite broad-brush. Complaints have been made, for instance, that assigning all commercial loans a 100 per cent risk weight ignores differences between companies' creditworthiness. While work is continuing on addressing important types of risk that are not covered by the accord this work is not complete. Given the great variety of national regulatory regimes it is not surprising that broad-brush rules would have been adopted. When supplemented with detailed implementation nationally, as has occurred with the capital accord, this is not necessarily a weakness. On the other hand, while not negating the evidence of increasing specificity over time in the banking regime, the continuing ambiguity or silence of the accord on certain important issues does indicate that significant weaknesses remain.

Learning

As noted in Chapter 2, Haas defines learning as "the process by which consensual knowledge is used to specify causal relationships in new ways so that the result affects the content of public policy." Objectives are interconnected and expanding. Decision-making style is analytical rather than eclectic or pragmatic as new problems are integrated into existing frameworks.

The Basle Committee has exhibited a remarkable degree of learning. Its major agreements and related reports reveal a logical progression in response to changes in the regime's environment, and in response to the generation of new consensual knowledge. Proactive initiatives integrated into a common set of goals characterize the Committee's work, rather than eclectic initiatives that are influenced by fragmented bodies of knowledge. For instance, despite the seriousness of the debt crisis the Committee did not get distracted from its central tasks, but rather integrated the problem by analyzing country risk as one aspect of prudential supervision.

There are a number of other interrelated indications of learning. First, the Committee has been able to correct its own errors and omissions, as in the shift towards home responsibility in the 1983 Concordat. Second, it has created ongoing mechanisms to deal with questions that emerge as a result of industry innovation. Third, participants have commented on the degree to which they have learned from each other. Fourth, new concepts such as incorporating off-balance-sheet items into risk weights have been proposed, tested and adopted, producing consensual knowledge where none existed previously. Fifth, the gathering of data has been modified as a result of the Committee's work, altering perceptions of reality. One example is the initiation by the BIS of figures on the global operations of multinational banks following the adoption of consolidated supervision as a principle. A second example is the reranking of banks by capital rather than assets in *The Banker*'s league tables.

Autonomy

Autonomy refers to the extent to which an institution can alter its own rules rather than relying on outside agents to do so. The existence of leadership socialization and recruitment mechanisms that reduce rapid turnover at the core of the system is an indication of autonomy.

The Basle Committee exhibits indications of a high degree of autonomy in its ability to insulate itself from external pressures such as industry lobbyists, politicians in the Group of Ten countries, and supervisors outside the Group of Ten. To some extent this reflects the ability of central banks domestically to insulate themselves from political pressures. At the same time, a number of the institutional features of the Basle Committee, including its secrecy, its exclusion of all outsiders from its meetings, and its sharp differentiation between members and non-members in its practice, all enhance its autonomy. The Committee's esprit de corps is an indication of a high degree of peer socialization.

On the other hand, the autonomy of the Basle Committee members from their national regulatory agencies is more constrained. Committee members are appointed by these agencies and are answerable to their superiors when they return home. Furthermore, the Basle Committee is ultimately responsible to the Group of Ten Central Bank Governors. At the same time many of the factors identified by Keohane and Nye (1977) and others regarding the ability of bureaucrats to develop increasing loyalty to their opposite numbers in other countries relative to their loyalty to their own state are present in the banking regime. Five factors are particularly relevant: (1) the meetings of the Basle Committee do not involve the Governors themselves; (2) the meetings are regular; (3) the meetings are in a location remote from the participants' home agencies; (4) the Committee can draw on a secretariat independent of individual home agencies; (5) the subject-matter of meetings is highly specialized information about bank regulation and may be too technical for central bank governors, whose main concern is monetary policy, to monitor in any detail. These factors all encourage the development of loyalties of Basle Committee members to the Basle process as opposed to their superiors back home. While it is not possible to obtain the information necessary to make a precise assessment of the degree of autonomy of the Committee from the Group of Ten Governors, accounts of the Committee's work indicate that the Group of Ten Governors have been limited to endorsing and encouraging the work of the Committee at key points, rather than controlling the process as it develops.

As indicated previously, the major failure of the Basle Committee to alter its own rules is represented by the bilateral US–UK capital-adequacy proposal. Once concluded, however, this bilateral agreement did not supplant the Committee. Instead the US and the UK returned to the Committee and finished negotiating the capital agreement. Monitoring and further implementation of the capital agreement has been carried out within the regime.

Conclusion: A Strengthening Banking Regime

Looking at the above indicators overall, there is significant evidence of a strengthening of the regime over the life of the Basle Committee. Each agreement has become more specific and more difficult to implement, and yet compliance has been widespread. In contrast to many international agreements, contrary interpretations of what constitutes compliance have not been a serious problem, in large part because the Basle Committee has set up mechanisms to continue developing and interpreting its agreements. The evolution of the Basle Committee's work also displays evidence of learning, including the creation of new consensual knowledge and the integration of new problems into a coherent policy trajectory. Autonomy, the ability of an institution to change its own rules, is the measure upon which the Basle Committee's performance is most mixed. On the one hand the Committee is remarkably well-protected from influence by politicians and lobbyists by its tight control over information and its exclusion of outsiders from its deliberations. Furthermore the most powerful state in this issue area relied on the Committee's work to an important degree. It will become apparent in Chapter 4 that the securities regime is quite different in this respect. On the other hand the temporary defection of the US and the UK in 1987 revealed the limits to the Committee's ability to transform its rules. While the defectors returned to the Basle process fairly quickly, it was the individual power of key states and not the multilateral process that was operative in the interim.

INTERNATIONAL BANKING AS AN INDUSTRY

It is now time to turn to an analysis of the structure of the industry which the banking regime seeks to regulate. As discussed in Chapter 2, the overall goal of this book is to analyze the relationship between interstate regimes and industry structures. If the hypothesis developed in Chapter 2 is correct then the strengthening of the interstate banking regime discussed above should be associated with an intensification of atomistic competition and a decay of private regimes in the international banking industry. As will become apparent below this is indeed the case. This section starts with the most quantitative evidence, such as concentration ratios. It then moves to more qualitative analysis of the intensity of competition, looking at factors such as pressures from substitute products. Finally, a qualitative analysis of the nature of private social institutions in each market is carried out.

Rivalry among Existing Firms

As discussed in Chapter 2, the following measures can be used to assess the degree of rivalry among international banks: concentration ratios, margins on international loans, profitability and territorial centralization.

Concentration Ratios

For commercial banks international market share can be assessed by the measuring the share of total world assets held by a specific number of the largest banks. These can be calculated from *The Banker*'s list of the world's largest banks, which are available from 1968. Although *The Banker* list is not restricted to international banking, the upper sections of this list can be used as a proxy, since, as *The Banker* ("International Banking Takes its Toll," 1984:107) comments, international banking is an area "which was pioneered by the bigger banks and which is still dominated by them."

Figure 3.3 presents concentration ratios for the top ten banks' share of total assets of the top 100 banks in *The Banker*'s list. Concentration dropped from just under 26 per cent in 1968 to just under 22 per cent in

Figure 3.3 International bank concentration (top ten share of assets of top 100 banks, 1968–90)

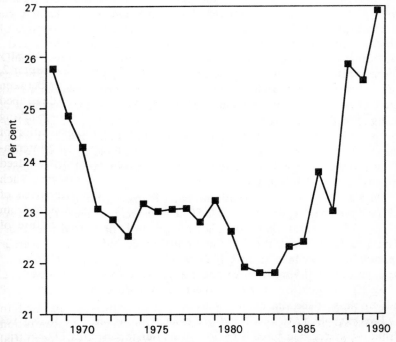

Sources: *The Banker*, various issues; *Moody's*; *Institutional Investor*.

1983. After 1983 concentration ratios began climbing, reaching just under 27 per cent in 1990.

This fits quite closely with the expected pattern. Declining concentration ratios in the period up to 1983 are an indication that the industry was becoming less oligopolistic – that the intensity of atomistic competition was increasing. It was during this period that the banking regime was being constructed and strengthened. Initial joint efforts of regulators to raise capital ratios began in the early 1980s and gathered steam as the decade progressed, culminating in the establishment and implementation of July 1988 agreement. After 1983 concentration ratios reversed their decline, increasing dramatically between 1985 and 1990. In short, this data on concentration ratios supports the hypothesis developed in Chapter 2.

Spreads on International Loans

Information on spreads on international loans is a useful measure of the intensity of competition, although this measure must be treated with caution. The spread between the cost of funds to banks and the interest rate that they can charge for loans is an important source of profits. Competitive pressures can be expected to reduce these spreads. One must be cautious in interpreting data on spreads, however, since spreads also reflect the riskiness of loans (Sarver, 1988:254). Spreads can increase as profitability declines and competition increases if risks are increasing and borrowers are defaulting. Another disadvantage of using spreads to assess profitability (Group of Thirty, 1982:28) is that large banks can access funds more cheaply than small banks, and that they can rely on sources of fee income not available to small banks. Thus profits of large banks may be imperfectly correlated with average spreads across the industry.

Data on spreads on international bank loans beginning in the early 1970s have been reported in the OECD's *Financial Market Trends*. As Figure 3.4 indicates, these spreads have generally decreased over time. The data from which the table was constructed indicate that average spreads have declined from a high of 149 basis points in 1976 to 52 basis points in 1990. Moreover, according to *Euromoney* (Darbyshire, 1991:34) margins for prime borrowers were reduced to as little as 10 basis points at the end of the 1980s.

Two exceptions to this trend are evident, however. The first is the dramatic increase in spreads to borrowers outside the OECD countries during the first half of the 1980s. The second is the increase in spreads

Figure 3.4   Spreads in international loan markets (in basis points)

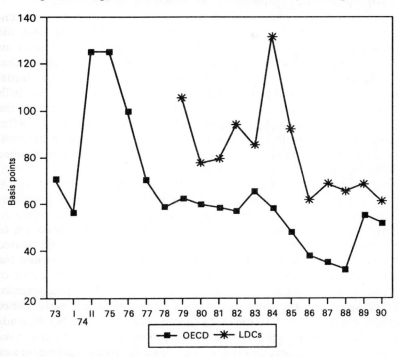

Source: OECD, *Financial Market Trends*, various issues.

to borrowers in OECD countries between the first and second halves of 1974.

The increase in spreads to non-OECD borrowers in the early 1980s can be attributed to greater perceptions of risk among bankers for such loans as a result of the LDC debt crisis, particularly following 1982 announcements by Mexico (August) and Brazil (December) that they were unable to make scheduled debt repayments (Sarver, 1988:264). Spreads to borrowers in OECD countries only increased moderately at this time. Thus increased spreads at this time were an indication of increased risk rather than decreasing competitiveness.

The increase in spreads to OECD borrowers in 1974 can similarly be attributed to perception of increased risk in the wake of the collapse of the Franklin and Herstatt banks in that year (Sarver, 1988:254). However, in this case, increased spreads may indicate a temporary respite from the tough competitive conditions that international banks were beginning to experience at the beginning of the 1970s. In 1973 demand for bank credits increased for a number of reasons, including increased demand for trade credits as a result of an acceleration of world trade, for dollars for speculation and hedging as the Bretton Woods monetary regime collapsed, and for loans to LDCs (Bank for International Settlements, *Annual Report*, 1974:160). This increased demand enhanced the power of banks in relation to their "buyers." LDC loans, which the BIS conservatively estimated as having doubled from $11 billion to $22 billion between 1972 and 1973, were particularly important in this respect, bearing "considerable fruit for the Eurobanks" (Bank for International Settlements, *Annual Report*, 1974:159). This increased demand at the time appeared to offer a solution to the competitive pressures that had developed in previous years due to declining demand resulting from tightening of exchange controls (Bank for International Settlements, *Annual Report*, 1974:159), and due to the entry of new banks into the Euromarket. The positive effect on bank performance was to prove transitory, however. This conclusion is reinforced by the consistently downward trend in international bank profitability.

The data on spreads supports the hypothesis. Like concentration ratios, spreads generally declined during the 1970s and early 1980s when the banking regime was being constructed and strengthened. This is a further indication that competitive pressures were increasing at this time. As with concentration ratios this downward trend was reversed in the 1980s after coordinated action on capital adequacy standards began (average spreads, not displayed in Figure 3.4, increased each year between 1987 and 1990). The upturn in spreads is less pronounced, and later, than the upturn in concentration ratios, however. Reasons for this will be discussed in the next section when profitability is measured, since that indicator also differs from concentration ratios in not turning upwards in the mid-1980s. The difference in timing for spreads is not significant given the fact that the overall trend is as expected on the basis of the hypothesis.

International Bank Profitability

Two separate measures of profitability are available: return on assets and return on shareholders' equity. As is evident in Figure 3.5 pretax profits on assets as calculated by *The Banker* have declined dramatically since 1970. The overall trend for profits on equity is more

Figure 3.5 International bank profitability

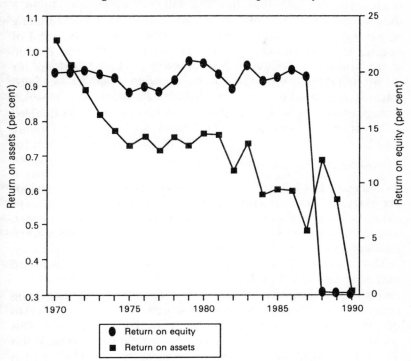

Source: *The Banker, Institutional Investor,* various issues.

complex. Between 1970 and 1987 this rose slightly but then dropped sharply in 1988. These patterns reflect the strategy pursued by banks during this period: rapidly expanding assets such as loans in order to make up for declining rates of returns on those assets as a result of intensifying competitive pressures. This rapid expansion of assets allowed banks to preserve the level of returns to shareholders that otherwise would have declined. This strategy was brought to an abrupt halt in 1988 as banks were forced to restrict asset growth and increase equity as a result of the 1988 Basle Accord. These patterns support the hypothesis in two ways. First, declining returns on assets indicate that competitive pressures were intensifying during the period in which the interstate regime was being constructed. Second, the severe drop in return on equity after the capital adequacy agreement of 1988 contradicts the view that the interstate regime was reflecting the interests of a powerful private regime. Any private banking regime would have as a central goal the preservation of returns on shareholders' equity since this represents the income received by the owners of the banks as a result of their investments. The story told by Figure 3.5 fits quite closely the hypothesis developed in Chapter 2: at a time of intensifying competitive pressures an interstate regime was created and strengthened in order to produce stability and order, even at considerable cost to the owners of the firms involved.

Territorial and National Centralization

As discussed in Chapter 2, both territorial and national centralization are likely to make the creation and reproduction of private regimes easier because of shared cultural experiences or regulatory contexts. Two data series on the international activities of banks are helpful in measuring these types of centralization.

The first is a BIS series which treats all activity originating from a particular territory as belonging to that territory, irrespective of the nationality of ownership of the banks. Thus international loans from subsidiaries of US banks located in London would be counted as part of the UK's share of international bank assets. This has been a traditional BIS method of categorizing international banking activity. Territorial centralization is likely to enhance the formation of private regimes independently of the degree of concentration by nationality of ownership because common sets of norms and rules can become embedded in a specific location.

Figure 3.6 displays trends in territorial centralization for the countries represented on the Basle Committee as measured by assets (such as loans). Europe's traditional dominance as symbolized by the term "Eurocurrency markets" is clearly evident. In 1973, for instance, more than 30 per cent of G-10 international banking was conducted from the UK, and over 50 per cent from other European members of the Group of Ten, for a total of over 80 per cent. Until 1984 the share of these European countries was in fairly consistent decline. The initial challenge came from US locations. This US challenge peaked in 1984. After 1984 the emerging challenge to European dominance was arising from Japanese locations. After 1988, however, this Japanese challenge eased off, with the continental European locations regaining some of their lost market share. These trends are consistent with the hypothesis

Figure 3.6 Market share by territory (share of Group of Ten assets)

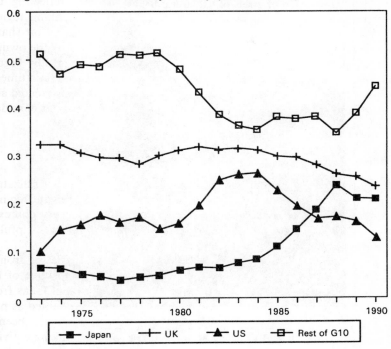

Note: The Group of Ten here includes Luxembourg.

Sources: Bank for International Settlements, *International Banking and Financial Market Developments*, various issues.

since there is a dispersion of international banking activity from traditional European locations over the period in which the interstate banking regime was being constructed and strengthened.[16]

The second series is based on the top ten international banks as listed in an annual listing of the top banks produced by *The Banker* and focuses on the distribution of the nationality of ownership among these top ten banks. Focusing on the top ten firms is useful because these firms are likely to be particularly important in shaping industry practices.

Figure 3.7 focuses on the top ten banks in *The Banker*'s annual listing. The first step in constructing this figure was to calculate the

Figure 3.7   Market share – top ten banks (share by nationality of bank ownership of assets of ten largest banks)

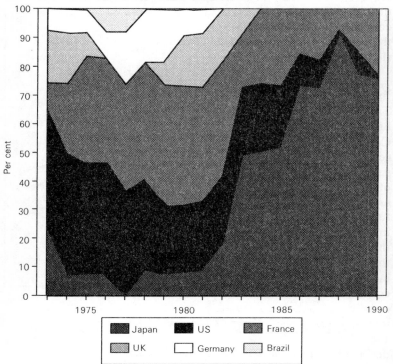

Note: The universe (denominator) is the total of the assets of the top ten banks appearing in *The Banker*'s annual listing.

Source: *The Banker*, various issues.

total assets of the top ten banks for each year. A share for each country appearing in the top ten was then calculated by adding the assets of all the banks with head offices located in that country and dividing this figure by the total assets of all top ten banks.

The most important feature of Figure 3.7 is the dramatic rise to dominance of the top ten by Japanese banks. This trend lasted to 1988 and then was reversed. Based on these figures alone, one might suspect that the market became highly concentrated at the end of the 1980s in the hands of Japanese banks. From the point of view of the ability of social institutions to be reproduced, however, it is not just concentration of nationality of ownership at particular points in time, but the continuity of this concentration that is important. On this dimension, the upheaval represented by the Japanese ascendancy is likely to have sharpened competition and made a private "regime" less viable.

Quantitative Analysis of Banking: Conclusion

Taken as a whole, the quantitative data indicates that international banking was becoming more competitive during the 1970s and 1980s. Concentration ratios, loan spreads, profits, and territorial and national centralization all declined in this period. This analysis therefore supports the argument developed in Chapter 2, that a strengthening of interstate regimes and an intensification of atomistic competition are associated. Other less complete statistics on international banking further support this conclusion. The Group of Thirty's 1982 report on international banking noted that the number of lending institutions in the syndicated loan market had increased ten-fold since 1972, and that the proportion headquartered outside Europe or North America had increased from one-eighth to one-third (Group of Thirty, 1982:28). In contrast to the picture that is sometimes painted of banks as constituting an omnipotent cohesive international ruling class which increased in power over this time period (Fennema and van der Pijl, 1987), the overall picture presented by the above data is one of declining profits, loss of control by the largest banks and dispersal of activity from traditional locations.

Qualitative Analysis

In this chapter qualitative analysis of the relationship between industry structure and the institutionalization of the regulatory regime has two distinct goals. The first is to supplement the quantitative statistics in clarifying the intensity of competition in the industry over time. The second is to look for evidence of intraindustry cooperation – a "private" regime – that is decaying as a result of this competition.

Qualititative Analysis of Competition

The quantitative statistics cited above, while useful, miss some other important indications of competition in international banking. First, they do not capture the degree of difficulty experienced by banks in retaining technological rents in these markets. Second, they do not directly address competitive pressures resulting from the threat of new entrants and substitutes and the bargaining power of suppliers and buyers, four factors identified by Michael Porter as contributing to competitiveness. Third, they do not indicate the perceptions of participants in the industry of the degree of competitive pressures. Such perceptions are important in explaining the impact of industry structure on regime institutionalization in a non-functionalist way. I will address each of these omissions in turn.

Pressures on technological rents   As noted in Chapter 2, technological innovation can be a weapon with which firms can counter competitive pressures. If the advantages of such innovation are rapidly dissipated, however, technological innovation can produce more aggressive competition. The high fixed costs of new technology can be a source of vulnerability and therefore lead to aggressive behaviour when those costs are not offset by higher revenues resulting from competitive advantages.

While it is difficult to quantify the competitive pressures associated with rapid dissipation of technological advantages, it does appear that such pressures did contribute to the increasing intensity of competition in international banking. Rapid technological innovation is generally associated with this industry over the past two decades. Important examples include the creation of new financial instruments and the computerization of "back-office" operations. There are a number of indications, however, that the costs of this technological innovation were not adequately offset by revenues.

A study carried out for the Group of Ten noted that many new instruments appeared to be underpriced, which may be in part due to "intense competitive pressures as individual institutions struggle to hold market share in changing markets" (Group of Ten, 1986:3). Three factors specific to the financial sector may have exacerbated the tendency to underpricing. First, new financial instruments are not generally patented (Group of Ten, 1986:200). Thus new products are quickly imitated and prices driven down before the risks involved are adequately assessed, and before the firm initiating the innovation has recouped development costs. Second, the increased computerization of the industry seems to have reduced barriers to entry rather than increasing them, perhaps because the knowledge involved in financial innovation, such as new mathematical formulas to estimate risk, is not embedded in any particular computer technology. Third, pricing is based on difficult predictions about future macroeconomic performance (Group of Ten, 1986:199–203). Furthermore, there does not seem to have been improvement over time: as the Group of Ten Report comments, "innovation has certainly not improved capacity to predict the longer-term future" (Group of Ten, 1986:202).

Although *mis*pricing may result to some extent from market failure related to imperfect information, an overall tendency to *under*pricing is only likely to occur in response to intense competitive pressures. Based on the information presented in the Group of Ten study one can therefore conclude that innovation was not successful in reducing competitive pressures, but rather has exacerbated them.

Accounts of particular new financial innovations further support the view that technological advantages are quickly dissipated in international banking. Loan syndication, which the Bank for International Settlements 1974 *Annual Report* (1974:159) called a "highly effective" new technique because of its ability to "remove virtually all limitations on the size of loans which could be handled by the market," allowing banks to satisfy new demands for credit from states, has subsequently led to massive underpricing in the sense referred to by the Group of Ten report.

The Group of Ten report offers a useful source of information on the new financial instruments developed during the 1980s. The report divides these into four: note-issuance facilities (NIFs):[17] swaps (interest rate and currency), options (foreign currency and interest rate) and forward rate agreements. Each of these instruments exhibited signs of maturity by the time of writing of the report in 1985.

The evolution of the market for interest-rate and currency swaps is illustrative. Trading in these instruments grew to a level at which an international market could be said to exist in 1981 or 1982 (Group of Ten, 1986:41). The value of the interest-rate swap market was estimated to have further grown to $100 billion by mid-1985 (Group of Ten, 1986:41–3) and $2 trillion by the end of 1989.[18] The range of fees for swap transactions declined from 50–75 basis points in 1982 to 12.5–25 basis points in 1984 and 1985 (Group of Ten, 1986: 41–3), and as low as 6–10 basis points by 1987 (Cooper, 1987:9; Price, 1987:79). Maturation is also evident in the replacing of bank hierarchies with arms-length transactions in these instruments. A wholesale market in swaps has developed, promoted by investment banks which aimed to make swaps tradable commodities. This interdealer market increased from 40 per cent of the market to 55 per cent of the market in 1984. The most standardized swaps are available for a bid/offer spread of 10–15 basis points (Group of Ten, 1986: 46). A 1990 analysis by *Euromoney* (Brady, 1990a:77) notes that the maturation of the swaps and options market has continued:

> Competition in the derivatives market is hotting up. Swaps and options have become commodities, the pace of innovation has slowed dramatically, and the market leaders are finding it increasingly difficult to differentiate themselves from each other.

Pressures from substitutes, new entrants, suppliers and buyers   As noted above, competitive pressures, in addition to rivalry among existing firms, can arise from the threat of substitutes and new entrants, and the bargaining power of suppliers and buyers. In international banking these pressures are evident in the process of securitization and in the institutionalization of the investment process.

Securitization refers to the replacing of the intermediating activity of banks with marketable securities. The bundling of mortgages into mortgage-backed securities and the shift by corporations away from bank loans as a source of finance to directly accessing capital markets through the issuance of bonds are two examples.

Securitization directly challenges the traditional raison d'être of banks. As the literature on imperfect information in banking makes clear, the hierarchical corporate structure of banks allows them to monitor closely the ongoing creditworthiness of borrowers in a way that is not possible in competitive markets where investors are dispersed.

There are three reasons generally given for securitization. First, the credit ratings of major corporations were higher than banks in the wake of the debt crisis, allowing them to access capital markets more cheaply than banks. Second, technological development has made information on borrowers widely available. Third, increasing volatility of interest rates has put pressure on banks to introduce more flexibility on the asset side of their balance sheets, a task which securitization of loans makes possible.

The process of securitization reflects and further increases the pressures on banks stemming from the four sources that are the focus of this section. Securitization is a threat from substitute products, which also involves the threat of new entrants. Securities firms and investment banks, which have traditionally specialized in marketable securities, are one set of new entrant. Corporate finance departments, which have begun carrying out many of the analytical functions previously the preserve of banks, are another.[19] The power of investors and borrowers is increased relative to banks because of the increased ease with which both can participate directly in capital markets.

The increased volatility of interest rates, while in part due to fiscal and monetary policies, also results from the deregulation of interest rates in country after country; a change which has increased the power of "sellers" relative to banks. Previously banks had a large source of cheap funds from deposits with interest rate ceilings. As alternatives became available to depositors, including certificates of deposit, cash management accounts, Eurocurrency accounts and Eurobond markets, pressures on banks to offer competitive interest rates grew.

The institutionalization of investment has also reduced the power of banks in relation to investors. The growth of both pension funds and mutual funds represent the growth of institutions that pool investors' funds. These institutions provide a hierarchical structure that allows the fund managers to assess alternative investment vehicles and to exert pressure on the firms with which they place their funds.

The competitive impacts of securitization are evident in Figure 3.8, which indicates the dramatic shift from loans to securities in international markets. The response of multinational banks to this trend is evident in the declining share of income from lending – from 75 per cent of income in 1982 to 64 per cent in 1987 (Clarke, 1987:229).

Although it is possible that banks will be able to offset these pressures to some degree by such strategies as entering securities markets, there is little doubt that securitization involved major new competitive pressures on international banking during the 1980s and that most of this pressure is unlikely to disappear since it involves the erosion of the specialized advantages involved in bank intermediation. The balance of power is continuing to swing towards borrowers and away from banks.

Perceptions of participants Prevailing perceptions of the competitiveness of international banking, as reflected in the most important journals and fora concerned with international finance, further support the view that the industry became considerably more competitive during the 1970s and 1980s, that this was related to the maturation of banking technology, but that this began to change as the banking regime became more effective. The following quotes provide examples:

Figure 3.8   International financial market activity by market sectors (billions of US dollars)

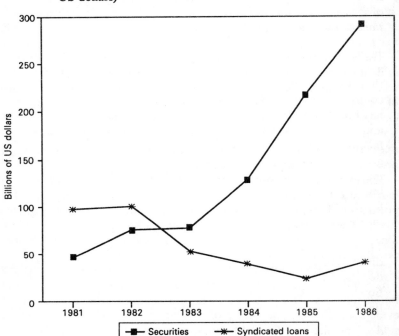

Source: Bank for International Settlements, *Annual Report*, 1987:108.

the new instruments and new markets threaten the profitability of banks' established business.... The new instruments, markets and flow of information have eroded spreads on some of the bank's traditional, and not-so-traditional, products. This is not uncommon in mature industries, where prices generally settle at a level which allows efficient producers to make reasonable, but unexciting profits, and inefficient producers go out of business (Dr. Andrew Bain, Group Economic Adviser, Midland Bank, 1987 Gilbert Lecture on Banking, published by The Chartered Institute of Bankers, 1987:32, 44).

The role of the international banks as an intermediary for large corporations has therefore largely disappeared. Where such corporations do borrow from the banks, the banks' profit margins are tiny, since lending money to a big corporation is a commodity which any of a large number of banks can easily provide (*Economist International Banking Survey*, [Hakim, 1984:57]).

Japanese banks came into this [off-balance sheet] market with aggressive pricing.... US banks tried to fight that trend but found that these products were ultimately viewed by the market as commodities; therefore they caved in on price. Consequently there has been a secular decline in the pricing of standby letters of credit and other commitments for perhaps the last decade. Many of these facilities are now priced at razor-thin levels ... banks don't earn a good return on equity in the most commoditized segment of the market. (James McCormick, president of First Manhattan Consulting Group, consultant to top banks, in response to this question from *The Bankers Magazine*: "Have banks been pricing their off-balance sheet commitments adequately?," 1988:7).

These new instruments have important consequences. They blur the distinctions between different segments of financial markets both domestically and internationally and they lead to increased competition.... An important part of the revolution is the "democratisation"[20] of financial markets, whereby oligopolistic market structures are replaced by competitive markets with relatively open access (Dr. Ian Cooper, Lecturer and Baring Research Fellow, London Business School, Introduction to the 1987 Gilbert Lecture on Banking, published by the Chartered Institute of Bankers, 1987:5, 27).

Competitive pressures in the market are expected to continue.... To the extent that capital requirements are effective, they should ultimately constrain expansion of lending when returns are inadequate (Group of Thirty [1982:29–30] referring to their survey of 111 commercial banks).

Many people think we have excess capacity in [the financial services industry] and that it is becoming a commodities industry. Let me compare the financial services industry to another commodities industry, the auto tire industry.... We have the same problem of overcapacity in this industry: insufficient assets for the existing number of institutions (Richard F. Syron, Morin Banking Center panel: see "Regulatory Strategies to Meet the Challenges of the Nineties," 1990:402).

Why have the world's banks juggled their way from one loss-making mess to the next – from third-world debt through leveraged buy-outs to the property bust? The reason ... is that they have lost their old advantages and skills in international lending, and the old benefits of working within government-blessed cartels. Bankers' prospects are grey (*Economist*, "Banks in Trouble," 1990a:21).

The market has been transformed by the [new capital] rules.... Customers used to laugh when we preached the gospel of profitability. Now they realize we are serious (Alan Moore, Director of Corporate Banking and Treasury, Lloyd's Bank, cited in Fairlamb, *Institutional Investor*, 1991:29).

The "Private" Regime

Given the increased intensity of competition in the international banking industry during the 1970s and 1980s, it is highly likely that intraindustry institutional arrangements for organizing international transactions became increasingly difficult to sustain; that a "private" regime eroded over this period. In order to confirm that this is the case, it is useful to look for changes in social institutions that organize international banking transactions.

In 1970, as the *Economist* (Hakim, 1984:S6) notes, "only a handful of British and French colonial banks and large American banks boasted international networks." Since then the social institutions that organize the market have undergone substantial change. There are two visible indications of these social institutions which will be addressed in turn: loan syndicates and intraindustry associations.[21]

Loan syndicates   The loan syndicate, which brings together sets of banks to participate in loans too large for any single bank to handle, is an important private source of institutional cooperation. An examination of the impact of these syndicates on the competitiveness of the industry is important in determining whether a private regime was decaying during the period being studied.

There are two indications that syndicates have not provided the type of social institution that would be needed for the most important banks to reestablish control over the market and increase their profitability. The first is the impact of the debt crisis on syndicates. The second is in the ability of new entrants, even in the area of new financial instruments, to use syndicates to gain entry to the market.

With the debt crisis there has been a shift in the goals of syndicates from arranging new credits to arranging rescheduling of existing debt. The institutional structure of these arrangements is quite hierarchical. A rescheduling can include as many as 500 banks, but negotiations are carried out by a steering committee made up of a small number of lead banks (Group of Thirty, 1982:13). Despite this structure, pressures eroding syndicate discipline are strong as each bank has an incentive to cheat by reducing its exposure immediately and individually, even if the interests of the syndicate as a whole are to impose a coordinated and orderly rescheduling on the borrowing country. Regulatory differences, including capital standards, contributed to conflicts within syndicates along national lines (Group of Thirty, 1982:13). Such problems led the International Banking Study Group of the Group of Thirty to comment in 1982 that most of its members "see a need for banks collectively to be better organized to handle their role in rescheduling more effectively" (Group of Thirty, 1982:15).

Note issuance facilities (NIF) began to involve syndicate-like techniques as the market grew in the 1980s (Group of Ten, 1986:20). In 1983 the institution of the "tender panel" was created for the distribution of NIFs. This was a group of underwriters who would bid for notes, which they would then place. The concept was extended in 1984 to involve "continuous tender panels", which allow the members to bid for notes at any time during the offering period. The two reasons for the adoption of this innovation indicate that it represents an erosion of the control of lead managers over the process. First, this innovation improved the terms for the borrower. Second, underwriters obtained improved access to the notes relative to managers.

In contrast to the Eurobond market, which will be discussed in the next chapter, there is no indication that the commercial banks have been able to use their syndicates to reverse the increasingly competitive conditions that they face. By the end of the 1980s in the Eurocommercial paper market, characterized by over-capacity and lack of profitability, only vague expressions of support for establishing a different syndication method were evident[22] – such a syndication method had already been put into place by the major firms in the Eurobond market, creating complaints by other firms that a cartel had been created and creating strong optimism among the main firms about the future of the market. In the syndicated loan market, an August 1991 report by *Euromoney* (Darbyshire, 1991:34) indicates that the market was characterized by pessimism, with the balance of power swinging towards the borrowers. This shift in power away from banks resulted in expectations that margins would be pushed downward. Moreover, according to one syndicator, the Japanese, revolting against being "stuffed" in syndicates by syndicate managers, intend increasingly to arrange their own deals.[23] Whether this is the reason or not, loan syndicates have been hurt by a significant drop in Japanese participation.[24]

Intraindustry associations The *Eurocurrency Handbook*, published by the New York Institute of Finance (Sarver, 1988:354–7) provides a directory of Euromarket institutions. The only likely candidate as evidence for the existence of a private regime is the Institute of International Finance (IIF) (Sarver, 1988:270–83). An organizing committee to set up the IIF was established in 1982. It involved 30 banks from Europe, Japan and North America. By January 1986 the Institute's membership included 182 banks and other financial organizations from 38 countries. It has a budget of $5 million and a staff of 35 (Sarver, 1988).

Despite its impressive membership size, the work of the IIF is quite narrowly focused on a single issue of concern to international banks – improving bank responses to, and assessments of, risks involved in lending to sovereign borrowers. Its articles of incorporation state that its primary objectives are

> to improve the timeliness and quality of information available on sovereign borrowers, to encourage communication among the major participants involved in the international lending process (governments and multilateral organizations and private lending institutions), and to foster a greater understanding within the financial community of the future of international lending (Sarver, 1988:270).

Its major products are country reports, a country database, and reports of special committees on other aspects of the relationship between banks and sovereign borrowers. By October 1991 the Task Force on the Regulatory, Accounting and Tax Treatment of Cross-Border Lending, involving two IIF staff members, had been made responsible for the issue of capital adequacy but had done very little on this central regulatory concern. More than three years after the publication of the Basle capital adequacy agreement, the IIF was still studying the accord and had issued no public statements concerning capital adequacy.[25] Finally, in September 1992 the IIF announced that it would become more active in mediating between large international banks and the Basle Committee (Acworth, 1992:6).

The IIF's impact on competitive conditions in international banking, therefore, has primarily been through the increased power it gives banks in relationship to "buyers." This impact is similar to that of the IMF in organizing relations between banks and sovereign borrowers. The IIF has, however, little ability to restrain competition by imposing rules on its member banks.[26]

Conclusion: Qualitative Measures of Competition in International Banking

Several points emerge from the above qualitative analysis of international banking which reinforce the conclusions that emerged from analysis of concentration ratios, profitability and spreads. First, technology is not protecting the top firms from competitive pressures. Technological rents are rapidly dissipated as new products are imitated and commoditized. Indeed technological developments are undermining the core expertise of the banks, providing suppliers and buyers with new leverage and substitute products. Second, the private social institutions that exist in the international banking industry are weak and ineffective. Loan syndicates have not been designed to exercise discipline over the industry and have even enhanced the power of new entrants. The banks' most important private organization, the IIF, has been fighting a rearguard battle against debtors and has done little to provide a private source of regulation for international banks.

CONCLUSION: INTERNATIONAL BANKING

The first section of this chapter demonstrated that the regime for international banking has displayed increasing strength since the creation of the Basle Committee on Banking Supervision in 1974. This was apparent in the degree of compliance by states with the regime, in the increasing specificity of the Committee's agreements, in the evidence of substantial learning and in the degree of autonomy of the regime with respect to state actors.

The overall picture for the industry which the interstate regime seeks to regulate is of an industry experiencing increasingly intense atomistic competition over this same period. No evidence of strong private social institutions was found. Thus the strengthening of the interstate regime was neither driven by nor associated with a strong private regime.

Some of indicators of intense competition, such as concentration ratios, began to reverse as capital adequacy standards began to be imposed by bank regulators. Because these were imposed at significant costs to the banks themselves in terms of the expensive new capital they needed to raise, and in terms of sharply declining returns on shareholders' equity, the picture is one of an interstate regime stepping in to organize an industry that had failed to organize itself.

In short, this analysis of international banking has supported the hypothesis developed in Chapter 2: the strengthening of this interstate regime was associated with increasingly atomistic competition and an absence or decay of a private regime, and not the reverse. The image of a few powerful banks controlling the industry and manipulating international institutions in their own interests is not an accurate one. International banking is instead characterized by the demise of old oligopolies, by the maturity of its basic technology and by a private sector that lacks organization. I turn now to the securities industry, where we will find a quite different picture. The significance of the conclusions from this chapter, along with those from Chapter 4, will be further developed in Chapter 5.

4 The Regime for Securities Regulation

In this chapter the relationship between the interstate regime for international securities centred on the International Organization of Securities Commissions and the structure of the international securities industry will be examined. Three major conclusions emerge from this chapter. First, this interstate regime has been strengthened to a degree that is surprising given the popular image of international securities markets as free and unregulated and the absence of these international institutions from the international relations literature.[1] Despite this strengthening the interstate securities regime is weaker than the banking regime. Second, like the banking industry, the securities industry has been characterized by increased levels of atomistic competition over the period in which the interstate regime has become stronger. However, unlike the banking industry, there is evidence of a relatively effective private regime in international securities markets, especially apparent in the strong sets of shared cultural norms of the Eurobond market and in the greater ability of bond syndicates to exercise discipline over markets than is the case in banking. Third, the securities industry therefore offers additional support for the argument, developed in Chapter 2, that the emergence and strengthening of an interstate regime is associated with increasing levels of atomistic competition in the corresponding international industry. This relationship is evident over time within the securities industry. It is also evident when comparing across the banking and securities industries: international banking has both a stronger interstate regime and a more atomised industry structure with greater competitive pressures than is the case for international securities.

The structure of the present chapter follows closely that of Chapter 3. As with the banking regime it is useful to first provide a brief overview of the process of globalization and of the basic features of the securities regime. A discussion of the structure and process of the regime will include a more detailed account of IOSCO's functioning, and will specifically address the role of the United States. This will be followed by an assessment of regime strength, using the same four indicators – compliance, specificity, learning and autonomy – that were used for the banking regime. These indicators will be compared not only over time, but also to the performance of the banking regime as analyzed in Chapter 3. The second part of the chapter, as in Chapter 3, involves quantitative and qualitative analysis of industry structure.

THE GLOBALIZATION OF SECURITIES MARKETS

Defining International Securities

A securities firm arranges direct financing between lenders and borrowers, in contrast to banks which intermediate between depositors and borrowers. A security can be defined as "any medium of investment in the money market or capital market" (Bannock and Manser, 1989:184). Like a bank loan, a security represents a contract between a creditor and a debtor involving a claim to a stream of future payments (Shearer, Chant and Bond, 1984:43). Unlike bank loans, however, securities are generally traded in markets.

Securities can be divided into two main types: bonds and equities. An equity, or share, can be defined as "one of a number of equal portions in the nominal capital of a company, entitling the owner to a proportion of the distributed profits and of residual value if the company goes into liquidation" (Bannock and Manser, 1989:185). A bond can be defined as "a contractual obligation of the borrower to make payments of interest and repayments of principle on borrowed funds at certain fixed times" (Fisher, 1984:13). The stream of payments to owners of equities therefore typically varies depending on the performance of the firm, while the stream of payments to owners of bonds is based on contractual obligations set out when the bond is issued. While bonds have generally been long term, short-term financial instruments that are otherwise similar to bonds, such as notes, can also be called bonds (Fisher, 1984:13).

Securities can be considered international if they are denominated in a currency other than that of the market in which they are sold, or if they are sold in a country other than the home of the issuer. A distinction has traditionally been made between "Eurobonds" and "foreign bonds." The distinction is summarized in Table 4.1. A similar distinction can be made for equities (Samuel, 1988–9:334).

Table 4.1   Eurobonds and foreign bonds

	Eurobonds	Foreign bonds
Underwriting syndicate is	International	Primarily from one country
Number of countries in which bond is sold	Many	One
Sold in countries where the currency is	Different than the bond's denomination	The same as the bond's denomination
Available in bearer form?	Always	Usually

Sources: Fisher (1984:13). For a more detailed breakdown see Benzie (1992:16).

Indicators of Globalization

The globalization of bond markets has preceded the globalization of equity markets. Foreign bonds have a long history. For instance, they were popular in the nineteenth century as an instrument through which European investors financed railway construction in the Americas, Russia and China, and industrial expansion in the United States (Fisher, 1984:15). Eurobonds are generally dated from a 1963 dollar-denominated issue for Autostrade. Autostrade operated Italian free-ways. Its Eurobond issue was underwritten by a European consortium and sold in Europe (Fisher, 1984:19). The Eurobond market developed in size and complexity throughout the 1960s and 1970s. In contrast, the Euroequity market has only started expanding rapidly in the 1980s.

The growth of the international bond market is evident in Figure 4.1. Total international bond issues increased from $3.2 billion in 1965 to $225.4 billion in 1986. This growth was substantially higher than growth in world output (international bonds as a percentage of world output grew roughly from 0.199 per cent in the mid-1960s to 1.29 per cent in the mid 1980s). Eurobonds, which are more international than foreign bonds, represented an increasingly large portion of international bond offerings. International bond markets also grew faster than domestic bond markets, as indicated by Figure 4.2.

The growth of the international equity market is evident in Figure 4.3 and Tables 4.2 and 4.3. Both the primary and secondary markets have grown over time, despite fluctuations, and appear to be recovering after the 1987 crash.

Figure 4.1 Relative growth of the international bond market (bond issues as share of world exports, world GDP, 1970–85)

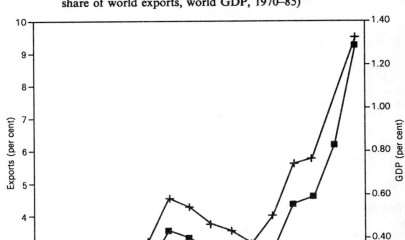

Source: IMF, 1988c:2–3; 1984b:2–3; United Nations, 1990:3; OECD, 1987:123–5; SEC, 1987:II–36.

There are a number of other indications of the globalization of securities markets that relate to changes in the institutional structure of markets. First is the linking of stock exchanges electronically. These include the link between the US National Association of Securities Dealers' Automated Quotation system (NASDAQ) market and the London market, NASDAQ and the Singapore market, the Singapore International Monetary Exchange and the Chicago Mercantile Exchange, the Sydney Futures Exchange and the Commodities Exchange of New York, the Boston Exchange and the Montreal Exchange, and the Toronto and American Stock Exchanges (Austin, 1987:225; Cox, 1987:200; Wall, 1989).

Figure 4.2 International bonds and G-5 domestic bond markets compared (international bond issues as a percentage of domestic G-5 bond issues)

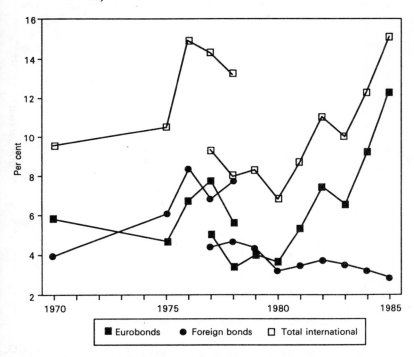

Note: For the G-5 domestic bond issue figures, the first series (1970–8) reflects net bond issues, and the second series reflects gross bond issues. Thus the two series are not directly comparable, since the denominator of the first series will be lower than the denominator of the second series, making the first series higher than if it too were based on gross issues. The first series is included, however, to indicate that the trends were similar in both periods. The figures for international bonds are gross figures.

Sources: OECD *Financial Statistics*, 13(1), 1979; OECD, 1987: 123–5; SEC, 1987:II–36.

Second is the increasing involvement of firms that trade securities in more than one market. For instance, in 1986 Merrill Lynch had more than 600 international account executives in 48 offices in 28 countries other than the US and Canada. Shearson Lehman/American Express

Figure 4.3   Gross cross-border flows of international equities (billions of US dollars)

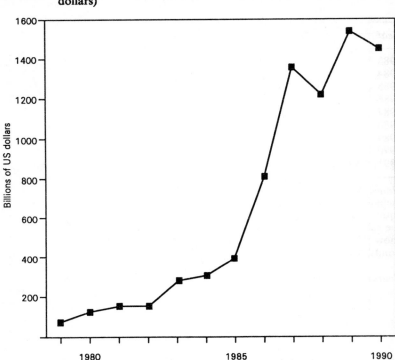

Source: Salomon Brothers International Limited (1990:9, 1991:28).

had 20 offices in 17 countries. All together US brokerage firms had more than 250 branches in 30 foreign countries, excluding Canada and Mexico.[2]

Third, equity markets have expanded in countries that have traditionally relied on other methods of mobilizing and allocating capital. In Japan corporations have shifted away from their traditional reliance on bank finance, with average debt-to-equity ratios of TSE-listed firms dropping from 2.75 in 1981 to 1.07 in 1991 (Emmott, 1991:S32). A similar shift occurred in France and Germany (Emmott, 1991:S41). This process is also evident in the spread of equity markets to Third-World and socialist economies. Stock exchanges have opened in the Soviet Union and China. As of 1988 there were 35 equity

Table 4.2   International equity offerings (billions of US dollars)

Year	Stock	Equity-related bonds	Total
1983	0.2	8.0	8.2
1984	1.2	10.9	12.1
1985	3.5	11.3	14.8
1986	11.8	26.9	38.7
1987	20.3	43.0	63.0
1988	8.5	34.1	42.6
1989	9.9	72.2	82.1
1990	15.1	24.0	39.1
1991, 1st half	14.6	23.0	37.6

Notes: Stock includes common and preferred shares. Equity-related bonds include convertibles and bonds with equity warrants. The dramatic decline in equity-related bonds in 1990 is due to the decline in the Japanese stock market, the major source of such securities. Figures for the first six months of 1991 show that recovery in international equity offerings, including equity related bonds, was under way.

Sources: Figures to 1987 are calculated from *Euromoney* and *Financial Market Trends* by SEC economists Chuppe *et al.* (1989:39). From 1988–9 the figures are from *Euromoney Annual Financing Report*, and the 1990 and 1991 figures are from Salomon Brothers International Limited 1991:21).

Table 4.3   International trading activity as a percent of total

Year	Cross-exchange	Cross-border	Total
1986	1.5	12.1	13.6
1987	4.5	11.9	16.3
1988	3.2	11.4	14.6
1989	4.7	13.0	17.7
1990	6.7	11.0	17.7

Note: Total share trading includes cross-exchange, cross-border and domestic trading. Cross-border are transactions on domestic markets in domestic shares for foreigners. Cross-exchange are transactions in foreign shares on domestic markets or specialist exchanges.

Source: Salomon Brothers International Limited (1991:28).

markets in developing countries with a capitalization of almost $360 billion, up from $67 billion five years previously (Sudweeks, 1989:70).[3]

Fourth is the increasing correlation of prices in equity markets, most evident in the global nature of the October 1987 crash. The mean correlation coefficient between US and nine other major equity markets increased from 0.35 in the 1975–9 period, to 0.43 in the 1980–4 period, to 0.62 in the 1985–8 period.[4]

Fifth is the modification of national securities regulation to facilitate global trading of securities. Since this involves the creation of new structures of global authority, it will be discussed more extensively below. These modifications range from removing barriers to the participation of foreign securities firms on domestic stock exchanges to the harmonization of regulations related to the issuing of new equity securities (OECD, 1990:20).

Reasons for Globalization

Many of the reasons for the globalization of banking apply as well to the globalization of securities markets. A general process of financial deepening, financial firms following corporate clients abroad, the use of private markets to finance balance of payments deficits in the post-Bretton Woods era, escaping domestic regulatory regimes, the desire of securities firms to profit from firm specific advantages, changes in computer and communications technology and the need for global corporations to overcome the constraints of small domestic financial markets have all have played a part in the globalization of securities markets.

There are additional reasons for the globalization of securities markets however. Some corporations seek to enhance global recognition through having their stock sold internationally. Privatization of very large state companies, particularly in Britain and France, has been an important stimulus to the globalization of equity markets since even these large markets would not have been able to absorb such large issues. The wave of corporate restructuring that has characterized the past decade has also stimulated global securities markets. Cross-border mergers and acquisitions grew from $39 billion in 1986 to $128 billion in 1990 (Salomon Brothers International Limited, 1991:15). Some analysts have seen the hierarchically organized multinational corporation as being replaced by more flexible forms of organization that rely on global securities markets.[5] Finally, the negative impact of the debt crisis on international banking has been a major stimulus to international securities markets as the credit ratings of many corporations became superior to those of banks and they could therefore raise capital more cheaply by going directly to capital markets. With the drying up of new bank loans to the Third World, securities markets have been touted by lending agencies as the solution to the debt crisis.

Despite the increasing globalization of securities markets, there are a number of factors which slow this process: differences in local regulations; the problem of clearance and settlement (for example ad hoc procedures for transferring stock certificates can make international trading more difficult and risky); the difficulty of preventing fraud internationally; and the potential for instability that results from an inadequate patchwork of international regulation. The single most serious setback for globalization, the 1987 market crash, highlighted the importance of many of these issues. Although the crisis was contained with the help of quick action by central bankers, the danger that failures in one market could potentially spread to other markets became clear.

In sum, the globalization of securities markets displays both similarities and differences to the globalization of banking. Like banking, and for many of the same reasons, the growth of international securities transactions has outpaced the growth of domestic markets. There are however, additional different reasons for, and obstacles to, the globalization of securities markets.

THE REGIME FOR GLOBAL SECURITIES

IOSCO's Main Features

As with banking, there are a number of international organizations and informal arrangements through which state regulators attempt to shape the global securities regime, including the International Organisation of Sercurities Commission (IOSCO), the European Community, the Group of Thirty, the Wilton Park Group, the International Society of Securities Administrators and the North American Securities Administrators Association Inc. (NASAA). None of IOSCO's competitors plays a comparable role in providing a global regime for regulating securities firms.[6]

IOSCO aims to be geographically comprehensive. As of 1991 there were 91 members, including state regulators, self regulatory agencies and international organizations from 60 countries (IOSCO, 1991b).

Although IOSCO began as an inter-American organization[7] it has moved quickly to overcome this limitation following its 1984 decision to become a global organization. It held its first annual meeting outside North America in Paris in 1986, and it admitted as members two key players from outside North America – Germany and Japan – in 1988.

IOSCO's Accomplishments

IOSCO aims to improve cooperation on the regulation of markets through information sharing, standard setting and enforcement. IOSCO's most important contribution is to the remarkable network of international agreements that has grown up to help securities regulators prevent international fraud. This section will show that IOSCO overstates its contribution and that much of this network has originated in US policies developed unilaterally at the domestic level. At the same time there are signs that the enforcement aspects of the regime organized around IOSCO are beginning to display an important degree of autonomy from IOSCO's member states, including the US. IOSCO's other work, while important, is more limited, either because it has not yet resulted in agreements, or because agreements are less integrated into a developing process. Two such projects, IOSCO's contribution to the multijurisdictional disclosure system and to capital standards, will be briefly analyzed here.

Enforcement and Information-sharing Agreements

The most important agreement arrived at through IOSCO is its Resolution on Reciprocal Assistance, adopted on 7 November 1986 in Rio and signed by 40 agencies from 35 countries as of 1991.[8] This "Rio Declaration," as summarized in IOSCO's 1990 Annual Report,

> calls upon members, to the extent permitted by law, to provide assistance on a reciprocal basis in the gathering of information related to market oversight and protection of investors against fraudulent securities transactions. Each signatory agency also designates a contact person who is responsible for the timely processing of all requests for assistance (IOSCO, 1990a:1).[9]

This resolution is important because of IOSCO's claim that it is "nothing short of the ancestor to almost all the Memoranda of Understanding in place today" (IOSCO, 1989a:1). The Memoranda of Understanding (MOUs) are a series of mostly bilateral agreements between securities administrators promoting cooperation in the enforcement of securities laws. In some cases these memoranda have necessitated changes in domestic regulations or laws to enable securities regulators to carry out their international commitments.[10] The Rio Declaration was supplemented by a 1989 Resolution on Cooperation, currently signed by 18 agencies from 16 countries, urging modification of domestic regulations or laws as needed to implement the Rio Declaration, as well as asking agencies to give consideration to the type of information they would want to exchange.[11]

As of September 1991 IOSCO had recorded 53 international agreements related to the surveillance of capital markets and enforcement of securities laws. These include the memoranda of understanding that have been signed in the wake of the Rio Declaration's call for greater cooperation between securities regulators in this issue area.

Two features of these agreements call into question IOSCO's claim to have played a major role in their development. First, a number of MOUs were signed between regulators in the most important securities markets before the Rio Declaration, including the agreements between the United States and Switzerland (1982), Ontario (1985), Canada (1985), Japan (23 May 1986), Cayman Islands (3 July 1986) and the United Kingdom (23 September 1986).[12] Second, and more importantly, the United States has been one of the partners in an overwhelming majority of the cooperative agreements and the MOU strategy can be traced to policies developed within the SEC for which IOSCO played a relatively unimportant role. In order to assess the significance of IOSCO's contribution to international enforcement I will first highlight the US role, and then turn to recent evidence of autonomy.

In the early 1980s the US SEC began to realize that its efforts to enforce securities regulations were becoming more difficult as a result of the globalization of these markets. It became increasingly apparent to the SEC that unilateral actions alone were inadequate for preventing fraud. For instance, some countries would not provide information to the SEC because they did not regard the activities in question as fraudulent. Denial of access to US securities markets can be ineffective, as for instance where the SEC is unable to determine the identity of those it wishes to prosecute, or where their subsequent activities do not take place in the US.[13]

The shortcomings of a unilateral approach were evident in the strong negative reaction in 1985 to a SEC "waiver by conduct" concept release (SEC, 1984; Greenstein, 1987).[14] The release suggested that purchase or sale of securities from abroad be taken as consent to the application of US laws regarding disclosure of information even where such disclosure is prohibited by the foreign country. US courts would have been able to rule on whether US law enforcement issues outweighed a foreign state's sovereignty interests. Most of the 65 comments received on the release were negative. In 1987 SEC Commissioner Charles Cox noted that "the SEC recognizes that this idea was poorly received and is committed to exploring different alternatives" (Cox, 1987:218).

Existing treaty arrangements for judicial cooperation were seen as inadequate because they are too general and inflexible for highly technical and rapidly evolving securities markets in which intense surveillance of legal activities is needed to detect illegal activities (Dupont-Jubien, 1987).[15]

Faced with these problems the SEC began to advocate the signing of bilateral memoranda of understanding with their counterparts in other countries. These MOUs seemed attractive for the SEC because they do not directly involve political leaders or legislatures, and are therefore more easily signed, more flexible and more tailored to securities offences.[16] Thus the MOU strategy grew out of existing US policies as a way to deal with the shortcomings of a unilateral approach.

The influence of the SEC over the MOU process is also evident within IOSCO. The 1986 proposal to set up an IOSCO committee to deal with enforcement was made by then SEC Chair John Shad, and was met with some concern on the part of Europeans regarding US influence.[17] Both the Rio Declaration and the 1989 resolution on cooperation were proposed by the United States.[18] A set of SEC proposals for the subpoenaing of evidence presented at IOSCO's 1988 annual conference were rejected as being too aggressive and incompatible with other countries' views of insider trading.[19] Despite this involvement of the US, there is no indication that the US itself regards the IOSCO process as central to its own policies. A 1989 speech by then SEC Chair David Ruder (1989:21) to IOSCO tacitly indicated that IOSCO was a secondary focus for the US in the MOU strategy:

> The SEC has been pleased with the extensive cooperation it has obtained from other foreign securities regulators within the context of its MOUs and hopes to continue to negotiate additional MOUs on a bilateral basis in the future. *In addition*, in order to attempt to

develop similar cooperative efforts in a multilateral setting, the SEC recently has supported an IOSCO Technical Committee resolution on this subject [emphasis added].

In sum, IOSCO's claim to have originated the increasing number of MOUs with the Rio Declaration cannot be supported, as indicated by the prior existence of MOUs, by the logical progression of prior US policy that led to a MOU strategy and by the failure of the SEC to attribute a role to IOSCO in its own MOUs.

At the same time there are indications that the MOU process has developed a momentum independent of the US and that the process is becoming more institutionalized. There are a number of indications of rapid growth of these MOUs as an instrument for regulatory cooperation. Table 4.4 displays the number of MOUs or similar agreements signed between 1986 and 1991, separating out those in which one partner was a US agency. Starting in 1990 the number of agreements that did not involve the US was greater than the number that did not. This indicates that their geographic spread is expanding, and that the momentum of the process does not solely depend on the initiative of the SEC.

The use made of existing MOUs appears to be increasing as well, as indicated by the increase in the number of international requests for assistance involving the SEC (see Table 4.5). Not just the SEC but foreign authorities as well appear to be using the MOUs.

Table 4.4   International memoranda of understanding and similar agreements between securities regulators, 1986–91

Year	1986	1987	1988	1989	1990	1991
Involving the US	2	1	5	3	4	5
No US involvement	0	1	1	0	15	16

Notes: A large proportion of the agreements not involving the US in 1990 and 1991 involved the UK as one partner. Exact figures for the distribution of these UK agreements between the two years is not available, and so these figures are estimated. Figures for 1991 go to 20 August. If two agreements are between the same two countries but involve different agencies then they are counted as two agreements, unless they were signed on the same day as part of a single process.

Source: IOSCO data tabulated by author.

Table 4.5   International requests for assistance involving the SEC

Year	SEC requests to foreign governments	Foreign requests to the SEC
1988	84	81
1989	101	150
1990	177	130

Notes: Figures include enforcement assistance requests, enforcement referrals and technical assistance requests. These figures must be treated with caution since requests to the SEC include more requests for technical assistance than is the case with requests from the SEC.

Source: SEC (*Annual Report*, 1991:24).

A further indication of the growth of the MOU process is its institutionalization within IOSCO. The MOUs are being monitored and assessed within IOSCO by the Technical Committee's Working Group on Enforcement and Exchange of Information, chaired by Jean-Pierre Michau of France. A list of general principles for use in negotiating future MOUs was adopted by the Presidents Committee in October 1991. This document represents a much greater specification of MOU principles than had existed previously.

A final indication of the growth of the MOU process is the modification of domestic laws to enable regulators to carry out their MOU obligations. This includes the SEC, which was authorized by Congress under Section 6 of the Insider Trading and Securities Fraud Enforcement Act of 1988 to use its compulsory powers to obtain information for foreign securities authorities. In addition, the SEC proposed legislation that would give it a battery of new powers, including exemption from the Freedom of Information Act of confidential documents obtained from foreign authorities, the ability to impose sanctions on the basis of findings by foreign courts and the authorization to conduct investigations abroad.[20] The legislation makes exercise of these powers contingent on the existence of a cooperative arrangement with foreign authorities.[21]

In short, while the MOU process originated in the US and was brought into IOSCO at the SEC's initiative, there are a number of signs that it has begun to develop a degree of autonomy. At the same time there are also some obvious limitations to the effectiveness of MOUs. In contrast to the Basle Committee on Banking Supervision, which started with the issue of information sharing and then went on to work multilaterally to begin to harmonize domestic regulations, the enforcement activities of the securities regime have a makeshift quality.

The Multijurisdictional Disclosure System

A second concrete initiative that is closely related to IOSCO's work is the multijurisdictional disclosure system (MJDS) which has been negotiated between the United States and Canadian regulators.[22] The goal of the MJDS is to make cross-border issues of securities easier through the mutual recognition by Canadian provincial and United States regulators of each other's disclosure requirements. Such a bilateral agreement was seen as a logical starting point for wider cooperation on regulating multinational issues because of the similarity between US and Canadian regulatory systems.

The MJDS, however, has its origins in a unilateral measure taken by the United States rather than in the discussions at IOSCO. Initial discussion of the alternative ways of harmonizing multinational offerings of securities was called for by a February 1985 SEC Concept Release. This release envisioned a program involving the US, the UK and Canada because of the similarities of their regulatory systems, with the system to be later spread to other countries. Indications are that IOSCO's role in the MJDS negotiations was minimal. A 1989 speech to IOSCO by then SEC Chair David Ruder (1989:13), in which the MJDS was discussed, makes no mention of an IOSCO role.[23]

Although the SEC claims that several countries have expressed strong interest in MJDS-like agreements, the suitability of the MJDS as a vehicle for multilateral convergence is questionable.[24] Even though the UK was dropped from the plan,[25] the negotiations over the MJDS took five difficult years. Although there is some indication that work is underway to extend the agreement to the UK and Japan, the US–Canada agreement appears to have taken more effort than was originally envisioned.[26] Furthermore, use of the system has been minimal to date (Munroe, 1991:13).

IOSCO has, however, contributed to future cooperative agreements on multinational issuance of securities through its massive international survey of existing disclosure regulations in 14 jurisidictions.[27] Discovering what differences exist is a necessary preliminary step before negotiation. Furthermore, in the very act of responding to the survey many regulators were forced for the first time to write down procedures that had been tacit.[28] Other IOSCO work on accounting differences will make negotiations on reciprocal disclosure documents easier in the future.[29] At IOSCO's 1988 Annual Conference, then SEC Chair David Ruder indicated that an IOSCO report on international offerings could serve as a blueprint for future negotiations on this issue between the SEC and other regulators ("Ruder Says Unreleased IOSCO Report," 1989:1438).

Thus, as with the MOU process but to a lesser extent, IOSCO has begun to lay the groundwork for a more institutionalized, multilateral approach to an activity initiated by the SEC for its own policy reasons.

Capital Standards

One of IOSCO's most important projects is an effort to establish common capital standards for securities firms, an effort which started in earnest with a report on this issue in 1989. If IOSCO were successful at establishing such standards it would be an accomplishment comparable in the significance of its effects and in the stature it confers on IOSCO to the Basle Committee's capital accord of July 1988. Unfortunately for IOSCO there are two features of these negotiations that are likely to preclude such an outcome.

First, much of the initiative in this issue area is coming from two other international institutions: the Basle Committee and the European Community. IOSCO's Technical Committee and the Basle Committee are working closely together on this issue but the process is being driven by pressures from the latter, which wants to make sure that its own standards are not undermined by a shift in financial activity away from banks towards more lightly regulated securities markets. Parallel work is proceeding in the European Community, but in contrast to the bank capital negotiations in which the EC followed the initiatives of the Basle Committee, in the securities negotiations the EC negotiations are much further advanced than those in IOSCO.

The second problem faced by IOSCO in its capital negotiations is the severe conflict that has stymied participants (Hobson, 1990:72–3). Most seriously, at IOSCO's Annual Meeting in October 1992 Richard Breeden, who was Chair of the SEC and of IOSCO's Technical Committee, announced his opposition to the proposals developed at IOSCO and downplayed IOSCO's importance, calling it a "clearing house of ideas and techniques" (Corrigan, 1992:24). The danger for IOSCO is more severe than conflicts that emerged in the Basle negotiations, not only because of the vehemence of Breeden's opposition, but also because of the greater complexity of the positions of the other major players.

In contrast to the Basle Committee, where the UK and the US worked together and ultimately moved forward the negotiations within the Committee, the leading players – the US, the UK and Germany – all have clashing perspectives. The UK is pushing for lower standards that take into account the ability of a large number of small UK securities firms to reduce risk through sophisticated hedging techniques. The Germans, whose securities business is carried out by large universal banks subject to the Basle standards, is pushing to bring standards more closely in line with those imposed on banks. The SEC, fearful that the 1987 market meltdown was heralding the next financial crisis, is determined to hold out for tough standards but is critical of perceived weaknesses in the Basle Committee's approach.[30]

The comments of a *Financial Times* journalist, while overstated, do indicate the stakes for IOSCO of this conflict: "If it fails to grasp this opportunity, then its hopes of acting as a leading force in the development of financial regulation around the world will come to nothing" (Waters, 1992b).

Other Accomplishments

IOSCO's other initiatives can be considered less noteworthy accomplishments because they are overly vague statements of intent, because there are important conceptual and technical questions that are not yet resolved, or because IOSCO is mainly a participant in work that is being done in other organizations. For instance IOSCO's Presidents Committee adopted seven "conduct of business principles" in 1990 (IOSCO, 1990a:8–9). Although these go beyond existing practices in many markets, were backed up by a somewhat more detailed IOSCO report (IOSCO, 1990b: Document No. 11) and involved review by IOSCO of their implementation, the vague wording of the principles weakened the significance of this accomplishment. On clearance and settlement, which IOSCO had listed as a priority, it is now the Group of Thirty and the International Federation of Stock Exchanges who are primarily responsible.

Structure and Process of the Regime

The internal structure of IOSCO is considerably more formalized than is the structure of the Basle Committee. The Presidents Committee, Executive Committee and Secretariat each have specific functions, as do the regional committees, the consultative committees and the Technical and Development Committees. IOSCO's annual reports spell out these functions and provide an organization chart linking the various committees. Most of its work is divided between its Technical Committee on International Transactions (TCIT), whose members are from the most developed securities markets, and the Committee on Market Development, which is primarily concerned with markets in the developing world and Eastern Europe.

On paper, power resides in the Presidents Committee, which is made up of the heads of all regular and associate member-agencies. It elects the executive committee and "has all the powers necessary to achieve the purposes of the Organization" (IOSCO, 1990a:14). In practice, because of its size, and because it only meets at Annual Conferences, the Presidents Committee is limited in its ability to act as a body. In contrast, the sixteen-member Executive Committee meets several times during the year.[31]

The power of the Executive Committee is reflected in the importance of its members. As Table 4.6 indicates, the administrators of the world's most important securities markets have been represented on the Executive Committee. Japan was elected to the Executive Committee the year after it was admitted to the organization, replacing Hong Kong on the expiration of its term. Five new members were admitted in 1991 in order to better incorporate regions of the world that had not been adequately represented on the Executive Committee.[32]

The power of the Executive Committee is also reflected in its ability to take major initiatives on its own prior to – or without – approval by the Presidents Committee. Such decisions include the creation of the TCIT in 1987, the creation of the Development Committee in 1989, the creation of the category of affiliate members in 1989, the decision to incorporate futures markets as an area of IOSCO's work and the approval of the program of annual conferences.

The Technical Committee is also designed to be more effective than the Presidents Committee since it only includes the most developed countries, and because its working groups are even smaller. In the original 1986 proposals for the Technical Committee, it was seen as taking responsibility for coordinating the work of IOSCO as a whole (Hawes, 1987:258). While this power was subsequently formally lodged in the Executive Committee instead, the Technical Committee continues to carry out this function as well because of the centrality of its work for IOSCO and the weight of its members in relation to the other members of IOSCO.

Table 4.6   Membership of IOSCO's Executive Committee

1991	1990	1989	1988	1987
Australia	Australia	Australia	Australia	Australia
France	France	France	France	France
Italy	Italy	Italy	Hong Kong	Hong Kong
Japan	Japan	Japan	Italy	Italy
Mexico	Mexico	Mexico	Mexico	Mexico
Ontario	Ontario	Ontario	Ontario	Ontario
UK	UK	UK	UK	UK
US	US	US	US	US
China–Taipai				
Germany				
Nigeria				
Poland				
Turkey				

Regional representatives:

Chile*	Brazil*	Chile*	Ecuador*	
India**	New	New	New	
Spain***	Zealand**	Zealand**	Zealand**	
	Sweden***	Sweden***	Sweden***	

 * Inter-American
 ** Asia–Pacific
*** Europe

Notes: Four members are elected each year for a two-year term. The dates refer to the year of the annual meeting at which the Presidents Committee conducted elections. The members appearing under that year were either elected at that meeting or were entering their second year, having been elected the previous year. At the 1991 annual meeting five new positions were added to the Executive Committee. Since securities markets are a provincial responsibility under the Canadian federal system, the Canadian participants in IOSCO are the provincial securities commissions from Quebec, Ontario and British Columbia. Although Quebec does not have a seat on the Executive Committee, Paul Guy's close connections with the Quebec Securities Commission has given Quebec a major input into IOSCO.

Sources: IOSCO Annual Reports and IOSCO, 1991b.

In addition to the committees referred to above, an important part of the work of the organization is carried out in its Montreal Secretariat, headed by Paul Guy, which prepares meetings of the above committees and ensures follow-up on decisions taken in them, as well as being heavily involved in organizing the annual conferences. With a budget of $235 500 in 1989 (IOSCO, 1990b:20), however, most of the work of the organization is only made possible by the decentralized contributions of administrators and staff of member agencies.

The Role of the United States

As with the Basle Committee, it is important to examine the role of the US to determine whether its influence undermines IOSCO's autonomy, and therefore its strength in general. US influence is clearest in the MOU and MJDS processes, but is also evident more generally. An example is the SEC's 1988 Policy Statement on the Regulation of International Securities Markets, presented by the SEC at IOSCO's 1988 annual conference (IOSCO, 1988b). While acknowledging that "regulators should be sensitive to cultural differences and national sovereignty concerns," the principles put forward match closely those governing the US system. Moreover, the statement claims that "the United States Securities and Exchange Commission believes it has a responsibility to assume a leadership role in international securities regulation. It considers the principles and goals contained in this Policy Statement to be central to achieving a truly global market system."[33] In general, statements by US securities regulators on the globalization of securities markets often ignore IOSCO.[34]

Although both IOSCO and the Basle Committee rely heavily on decentralizing tasks to their member agencies, the supranational resources available to the Basle Committee through the expertise at the Bank for International Settlements are much more substantial than those available to IOSCO through its Montreal Secretariat. The sheer quantity of resources, such as lawyers and research capacity, that the SEC can provide relative to other agencies contributes to SEC influence.[35] The historical legacy of IOSCO's origins as an inter-American organization also contribute to US influence.

The differences in the mandates given to US regulatory agencies by Congress with respect to international cooperation are additional indications of the weaker commitment of the US to the multilateral process in the securities regime. As with banking, there was a congressional mandate for greater attention to be given to international cooperation: the Financial Modernization Act of 1988 called for a study on the harmonization of the regulation of banking and securities organizations, including the international dimension (US Senate Committee on Banking, Housing and Urban Affairs, 1988:72–

3). The mandate is both weaker and later than was the case with the International Lending Supervision Act of 1983, which explicitly directed regulators to develop cooperative arrangements.

Overall, US actions with respect to international securities regulation appear to be driven by the desire to find an effective way to carry out national goals with little predisposition to support a multilateral regime except when unilateralism has failed. This attitude of the US is related to the desire of policy-makers and industry participants to prevent further erosion of the United States' share of worldwide market capitalization, which declined from 55 per cent to 31 per cent between 1982 and 1989.[36] Regulations in the US are stricter than in many other countries, making foreign markets more attractive for some investors and borrowers. If international regulations were more harmonized some of this migration of capital markets away from the US might be prevented.

The influence of the US over IOSCO is offset by some indications of a more genuine multilateralism however. The MOU process in particular has developed a degree of autonomy as agreements not involving the US have been signed, as the US has had to cede elements of sovereignty and as the principles underlying the MOUs have been codified at IOSCO. Despite the SEC's ability to block capital negotiations in 1992, the very fact that a set of proposals could develop at IOSCO which differed to such a degree from US goals is an indication of a degree of autonomy. The leading role of two international institutions – the Basle Committee and the EC – in establishing international capital standards testifies to a degree of US weakness, although not to IOSCO's strength.

Assessing the Strength of the Securities Regime

Like the Basle Committee, IOSCO is well-suited to the application of regime analysis. Although IOSCO has some features of a supranational international organization that are lacking in the Basle Committee, such as formal voting by a general membership on resolutions, it, too, does not have the authority to force its members to follow its injunctions. As is the case with the Basle Committee, treating IOSCO as a social institution that may contribute to the convergence of expectations around a common set of principles, norms, rules and decision-making procedures, allows us to understand better its role in generating international cooperation.

As in analyzing the banking regime, the four indicators to be used to assess the strength of the securities regime are: (1) compliance, (2) specificity, (3) ability to learn and (4) autonomy. In doing so I will compare the securities regime with the banking regime on each dimension.

Compliance

Assessing compliance with the injunctions of the securities regime is much more difficult than for the banking regime, an indication in itself that the securities regime is weaker than the banking regime. There are three reasons for this difficulty. First, some of the agreements have not been in place for long enough to assess them. Second, the wording of the agreements are not as specific as are the major agreements of the Basle Committee, and it is therefore more difficult and less worthwhile to discern violations. Third, there is no public institutional arrangement for monitoring compliance. In the banking regime there are a number of sources of information on compliance: Basle Committee publications, national authorities, IMF and OECD publications and the trade press. In part the interstate securities regime has not developed enough for the devotion of resources to monitoring compliance to be worthwhile.

The number of agencies that have signed agreements can be a partial indicator of compliance. Of IOSCO's 91 member agencies, 40 had signed the 1986 Resolution on Reciprocal Assistance and 18 had signed the 1989 Resolution on Cooperation. To a small degree these surprisingly low figures can be explained by the rapidity of IOSCO's expansion (with eleven members added in 1991 for instance) since some of the agencies may not yet have had time to consider the resolutions. Overall, however, the figures are an indication of lack of enthusiasm for one of the most important features of the regime.

The number of MOUs signed is a more positive indication of strength since they have increased significantly over time, despite the greater commitment involved in carrying out MOU negotiations, and in the language of the MOUs. At this point, agreeing to the 1986 and 1989 Resolutions involves signing a document that has already been produced, while arranging a new bilateral MOU involves initiating negotiations.

There are also examples of enforcement actions that would not have been possible without an MOU. The fact that the agencies involved exchanged the required information is an indication of compliance.

Three SEC lawyers noted in a 1988 article (Goelzer, Sullivan and Mills, 1988:88) that "the [Securities and Exchange] Commission's experience with MOUs illustrates their effectiveness in securities enforcement. For instance, the Swiss MOU has enabled the Commission to trace and seize assets which were heretofore untouchable."[37] Similarly, the Senate Committee on Banking, Housing and Urban Affairs reported that "MOU's have provided an effective and efficient means of obtaining information" (cited in Jiminez, 1990:305).

In addition to the commitment of individual states to IOSCO's *agreements*, the degree of commitment to IOSCO's *process* is also an indication of compliance. To use Hirschman's often cited alternative forms of influence, "loyalty" and "voice" are indications that the organization is a more important locus of decisionmaking than is the case when "exit" predominates. The conduct of the US with respect to the banking and securities regime displays different degrees of commitment to the multilateral process. As noted above, the US has been less dependent on the IOSCO process in the pursuit of its goals than it has on the Basle process. In the securities regime many of the policies were initiated from within the US state, while the Basle Committee's risk-based capital approach originated in Europe and was developed to a greater degree within the Basle Committee itself. The most serious defection of the US from the Basle process was the short-lived bilateral accord with the UK. In contrast, the MOU process has relied on bilateral agreements from the beginning.

In sum, it is clear that compliance with the securities regime is less developed than is the case with the banking regime, but that it has been expanding over time.

Specificity

Specificity refers to the degree to which actor expectations are clearly specified in the form of rules. On this dimension, the banking regime is clearly far stronger than is the securities regime.

While both regimes have explicit, but very general, sets of overall goals, the Basle Committee has additionally been responsible for highly specific international agreements, while IOSCO has not. Although it is an important issue (OECD, 1988:19) there is not yet agreement on the division of responsibility between home and host supervisors for securities firms. The Rio Declaration, the conduct of business principles, and the other resolutions of IOSCO are far less specific than either the Concordats or the capital agreement.

While the MOUs themselves, and the multijurisdictional disclosure system, are much more specific than the Rio Declaration, these texts have been negotiated bilaterally, outside the framework of IOSCO. In most of IOSCO's priority areas considerable work needs to be done before its resolutions can even approach the level of specificity of the first Concordat.

Despite this weakness of the specificity of the securities regime in comparison to banking, there is evidence of higher levels of specificity in the securities regime over time. IOSCO has produced a number of increasingly detailed reports, some of which have been approved by the Presidents Committee. These reports contribute to the coordination of expectations. For instance, at the 1990 annual meeting the working party responsible for information sharing and enforcement tabled a 30-page report on the lessons learned from the MOU experience. At the 1991 annual meeting a more succinct three-page listing of ten principles for MOUs was approved by the Presidents Committee. While the approval of the Presidents Committee is not as significant as the signing of a multilateral agreement, it is an important indication of a degree of consensus that had not previously existed. In the capital standards negotiations the issues have also been specified with ever-increasing levels of detail, although this accomplishment was threatened by the SEC actions in 1992.

Learning

The work of both IOSCO and the Basle Committee has evolved considerably over time. In the case of IOSCO important developments have been made in increasing shared understanding among supervisors of the problems associated with the regulation of international markets. Consensus on some practical and conceptual issues has developed. These shared understandings are far less specific and integrated into an overall conceptual framework than is the case with the Basle Committee, however. The Basle Committee's work has been much more proactive, taking initiatives requiring concrete changes in response to emerging problems. It has built on past experiences, as is most evident in the way in which the the revised Concordat responded to problems that had emerged in the first. Current efforts to actively apply the capital accord to new financial instruments as they emerge also indicate a capacity to learn.

IOSCO's work remains fragmented into distinct functional subject areas. New projects are taken on, and old ones finished, without a sense that they are being integrated into a developing framework requiring concrete changes in the actions of states. IOSCO has been much slower than the Basle Committee to focus its priorities. Both its working parties and its workshops at annual conferences have addressed a variety of functional subject areas with no clear prioritization between them (see IOSCO's Annual Reports).

Moreover, there are two areas to which IOSCO has devoted considerable energy, even though the leading role in developing greater international cooperation in these areas is being played by other international organizations – an indication of lack of focus. This is the case for clearance and settlement and accounting and auditing standards. In another example of lack of focus, an IOSCO report on the October 1987 crash – an event about which a number of other studies were being made – was produced by the French Commission des Operations de Bourse, but was not published because the Technical Committee decided it would create more problems than it would solve ("IOSCO Drops Overview," 1988:1585).

There has been some discussion in IOSCO of organizational changes that would address the lack of focus in the organization's work. For example, in 1990 the Technical Committee reduced the number of its working parties to four, folding accounting and auditing and multinational offerings into one of these working parties, and dropping clearance and settlement as a separate focus. Despite such changes IOSCO's work remains considerably less focused and integrated than is the case with the work of the Basle Committee.

Autonomy

Autonomy refers to the extent to which the institution can alter its own rules rather than relying on outside agents to do so. The existance of leadership socialization and recruitment mechanisms that reduce rapid turnover at the core of the system are additional important indications of autonomy.

Superficially IOSCO appears to be more autonomous than does the Basle Committee. IOSCO's Presidents Committee is the final authority on rule changes, and the Executive Committee has considerable latitude to take initiatives on its own. In contrast, the Basle Committee is a Committee of the Group of Ten and its major initiatives must be endorsed by the Group of Ten Central Bank Governors. IOSCO has its own secretariat, while the Basle Committee relies for its secretariat on another organization, the Bank for International Settlements.

However this apparent greater autonomy of IOSCO is deceptive. Analysis of these formal relationships of authority must be supplemented with the more informal and unstated institutional relationships that have developed. In both organizations, the impact of policy goals of individual states developed at the national level is relevant. The differences in the conduct of the US towards the two institutions, as discussed above, indicates that the banking regime has more autonomy from the US than is the case with the securities regime.

The adequacy of the institutional arrangements for decision-making and dispute resolution also differ in the two regimes. The Basle Committee, despite its less elaborate organizational structure, has been able to rely on strong sets of shared understandings to a much greater degree than has IOSCO. This is not surprising given the smaller and less diverse character of the membership. In the banking regime decision-making has remained insulated in the Basle Committee, with supervisors from outside the Group of Ten involved through distinct structures such as the Offshore Group. In contrast, IOSCO's Presidents Committee involves members from all regions of the world.

Socializing mechanisms are also less developed in the securities regime than in the banking regime. Both institutions train supervisors from developing countries, but the Basle Committee does this at special workshops in Basle, while IOSCO places people in national securities agencies. The Basle Committee's *Report on International Developments in Banking Supervision* provides a much more coherent regulatory worldview than do IOSCO's annual reports.

As indicated in previous sections, there is some evidence of a developing autonomy of the securities regime, as for instance in the MOU process. At the same time, it is clear that the securities regime is less autonomous than the banking regime.

The Interstate Regime: Conclusion

The above analysis of compliance, specificity, learning and autonomy has indicated that the interstate regime for regulating securities markets has grown stronger over time, but is weaker than the interstate regime for regulating banking centred on the Basle Committee. The next step, therefore, is to analyze the structure of the international securities industry. If the argument developed in Chapter 2 is to be supported I should find an increasing degree of atomistic competition at the industry level and decaying private regimes to be associated with the strengthening of the interstate regime chronicled above. I should also find less atomistic competition and stronger private regimes than was the case in international banking. As will be apparent in the ensuing pages, these trends are indeed apparent in the securities industry. It is to this topic that I now turn.

INDUSTRY STRUCTURE

As with the banking industry in Chapter 3 the following analysis of the structure of the international securities industry starts with quantitative analysis of the degree of rivalry among existing firms. This is followed by more qualitative analysis of the impact of technological change on competition, and of the social institutions that structure the industry.

Rivalry among Existing Firms

The quantitative measures available for assessing the intensity of competition in the international securities industry differ from international banking. There is no historical series comparable to *The Banker*'s on the size and profitability of international securities firms.[38] Statistics compiled by *Euromoney* on the most active firms in the issuing of Eurosecurities are, however, available from the start of the Eurobond market in 1963.

Concentration Ratios

In analyzing concentration ratios in international securities markets I will be looking at the top organizers of new bond issues[39] rather than using assets as a criterion. In part this is because of lack of data on the assets of securities firms, as noted in the above footnote. It is also more relevant theoretically, however, since the key function of securities firms is to arrange the provision of funds to borrowers through finding purchasers for their bonds, rather than to provide funds from the securities firms' internal resources. Thus the organizational function rather than the size of the funds provided is more relevant. Focusing on the organizers of new issues is also relevant because these firms are in the best position to exert control over the market.

There are two particularly important organizing positions for which data on market shares is available. The first is the the position of lead manager. The lead manager is responsible for organizing the issue. Large issues typically have a team of other managing firms that share the responsibility and are called co-lead managers. The second position is the "bookrunner." This is the firm responsible for keeping track of the financial accounts related to the bond issue. This function is usually carried out by the top manager in a syndicate.

Unfortunately there is no single data series for either of these positions that extends from the beginning of the Eurobond market in 1963 to 1990. *Euromoney*, which is the best source of information on individual firms in the Eurobond market, focused on lead managers up until the middle of the 1980s, and on bookrunners thereafter. This data was used to construct Figure 4.4.

Figure 4.4 presents the market share of the top ten firms and of the top five firms from 1963 to 1990. The share of the top ten lead

Figure 4.4   Eurobond market shares, top 5 and 10 lead managers and bookrunners, 1963–90

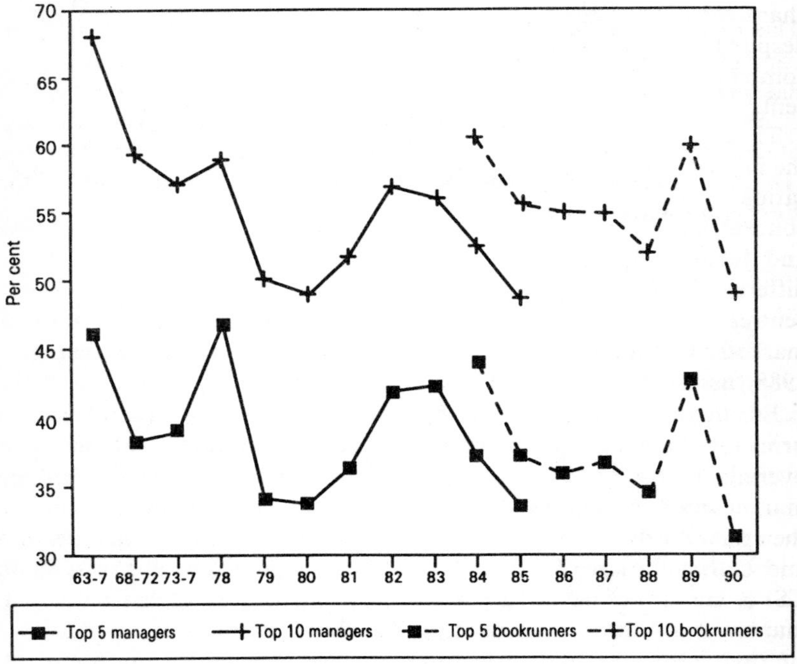

Note: See text for explanation of break in series.

Sources: *Euromoney*, various issues; Kerr, 1984.

managers and co-lead managers of Eurobond issues is used between 1963 and 1985. The share of the top ten bookrunners is used between 1984 and 1990. Concentration ratios for bookrunners are higher because there is only one firm responsible for running the books per issue, whereas there has frequently been more than one manager. Although the share of managers and of bookrunners are different in 1984 and 1985, the two years where both series are available, the direction of change in the concentration ratios are similar. One can therefore assess the direction of change in the concentration ratios for the entire historical period.

Two characteristics of the Eurobond market stand out from these figures. The first characteristic is that the overall trend of these concentration ratios over time is clearly downward, although this trend was temporarily reversed in 1978, 1981, 1982 and 1989. For instance, the share of the top ten managers declined from over 68 per cent in the 1963–7 period to 49 per cent in 1985. The second characteristic is that these ratios have been, and remain, quite high, despite the decline. For instance in 1990 the top five bookrunners had a combined market share of 31 per cent, while the top ten had 49 per cent.

These figures considerably understate the degree of concentration of the market because they do not indicate the much higher concentration ratios in particular segments of the market. Table 4.7 indicates concentration ratios for the top bookrunners for specific currencies and features. These submarkets are distinguished not only by the different firms that dominate them, but also by differing geographic centres, differing barriers between Eurocurrencies and their domestic markets, and persistent variations in interest rate features (Sarver, 1988:163–6).[40]

Furthermore, the market is segmented by type of client, with specific firms retaining a greater market share of these submarkets than of the overall market, as is evident in Table 4.8. This table compares the market share of selected firms in their specialized client segments with their share as lead managers in all issues for this year (1989). Nomura and Daiwa together dominated 38 per cent of the corporate market, CSFB and Morgan Stanley dominated 34 per cent of the sovereign market and Deutsche and Salomon dominated 45 per cent of the supranational market.

In sum, international securities markets have traditionally been highly concentrated, and remain so today. While this is evident from concentration ratios in the market as a whole, it is even more striking in

Table 4.7   Concentration in Eurobond market segments, top 5 and 10 lead managers and bookrunners, 1990

| Instrument | *Share of top firms (no. of firms)* | | | |
	1	*3*	*5*	*10*
All issues	9.2	22.2	31.4	49.1
Euro-dollars	15.8	30.8	43.2	66.3
Euro-C$	16.1	41.1	59.6	84.7
Euro-Dkr	100.0	–	–	
Euro-DM	36.0	57.5	71.3	88.4
Euro-Ecus	25.1	48.4	63.4	86.2
Euro-FF	44.1	74.0	95.5	95.5
Euro-lire	26.7	72.3	88.4	–
Euro-LuxF	25.0	57.5	76.9	96.5
Euro-markka	49.2	78.3	92.8	–
Euro-NZ$	56.5	100.0	–	–
Euro-Skr	23.5	70.5	100.0	–
Euro-sterling	19.1	48.3	64.6	88.2
Euro-yen	20.8	49.3	65.8	83.1
Matadors	45.3	85.4	97.2	–
SFr for. bonds	24.8	64.0	71.0	84.3
Asset-backed	22.5	47.5	64.5	91.6
Convertibles	18.7	46.3	63.2	88.8
Euro-FRN/VRNs	9.5	22.7	32.5	52.6

Note: Each column of numbers refers to the share of the market controlled by a specific number of top firms. For instance, the first column presents the share of the top firm, the second presents the share of the top three firms, and so on.

Source: *Euromoney Annual Financing Report*, March 1991, various tables.

Table 4.8   Client submarket share

Firm	*Overall share (percent)*	*Submarket*	*Share of submarket (percent)*
Nomura	13.9	Corporates	26
CSFB	6.6	Sovereign	13
Daiwa	7.2	Corporates	12
Deutsche	4.1	Supranational	30
Morgan Stanley	2.9	Sovereign	21
Salomon	2.8	Supranational	15

Source: *Euromoney*, March 1990:4,8.

more specialized segments of this market. At the same time these concentration levels have declined significantly over the years in which the Eurobond market has been in existence.

Spreads and Profitability

No measure of the spreads and profitability of international securities transactions comparable to figures provided by the OECD and *The Banker* for international banking are available. Three sources of information help provide a picture, however: trends in fees on new issues of Eurobonds, perceptions of participants and data on profitability of US broker–dealers.

In the primary market for Eurobonds, securities firms receive their income from fees for management, underwriting and selling. Traditionally these fees are determined by dividing the total payment for handling the bond, called the total gross spread, into these three categories. The total gross spread is expressed as a percentage of the principal amount of the issue (Fisher, 1984:60).

The managers, who organize the issue, have the most control and prestige over the process. Underwriters, who accept some of the risk that the bonds will not all be sold by agreeing to carry unsold bonds on their books, are the next rank down on this hierarchy. The lowest rank are the sellers. The ranking is evident in the display of firm names in tombstones – the printed announcements of bond issues in newspapers and journals – and in the share of the total gross spread that is allocated to each activity.

The total gross spread has been steadily declining. In the first decade of the market, new issue spreads were virtually fixed at 2.5 per cent (Kerr, 1984:104). After 1974 the traditional spread dropped to 2 per cent (Kerr, 1984:105), and by 1980 to 1.875 per cent (Muehring, 1989:80). While this nominal spread continued to characterize the market for a number of years, the actual amount of fees available was being reduced by competitive pressures as managers allowed issuers to offer yields that were so low that the bonds could only be sold by squeezing the fee income and reducing the price of the bond to investors. *Institutional Investor* (Muehring, 1989:80) noted: "as a result, of course, with no one else to lift a few basis points from, the underwriters turned on themselves in a vicious zero-sum game that tore the market to shreds."

In response to this pressure on gross spreads the major Eurobond securities houses began to abandon the fiction that standard commissions were 1.875 per cent. Following this move commissions dropped as low as 0.25 per cent. According to *Institutional Investor* (Muehring, 1989:83) it is likely to remain at that level for institutional sales of bonds from the top issuers, ranging up to 0.875 per cent for bonds that involve the more expensive process of retail sales. The important institutional changes that accompanied this price change are discussed further below.

While historical data on the profitability of the Eurobond market is not available, comments by observers and participants indicate that declining spreads produced downward pressures on profits. As *Institutional Investor* comments,

> The profitability of the market's core underwriting and trading activities has been effectively hollowed out by the intense competition of new players entering the primary market with grandiose ambitions of fame and fortune (Muehring, 1989:80).

Or as *Global Finance* comments, in response to its own rhetorical question about whether there is overcapacity in the global securities business,

> In the three global centers of finance, London, New York and Tokyo, the answer appears to be a resounding yes, at least if one looks at the declining rates of return on capital for investment banks operating there (Casey, 1990b:38).

Another source of information on profits of securities firms is SEC data on US broker–dealers. Although these are domestic rather than international firms, there is likely to be some correlation between profits in the two markets.[41] Given the quality of SEC data on these firms it is worth examining these trends to supplement the quantitative analysis above.

Figure 4.5 indicates historical trends in the profitability of US broker–dealers registered with the SEC, based on data provided in various SEC annual reports. The basis of SEC data changed in 1981 from consolidated to unconsolidated reporting, and while reworked data was provided back to 1976, data for earlier years is not available. Thus the earlier series differs from the later series. As indicated by the years for which both series are available, the differences do not preclude rough comparison. Figures on the number of registered firms are also available for the later period. The SEC data indicates

Figure 4.5   US broker–dealer performance (1970–89)

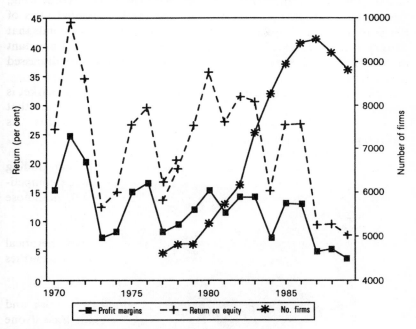

Source: SEC *Annual Report*, various issues.

that the general trend in both profit margins and return on equity has been downward over time. For the years for which the number of firms is available, there is a clear upward trend, indicating a continuous process of new entrants despite declining profitability. This trend began slowing at the end of the 1980s. This data reinforces the conclusion that profitability in international securities markets was declining over the 1970s and 1980s.

Geographical Concentration

As with international banking it is useful to examine geographical concentration because the social institutions involved in private regimes are likely to be sustained by cultural and spatial stability and homogeneity. Unlike banking, however, data is only available on concentration by nationality of ownership.

Figure 4.6 presents trends in the concentration of the Eurobond market by the nationality of the ten most important firms (with "important" referring to the top lead managers or bookrunners in the Euromoney *Annual Financing Guide* listings). The market has gone through three distinct phases. In the first phase Germany was dominant in these listings. In the second phase the United States dominated. In the third phase Japan displaced the other two's firms; the third phase is less clearly dominated by a single country however.

Figure 4.6   Market share among the top ten Eurobond firms (share of issues by nationality of ownership of firm, 1963–90)

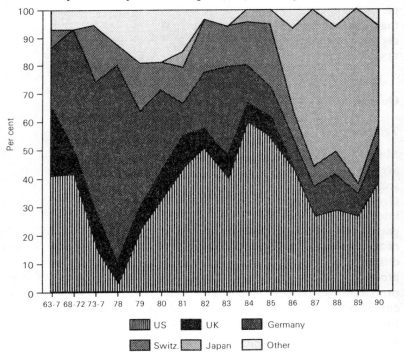

Note: The universe is the value of new Eurobond issues handled by the top ten Eurobond firms (lead managers for the earlier period, bookrunners for the later period). A nation's total consists of the value of issues handled by all firms in the top ten ranking of that nationality.

Sources: *Euromoney Annual Financing Guide*, various issues; Kerr, 1984.

As was the case with the territorial and nationality concentration of banking, the rise of Japan and less clear dominance of a single nationality over the top firms is likely to have increased competition. The greater stability and concentration of the Eurobond market in general is evident, however, in the greater domination of the market by firms from a single country in earlier phases.

Taken as a whole, the quantitative data indicates that the intensity of competition was increasing during the 1970s and 1980s. This is the trend that one would expect since the interstate regime was emerging and strengthening during this period. Comparison of the intensity of competition in the banking and securities industry is more difficult since the indicators are measured differently. While the evidence of persisting high levels of concentration in the securities industry suggests that competitive pressures have not been as severe as in banking, it is necessary to look at quantitative indicators to provide a better basis upon which to compare. It is to this task that I now turn.

Qualitative Analysis

Technological Rents

Much of the analysis of the speed with which technological advantages are dissipated in international banking applies to international securities. While the new financial instruments addressed by the Group of Ten Report are produced and traded by the major international commercial banks, the major securities firms are engaged in trading most of the same instruments. While the specialization of the two types of financial firms in these new financial instruments differs to some degree the factors contributing to a rapid product lifecycle are similar. As with international banks, the technology produced and traded by securities firms cannot be patented, is not embedded in a material product, is more easily imitated by non-financial firms as computerization proceeds and rests on predictions of the future, all of which make accurate pricing difficult.

There are, however, some important differences between the technological dynamics in the two industries. Securities firms appear to be better positioned to take advantage of the overall direction of technological development in a period characterized by securitization because of their traditional focus on the techniques associated with marketable securities (Hakim, 1984:S40; Rohlwink, 1987:26–8).

When banks attempt to participate in securities markets they are likely to diversify into the most commodified segments of these markets. The fate of the Eurocommercial paper market, which had involved both banks and securities firms, is noteworthy. By 1989 the *Bank of England Quarterly Bulletin* (May, 1991:234) had noted, "the intense competition and relative unprofitability of this market caused some securities houses to withdraw from the market" (see also *Euromoney Annual Global Financing Report*, March 1990:26). As an investment banker (Chu, 1988:60) noted,

> [i]f commercial banks are ever to achieve significant market share in the future, it is likely to be in such areas as interest rate swaps, currency swaps, commercial paper, or mortgage-backed securities, where high volume is required and transactions are extremely commodity-like in nature ... the highly personalized value-added core businesses ... require other special qualifications that large commercial banking organizations do not possess.

The rapid expansion of international equity markets in recent years has provided securities companies with an opportunity to forestall the impact of competition which will be difficult for banks to move into. This area, which includes cross-border mergers and acquisitions,[42] involves more highly specialized knowledge than do the bond or loan markets. *Euromoney* (Evans, 1989:72) notes that

> the established players believe the barriers to entry are high enough to keep out the riff-raff. You probably need genuine end placement power, enough capital to be a continuous market-maker and a decent research department to be in Euro-equity syndicates – that's a costlier infrastructure than for debt underwriting.[43]

The technological inequality between banks and securities firms is evident in the interactions between the two types of firms in countries where the two industries have traditionally been separate. Trade journals indicate that banks have attempted to compensate for their lack of knowledge of the securities industry by luring experts from securities firms, whose salaries have often been higher than their counterparts in commercial banks (Casey, 1990a:63); Garten, 1989:527). No comparable indication of recruitment of bank experts by securities firms exists.

Offsetting these advantages of securities firms is their entrepreneurial and individualistic culture, which allows individual employees rather than the firm as a whole to appropriate technological rents. These employees can easily leave and set up competing firms or join commercial banks if this appropriation is threatened. In addition, some banks can draw on their corporate client base and expertise in lending activities, which can be translated into underwriting of corporate notes (Casey, 1990a:62). Moreover, banks may be able to play to their advantage their expertise in operational infrastructure associated with the payments system (Evans, 1986:9).

While securities firms do appear to have an overall technological advantage over banks, both industries have experienced an erosion of their ability to appropriate technological rents. As a senior managing director of one bank-owned securities firm put it, with reference to the Federal Reserve's relaxation of restrictions on bank participation in securities markets:

[t]hey let us into these wonderful markets that had been lucrative in the past but by the time we got into them were extremely well spoken for, dominated by a few leading houses with margins generally much tighter than they used to be (cited in Casey, 1990a:64).

Or as a banker put it in the same article, "It's like saying, 'Congratulations, we'll let you into the party.' But it's three in the morning and all the liquor's gone" (Casey, 1990a:60).

In short, the impact of technology in international securities markets, as in international banking, has been to increase, not decrease, the intensity of competition. As with banks much of the specialized knowledge of securities firms is being codified and sold through electronic networks. The impact of technological change on securities firms has been less severe than is the case with banks however. The overall trend towards securitization has made the specialized knowledge and organizational culture of securities firms more valuable, while bank products have become commodified. This has allowed leading securities firms to retain better control of securities markets and minimize the competitive threat from new entrants.

These trends further reinforce the argument developed in Chapter 2. The interstate securities regime emerged and was strengthened during the 1970s and 1980s, the period in which the intensity of competition was increasing. Furthermore, the securities regime was less developed than the banking regime during this time period, which corresponds to more intense competition in the banking industry compared with the securities industry.

Pressures from Buyers and Suppliers

International securities firms are threatened to some degree by the entry of large commercial banks into the securities business from markets where such entry had previously been forbidden. As noted above, however, securities firms enjoy a technological advantage over banks, reducing the threat of entry to some extent. Indeed, in the most important of such markets, the United States, banks have been very slow to make use of the enhanced securities powers they have been given (Casey, 1990a:60–5). Thus the threat to securities firms from banks is much less than is the threat to banks from securities firms.

Securities firms are, however, facing severe competitive pressures from "buyers" and "suppliers." The suppliers of funds (investors) are becoming increasingly institutionalized, shifting bargaining power to investors and away from securities firms. Many buyers of funds (issuers) have been able to master the required technology to displace securities firms entirely. This shift in power away from securities firms is evident in a number of interrelated developments. These include the increasing popularity of "private placements," in which corporations bypass securities firms entirely and place securities directly with institutional investors; the widespread electronic dissemination of information previously controlled by securities firms;[44] the pressures that both buyers and sellers have been able to put on the spreads in Eurobond markets; the increased tendency of large corporate borrowers to shop around in search of the lowest priced securities firms; and the destruction of the anti-competitive mechanisms by which international securities firms have traditionally been able to enhance their profits, including deregulation of brokerage fees in London (1986) and New York (1975).

The threat posed to securities firms by these developments is evident in the hostility of these firms towards General Electric Credit Corporation (GECC) which has eschewed long-term relationships in the Eurobond market and has aggressively sought out the cheapest rates from securities firms (Frank, 1988b:26). After giving a mandate to LTCB International, a newcomer in the market, on the basis of pricing, the reaction was especially severe:

the issue has been boycotted by the market; the big boys have decided (in an unusual display of unity) that they are not prepared to lose money by underwriting what they see as a mispriced deal. . . . Others reckon the latest GECC transaction was a brilliant piece of financial management; the company has cut through the inner circle of the market's most prominent houses and achieved highly attractive funding (Frank, 1988b:26).

In sum, while securities firms do not face as severe a threat from commercial banks entering their market as banks face from securities firms, they have faced serious competitive pressures from suppliers (investors) and buyers (borrowers). Once again, therefore, there is evidence that international securities markets have become subject to more intense competitive pressures during the time in which the interstate regime was strengthening.

The Private Regime in the Eurobond Markets

While the above sections have established that the intensity of competition was increasing in international securities markets, but that this competition was not as severe as in international banking, the analysis has not yet focused directly on the social institutions which would provide evidence of a private regime. It is to these social institutions that I now turn.

The surprisingly high degree of concentration in primary Eurobond markets is one indication of the potential for interfirm collusion and cooperation. As noted above, the market share of the top two or three firms in these submarkets ranges from 30 to 100 per cent.

Historical accounts of the Eurobond market confirm that such collusion and cooperation have played an important part in allowing the market to function. The social institutions involved in the private regime are evident in the importance of reputation, in the structuring of syndicates and in the development of the market's self-regulatory organization: the Association of International Bond Dealers, now renamed the International Securities Markets Association.

The reputation and size of both issuers and underwriters of Eurobonds are key factors that provide stability in the market. Fisher (1984) lists the following criteria that determine whether issuers will be accepted in the Eurobond market: whether corporations and governments are from the industrialized countries; whether corporations are rated BBB and above by Moody's or Standard and Poor's; whether the corporate name is well known; and whether corporations have $400 million or more of revenues, $400 million of total capitalization and $25 million or more net income. The top issuers generally consist of the largest corporations and most stable states or state agencies in the world.[45]

Reputation and relationships among a small number of individuals and firms have been important for the securities firms, although there has been a gradual erosion over time of these informal social institutions. Kerr's *History of the Eurobond Market* (1984) gives numerous examples of this.

Kerr (1984:7) notes of the early market, "That it grew so rapidly is because of the foresight of a small group of very talented men." His description of the relationships in these markets is revealing:

> The selection of underwriters and co-managers often depended on the whim of the senior partners or directors of the lead manager. Old client relationships were rewarded with underwriting invitations in the full knowledge that the client had little or no placing power in Eurobonds but would be in a position to offer reciprocal business in other areas (Kerr, 1984:103).

The secondary market was run by a similarly small and cosy community involving a few securities firms. One firm, White Weld, dominated this trade with a lead over others "by a long head and most of the tail as well," according to one of its traders (in Kerr, 1984:84). Even by 1975 the secondary trading community consisted of somewhere between four and nine firms (Kerr, 1984:86). Kerr (1984:87) describes its centre, in London, as a "close-knit community, particularly among the professional market-making houses."

Given the closeness of the Eurobond community, it is not surprising that it has been possible for strong sets of norms governing the conduct of participants to emerge. In a study of legal practices in the market, Rich (1980:509) noted that lawyers' "solutions exhibit surprisingly uniform characteristics.... The result is an *effective norm of international practice*, divorced from any individual municipal law, which poses potent commercial restraints and approaches the status of *transnational law*" (emphasis added). States have been surprisingly willing to cede sovereignty to the Eurobond community, allowing participants to freely select their choice of which country's law would apply in contracts, and waiving sovereign immunity when states were issuers.[46] Rich (1980:519) provides a number of examples where the

Eurobond market's "established norms of practice prevailed over contradictory municipal law provisions."

Over time this cozy community was transformed into a more competitive market, although a number of institutional innovations have been made in an attempt to resist this evolution.

The initial challenge to the cozy community came in both the primary and secondary markets from US firms that used aggressive competitive techniques unknown in Europe (Kerr, 1984:87,103). The reaction to Salomon's entry into the London secondary market in 1975, which involved techniques such as promises to better competitors' fees by one-eighth of 1 per cent, is described as one of "shock" (Kerr, 1984:87–8).

Institutional techniques to restrain competition centred around consortium banks and syndication practices. Four consortium banks were set up by four sets of securities firms and commercial banks, which constituted the consortium's shareholders, to act as exclusive trading houses for those firms.[47] Shareholding firms began cheating on their commitment to the consortium banks however, keeping the most profitable trades for themselves (Kerr, 1984:86). By the mid-1970s all four consortia were in trouble, and now none exists.

The bond syndicate has been an important source of order in the primary Eurobond market. Discipline is a key but elusive goal of bond syndicate managers. A key role of the syndicate is to stabilize the price of new bonds by only selling at an agreed price, and by agreeing to buy any bonds selling below that price. Without this stabilization many new issues would trade at a lower price, harming the issuer (when it comes to the market at a later date for a subsequent issue) and the underwriters (who have made commitments that the issuer receive a prearranged price). The lead managers seek to involve other firms in the syndicate, preferably in a subordinate role, while preventing any of these firms from selling the new bonds below the price agreed upon by the syndicate. Subordinate members of the syndicate have an incentive to cheat on the agreement, both to unload their own bonds quickly or even to sell their bonds to the lead manager.

The techniques for maintaining syndicate discipline have been weakened over time. Initially lead managers were able to keep track of bond serial numbers and punish violators by excluding them from future syndicates. With the establishment of clearing houses, however, this monitoring technique was lost (Kerr, 1984:105).

A further blow to lead manager control was the emergence of the "grey" market in 1978 (Kerr, 1984:88). This market was created by

Stanley Ross, who left a leading trading house to form his own firm, and who began quoting publicly on Reuters screens the prices at which bonds were trading between the major firms during syndication. Making these prices available put tremendous pressure on the syndicates as purchasers of the bonds could demand better prices. The reaction of lead managers was hostile. Kerr (1984:89) cites Ross:

> "I was under no misapprehension about the hornets' nest I might be stirring up, even if I was not prepared for the degree of aggressive hostility which our move provoked." He recalled one conversation with a leading syndicate manager who screamed "we don't care how you trade, or at what discount, Stanley – just take that bloody price off the screen".

Efforts to kill the grey market included unsuccessful proposals by threatened firms to ban it at the Association of International Bond Dealers annual general meeting in 1979. The grey market has subsequently become an accepted part of the Eurobond markets.

In the face of the breakdown of syndicate discipline, the major securities firms involved in the primary market moved to regain control of the issuing process by restricting the number of participants in syndicates, or eliminating syndicates entirely, with a single firm buying the entire deal.[48] These changes were codified to a degree in 1980 with agreement upon a set of written guidelines by the major firms (Kerr, 1984:107).

Over the 1980s this effort to reestablish control – the "Revenge of the Big Players" as *Institutional Investor* (Muehring, 1989:81) puts it – continued to develop, with a tight-knit group of the same firms beginning to negotiate and agree in advance a binding contract stating a single price at which they would sell the bonds. Both the legal obligation and the small size of the group help in ensuring compliance: "Enforcing law and order is easier for the lead manager in a smaller syndicate simply because miscreants are easier to spot and punish" (*Institutional Investor*, Muehring, 1989:81).[49] Securities firms are forced to establish internal controls as well to make sure that their sales forces do not violate the agreements (*Euromoney*, Global Finance Supplement, March 1991:2).

> The big underwriters are determined to shift the balance of power in the market away from issuers and investors and back to the intermediaries, that is, to them. *Then* maybe they can make a little

money again ... marginal players are going to be driven out of the market (*Euromoney*, Global Finance Supplement, March 1991:79–80).

Not surprisingly, these practices have led to complaints:

> Some lead managers are concerned that certain practices in the newly profitable Eurobond market smack of price-fixing and cartels.... Others complain about a "big seven" which has begun to control the new issues business. This comprises the members of the market practices committee of the International Primary Markets Association (*Euromoney*, Global Finance Supplement, March 1991:4).[50]

The rapid expansion of the Euroequity market has provided the core firms with a further opportunity to restablish control over the market. As noted previously, the specialized knowledge involved in this new market provides a substantial barrier to entry. The area is highly profitable, with fees ranging from 3 per cent for a large privatization to 7 per cent or more for a small offering (Evans, 1989:74). Syndicate discipline has been strong. *Euromoney* (Evans, 1989:74) notes that the market looks as though it is "avoiding the squabbles over syndication methods that plague Eurobonds."

The private regime: summary This discussion of the evolution of the Eurobond market has revealed a set of social institutions that are strong enough to merit the label "private regime." Although there are important examples of defections and cheating from Eurobond social arrangements, overall a pattern of surprisingly tight control of the market by a few firms is evident. Standards are as high as in relatively tightly regulated domestic markets, such as the US. Techniques of discipline and control have been strong enough to elicit complaints from those firms at which they are aimed. Syndicates are highly structured with developed interconnected roles as evident in the hierarchy of managers, underwriters and sellers. Defectors from the regime can be punished through exclusion from future deals. Commitments in the Eurobond market are quite explicit. This is true of general rules governing the operation of the market, such as with the criteria for acceptable borrowers and the syndication rules developed in 1980. It is also true of the large body of more detailed procedures that have become accepted as common practice in the market, as evident in guides such as Fisher (1984). Such level of detail in regime rules and procedures would be remarkable if it were present in an interstate regime.

Considerable learning and self-transformation of the institutions of the market are evident in the efforts of the largest firms to reestablish control in the 1980s. Although there are connections to state enforcement powers, as in the reference to domestic laws in bond contracts and the granting of the Association of International Bond Dealers certain statutory powers in London at the end of the 1980s, in general the evolution of the regime has been driven by private sector initiatives. Firms have generally chosen the country from which laws are incorporated into bond contracts. The informal practices of the market were generated over the years from patterns of close interactions of key firms. In short, if the firms in the Eurobond market were states the term "regime" would be quite appropriate for referring to the sets of social institutions binding them together.

It is clear, however, that there have been continuous challenges to the private regime since the creation of the market in 1963, as with, for example, the grey market. Indeed it is not clear that the present major effort by the largest firms to reassert control will succeed. Like international banking, competition has intensified since the earlier years of the market. Unlike banking, however, a strong private regime has been able to work continuously to offset the effects of this competition.[51]

CONCLUSION: INTERSTATE AND PRIVATE REGIMES IN INTERNATIONAL SECURITIES MARKETS

As with international banking, the international securities industry has been characterized by intensifying competition over the period in which the interstate regime centred on IOSCO was created and strengthened. The increased competition was evident in quantitative measures such as concentration ratios for managers and bookrunners in the Eurobond market, the fee structure of new Eurobond issues and the profits of US broker–dealers. Technological change in international securities markets has increased the intensity of competition. As with banks much of the specialized knowledge of securities firms is being codified and sold through electronic networks. Also like banks, securities firms increasingly face more powerful customers as institutional investors replace dispersed retail investors and as large corporations master the knowledge involved in selling securities.

The factors offsetting this increased competition are much stronger than is the case in international banking however. Despite declines in concentration ratios, the market remains highly concentrated, especially when market segmentation is taken into account. Securities firms are better positioned to take advantage of the trend towards securitization than are banks. The arranging of new securities issues remains highly specialized and is more resistant to commodification than are the activities of international commercial banks. Securities firms are also benefiting from the emergence of global equity markets, which require even more specialized knowledge than do bond markets.

The most important offsetting factor, however, is the existence of a relatively strong private regime in international securities markets. This regime displays many of the attributes that one would look for in a strong interstate regime. A strong set of social institutions has developed over the three decades in which the Eurobond market has been in existence. These have centred around the organization of syndicates, but are also evident in such institutions as the Association of International Bond Dealers. In contrast to the banking industry, there is evidence that this private regime may be able to successfully cope with some of the competitive challenges with which international securities firms are faced.

This chapter's analysis of international securities institutions and industry adds to the support given by the case of international banking to the argument developed in Chapter 2. As with banking the strengthening of an interstate regime has been associated with an increase in the intensity of atomistic competition. Furthermore, in comparing the relationship between industry and regime across the two industries the argument is also supported. The interstate securities regime has lagged behind the banking regime in terms of timing and strength while securities markets have experienced less intense competitive pressures and have been organized by a private regime to a greater extent. I will look further at the differences between these two industries, and at the nature of the link between industry structure and interstate regime, in the next and final chapter.

5 Conclusion: Industry and Regime

The task of this concluding chapter is to draw out the theoretical significance of the conclusions of the more empirically oriented work in Chapters 3 and 4. These chapters established that the strength of interstate regimes is associated with an intensification of atomistic competition in international banking and securities markets. The related proposition, that an absence or decay of private regimes is associated with the strengthening of interstate regimes, was also supported by more qualitative analysis of the social institutions involved in the two industries. After a brief reiteration of the theoretical arguments developed in Chapter 2 the present chapter will further address a key issue regarding the link between industry and regime: is the relationship described by Chapters 3 and 4 a causal one?

The argument of this chapter involves three parts. First, is a general claim about causation: event B can be said to cause event A if it can be shown that human agents, empowered and constrained by social structures, were led by B to alter their conduct to bring about A. Second, this model of causation will be applied to the international banking and securities regimes. Changes in the structure of these two industries can be said to cause changes in the strength of their respective interstate regimes if it can be shown that regulators perceived changes in industry structure as a problem to which changes in the regimes were designed to respond, and if they had the ability to bring about these changes. Evidence will be presented to indicate that such a process did occur. This model of causation, which is derived from structuration theory, differs from others popular in the study of international relations, such as realism, which looks at state interests without reference to industry structures or the motivations of particular actors within the state, such as bank regulators. The third part of this chapter will indicate the advantages of this causal explanation in comparison with alternative approaches.

METATHEORY AND THEORY REVISITED

In order to establish that there is a *causal* link between industry structure and interstate regimes it is necessary to return to some of the metatheoretical[1] concerns of Chapter 2. As will be further discussed below, causation is not directly observable, but rather is established theoretically by linking an observed relationship to a more fundamental force upon which a primordial quality is conferred by metatheoretical assumptions. In this chapter this will be done by developing an understanding of causation based on a structurationist metatheory. In this section I will briefly review the metatheory and theory, developed in Chapter 2, that served as a framework within which the more empirically oriented work in Chapters 3 and 4 was organized.

This book has been based upon and sought to strengthen further the general metatheoretical assumption that social life is densely institutional and the more specific metatheoretical assumption that markets are socially constructed and require an institutional framework if they are to function. These metatheoretical assumptions draw our attention to regimes and other social institutions and challenge the view that markets are natural forces that operate best when they are free of institutional contrivances. Chapters 3 and 4 have highlighted the role of international institutions – both interstate and private – in the organization of international banking and securities markets. These metatheoretical assumptions also led us to examine the role of industry structure, going beyond the treatment of industries as institutionless markets. While this does provide further evidence for the relevance of an institutionalist metatheory, it cannot prove or disprove such metatheory. As has become increasingly evident in international relations theory, metatheoretical frameworks, or paradigms, involve large-scale, fundamental, integrated, world-views that cannot be proved or disproved by an empirical test (Lapid, 1989).

This institutionalist metatheory provided a framework within which more substantive hypotheses were developed and subjected to empirical tests, a task which was carried out in Chapters 2, 3 and 4. Based on the assumption that markets require social institutions if they are to function, two alternative opposing hypotheses were elaborated in Chapter 2: first, that interstate regimes were associated with atomistic market structures involving intense competition and decaying private regimes, and second, that interstate regimes were associated with oligopoly and strong private regimes. Chapters 3 and 4 supported the first of these hypotheses, examining banking and securities industries individually over time, and together by comparing across industries. While it was in the background in Chapters 3 and 4, metatheory was important in these two empirically oriented chapters in providing a basis upon which to treat seriously social institutions and industry structure. A less institutionalist metatheory might have ignored such theoretical entities.

The development of substantive hypotheses in Chapter 2 did not simply rely on metatheory, however. Chapter 2 drew on a variety of substantive theories, which have been subjected to a variety of empirical tests in other issue areas and are based on disparate metatheories, including the analysis of domestic regulation of industries, corporatism, the new institutional economics, analysis of financial markets and neo-institutionalism. Unlike the use of metatheory, however, which grounded these hypotheses in untestable philosophical assumptions, these substantive theories strengthened the argument that interstate regimes and industries were related by showing the relevance of such a relationship in a variety of similar issue areas.

Establishing Causation

In addition to its role in developing and testing hypotheses about the relationship between industry structure and the formation of interstate regimes, metatheory is also vital in establishing that this relationship is *causal*. The empirical work of Chapters 3 and 4 has only confirmed that for these cases the strengthening of interstate regimes is associated with atomistic market structures and decaying private regimes. In order to establish that changes in industry structures *cause* the strengthening of regimes it is necessary to return to metatheory.

As with the development of hypotheses, establishing causation does not necessarily only rely on metatheory, however. Metatheoretical arguments can be supplemented by comparing substantive theories. Once a degree of causation is established between industry structure and the strengthening of interstate regimes, then this explanation can be compared with explanations provided by alternative substantive theories. In this chapter the explanation for the strengthening of interstate regimes developed in this book will be compared with three such alternative theories: hegemonic stability theory, transactions costs theory and epistemic communities approaches.

The notion of causation is surrounded by controversy both within the discipline of international relations and in the philosophy of science more generally (Dessler, 1991). The behavioural revolution of the 1950s and 1960s downplayed causation in favour of correlation, seeing the former as metaphysical and unscientific. Explanations were adequate if they subsumed an event under more general laws, which were themselves simply empirically established patterns of covariance. From this perspective one could explain the strengthening of the interstate regimes discussed in this book as resulting from changes in industry structure only by first establishing that such a relationship between regime and industry structure exists in a significant number of other cases.

While further research to determine whether a similar relationship exists in other issue areas is very useful, such research is neither sufficient nor necessary to claim that industry structure can explain the strength of interstate regimes for regulating finance. This is because of the shortcomings of correlational knowledge. An empirically observed covariance cannot by itself establish that changes in one variable are caused by changes in another. As Dessler (1991) notes, by itself the well-established relationship between barometers and thunderstorms does not offer a satisfactory explanation of the latter – barometers do not cause thunderstorms. Causation is only established with reference to more fundamental conceptions of the driving forces in nature and human society. These driving forces are not directly observable and cannot be verified through empirical testing but rather come to be seen as important through the role they play in large-scale philosophical frameworks, or paradigms. In other words, the connection between these forces and events is established through the use of metatheory.

Two examples from international relations theory are useful in clarifying this point. Although each contains innumerable variants, realism and liberalism are two paradigms that offer coherent world views and specify fundamental driving forces in human society. For most realists, self-interested, power-seeking states are the most fundamental actors. The hunger of states for power is fundamental. For most liberals the search for knowledge, the "cognitive imperative,"[2] is fundamental. In contrast with realists, for whom knowledge is a weapon manipulated by the powerful, liberals see interests as shaped by learning. For each paradigm an explanation can be considered adequate if it demonstrates how observed outcomes could be attributed to such fundamental forces. While such an explanation provides additional support for the relevance of these fundamental forces it does not prove that they exist. Belief in their existence derives from much broader features of the paradigm, such as its internal coherence, its historical record and its normative implications.

Entering into the ongoing debate about the relative merits of specific international relations paradigms, about the merit of the concept of a paradigm itself and about the criteria for selecting theories in a metatheory that takes paradigms seriously, goes well beyond the scope of this book. Here it is sufficient to specify a particular metatheory – structuration theory, the merits of which have been extensively discussed elsewhere[3] – and to show how the forces specified by this metatheory can be drawn upon to impart causation to the observed relationship between industry structure and the strength of interstate regimes that was established in previous chapters.

A Structurationist Approach to Causation

From a structurationist perspective neither deep structures operating behind the backs of human agents nor individual intentions provide adequate explanations of events. For the structurationist individuals are knowledgeable agents who must operate through sets of social institutions in pursuing their goals. These institutions are the resources upon which such agents call. They also shape the identities and constrain the choices of these agents. These institutions do not originate from a mysterious deep structure, but rather are generated as the intended and unintended consequences of the practices of agents, and are solidified through time through a process of routinization.

The knowledgeability of agents means that agents are motivated by reasons which they can articulate to themselves and others. Even if their actions have unintended consequences, these motivations are an important part of the explanation. Purposive behaviour is a key aspect of causation in human affairs. In the present issue area, this implies that the strengthening of an interstate regime needs to be perceived by regulators as a practical solution to problems associated with intense atomistic competition. Similarly, the regulatory instruments involved in the regimes need to be shown to be the best available ones given the existing development of social institutions in the industry.

To identify the structures that constrain agents as analyzed in structuration theory it is useful to look at both instruments and roles. Choice is constrained by the status of the existing social institutions through which agents must operate. Thus the last point in the previous paragraph speaks of constraint as well as choice. The concept of role implies that actors are empowered and constrained by the mutual expectations that define their identities. The perceptions of regulators involved in creating the regime need, therefore, to be compatible with their roles as regulators. This last point provides a more sophisticated tool with which to analyze the actions of regulators than is provided by crude applications of rational choice theory that claim that regulators are only concerned with maximizing the revenues of their bureaucracies. This crude view ignores the importance of legitimacy in empowering regulators. Regulators must cope with challenges from legislative review committees, industry and consumer lobbyists, and the general public. While regulators may not cope and be captured or disbanded, or may successfully cope by insulating themselves from these pressures, the value of being able to demonstrate that a mandate is being pursued is likely to be high. This limits the choice of goals by regulators. This does not mean that regulators are assumed to be selflessly serving the public interest, but rather that they are constrained by the need to operate through existing institutions no matter which goals they wish to pursue.

In short, it is important to trace the connections of variables through the perceptions of agents (regulators in these cases) concerning the purposes of their practices and through the constraints imposed by structures, which include the availability of institutional capacity (the effectiveness of alternative regulatory tools) and the need of agents to empower themselves through calling upon their roles (regulatory mandates). Having briefly reviewed the reasons for examining these with general reference to regulators, I now look at each, first in international banking and then in international securities.

STRUCTURATIONIST CONNECTIONS: BANKING

Perceptions

As discussed in Chapter 3, the stated purpose of the Basle Committee is "to help ensure bank solvency and liquidity by promoting discussion and co-operation between those responsible for the supervision of banks and foreign exchange markets in the Group of Ten countries, Luxembourg, and Switzerland" (BIS, 1984:56). In the course of negotiations over capital standards this concern with solvency and liquidity was supplemented with a concern for the "competitive inequality" created by differences in the regulatory burden for firms across countries (BSC, 1988a). A superficial reading of the stated goals of the Basle Committee would indicate that its primary goal was merely to enhance the stability of the international banking system, a straightforward extension to the international system of the purposes, by definition, of domestic prudential supervision. Yet this reading is inadequate, since it does not provide the supervisors' explanations of why instability had become a problem, nor does it explain why a second goal, competitive equality, was adopted.

Statements by the Committee and its chairs, as well as the work taken up by the Committee, indicate that threats to the system's stability were attributed to a number of sources, including the collapse of the Herstatt and Franklin Banks in 1974, declining capital ratios, off-balance sheet commitments, problems with country exposure and money laundering. While these are important, they are useful more as descriptions of the way in which the underlying problem developed, rather than serving as parsimonious explanations of a process that is long-lasting enough to have merited the sustained attention of the Committee since 1974.

It is not difficult to find statements by the Committee or its Chair indicating that the intensity of competition and declining profitability in international banking had contributed to increased risks and activities of banks that are dysfunctional for the banking system as a whole. As Cooke noted in 1981:

> In some degree it is the responsibility of supervisors to protect bankers from themselves. We live in a very competitive world and competition not infrequently impels actions which are marginal to management's own perceptions of prudent banking. It is all a matter of balance and the supervisors must see that the scales do not tip too far (Cooke, 1981:21).

In the same speech Cooke clearly linked the need for capital adequacy standards that take into account the need for competitive equality and the need to restrain competition:

> It may be argued that market forces should be allowed full rein to bring about necessary restraint on banks' businesses. The trouble with that view is that the perception in the market of capital inadequacy is likely to arrive for some banks at a time when they are no longer in a position to remedy the situation.... Recently competitive pressures have squeezed margins for a lot of business in

international markets. One aspect of this squeeze may well have been the capacity of banks with relatively liberal capital requirements to expand their book. This may have kept margins tighter than they would otherwise have been, impairing the effective operation of market forces and operating to the detriment of the earning capacity of the international banking community at large. This then is one argument for bringing national practices on capital more into line in the interests of the system as a whole (Cooke, 1981: 22).

Concern in the Basle Committee over profitability of banks was evident as early as 1979, when a survey to assess trends in profits was initiated (BSC, 1983a:5). Pecchioli's 1983 study of the policy issues related to international banking for the OECD noted that

> International profitability has been a subject of debate in banking and official circles for some time, but has gained in topicality in view of evidence of a structural deterioration of banks' balance-sheet structures.... Stiff competition may have forced some banks to aim an an excessive scale of international activity relative to their underlying financial strength (Pecchioli, 1983:44–5).

In 1985 the Basle Committee (1985a:14) remarked that "profitability of banks is a matter of prime concern to supervisors, and recently the Committee has begun to review in a structured manner the profits experience of banks in member countries and the factors which affect them." Pecchioli, in his 1987 study on international prudential supervision for the OECD, noted the connection between greater bank profitability and stricter capital standards (Pecchioli, 1987:117).[4] Federal Chair Paul Volcker, in explaining his support for the Basle process to Congress, noted that "I am concerned that competitive pressures may have eroded spreads on some of these instruments to the point that banks are not being fully compensated for the credit risks involved" (US House of Representatives, Committee on Banking, Finance and Urban Affairs, 1987:8). More recently, Peter Hayward (BSC, 1991:8), Secretary of the Basle Committee, indicated that in his view profitability was negatively correlated with deregulation rather than with greater regulation: "It is my perception that, in virtually all countries, it is in fact deregulation rather than its absence that is impacting on profitability by opening up competition."

Both the expansion of offshore centres and the expansion of lightly capitalized Japanese banks can be seen as aspects of threatening competition to which increased supervision and regulation was the answer. Both the Concordat, which aimed to eliminate gaps between national supervisory systems, and the capital agreement, which aimed to set out more specific standards for an acceptable level of supervision, clearly offered responses to these threats.

In short, there are clear indications that banking supervisors saw declining profits and intense competition as contributing to the instability that they were committed to reducing.

Tools

Why were these particular tools chosen? In order to consider this question, it is necessary to first suggest alternative tools, and then explain why they were not adopted. Five of the most plausible alternative tools are: (1) increasing unilateral national supervision; (2) encouragement of a private cartel, or private regime, involving the largest banks; (3) restraint of competition through protectionism; (4) the use of alternative supervisory tools such as deposit insurance, lender of last resort facilities, and moral suasion; and (5) greater reliance on market forces.

All of these alternatives are inadequate, however, either because they do not effectively address the problems with which regulators were concerned, or because they rely on institutional preconditions that are not present. Unilateral national supervision, protectionism and informal moral suasion were tools of the era before banks had become international, and had already proved inadequate to the task. Given the rapid dissemination of technological advantages, the challenge from new entrants and the fact that there was no indication that a private regime was developing autonomously,[5] it is not surprising that this option was not adopted.

There are a number of reasons why the development of rules by treating banking as trade in services and incorporating quasi-protectionist measures in such fora as the Uruguay Round was an unrealistic option. Trade negotiations aim to increase competition. Trade negotiators are often ill-equipped to deal with the highly technical nature of financial markets. Bank supervisors, with their developed regulatory and supervisory tools, are not located in trade ministries or foreign ministries, the agencies traditionally concerned with trade negotiations (see comments of SEC Chair Breeden in "Administrative Conference of the United States Colloquy," 1991:371).

Deposit insurance and expanded lender-of-last-resort facilities may, under certain conditions, increase stability, but they also tend to increase competition as market discipline over risk-taking is reduced.[6] Greater reliance on market discipline, while advocated by some academic economists and bank lobbyists (Shaw, 1988), has generally been seen as an inadequate solution by regulators due to the inability of the market institutions to facilitate the exercise of discipline by depositors over banks. Indeed, internationally there appears to be an emerging consensus among supervisors that supervision needs to be intensified rather than weakened as markets are deregulated (IMF, 1991a:14). In the international context, a state that allowed banks to fail would see international banking business move beyond its borders – if not immediately, on rumour of problems – with the speed of an electronic payment transfer (Lovett, 1989:1382).

In comparison with these alternatives, the two tools adopted by the Basle Committee appear particularly well-suited to the existing institutional preconditions for supervisory action. The Concordat, by extending home-office supervision to foreign offices of international banks, built on the existing supervisory capacity, which is national and located in the agencies represented on the Committee. Capital adequacy standards were amenable to the degree of formalization necessary if an agreement was to be monitored effectively and compliance enforced. Furthermore, these agreements allowed restraint of growth, without violating principles and norms against protectionism.

Institutionally the capital adequacy agreement much more effectively disciplines the firm than do more informal or specific regulations. By using market pressures, capital adequacy standards have forced firms to modify their internal controls without requiring supervisors to do the impossible task of detailed monitoring of bank operations. As noted in Chapter 3, since the agreement there have been widespread reports of banks instituting new internal controls to ensure that capital is allocated to uses with appropriate risks. This has forced many banks to monitor risk/return trade-offs on specific categories of lending for the first time. Furthermore, capital adequacy has become a key criterion in the market's assessment of bank performance, as evidenced by the new attention given to capital adequacy by ratings agencies and *The Banker*'s league tables. Market discipline exercised through bank stock prices is therefore now linked to capital adequacy. Finally, the stress on capital adequacy shifts the costs of bad management onto shareholders rather than deposit insurance systems.

Roles

Important limits have been put on bank regulators as a result of their need to call upon their roles as a source of empowerment. Bank regulators have justified their activities as contributing to stability, which is their mandate domestically and internationally. In the past two decades this mandate has been altered from one permitting the explicit restraint of competition, to one which promotes greater reliance on market forces. The consensus to this effect, represented in the OECD's 1989 report on *Competition in Banking*, as well as the current trend towards reducing protectionism in banking detailed in that report, are indicators of this. Thus regulators are precluded to an important degree from proposing solutions that involve strong interference in domestic market forces (as in interest rate ceilings for instance) or which involve protectionism (as with prohibiting bank entry on other than prudential grounds).

Ideologically, both the Concordat and the capital agreement fit well with what was ostensibly the principle mandate of bank supervisors – to enhance the stability of the system – while also restraining competition, a goal more difficult to incorporate into the existing supervisory institutions, especially in the current period.

As will be apparent when comparing theories, alternative explanations that require regulators to act in some assumed national interest without regard to their specific mandate are unrealistic. For instance, while reducing Japanese expansion was both a goal of important Basle Committee members and an outcome of the Basle process, this goal was expressed in general terms as the need to reduce the contribution of overly light regulation to excessive expansion, or to improve competition by evening out the regulatory burden. For instance, as Federal Reserve Chair Paul Volcker said in a testimony about the US–UK bilateral agreement:

> The need for parity of capital standards on an international basis is no less pressing. And, of course, as I have indicated before, that is an important objective of the US/UK proposal. The prospect of international banking organizations operating throughout the world with vastly different capital requirements and capital resources is not, in my view, in the best long-run interest of sound, stable, and competitive international banking and financial markets (US House of Representatives Committee on Banking, Finance and Urban Affairs, 1987:8).

Perceptions, Tools and Roles of Banking Regulators: Summary

The above discussion has established that the major stated goal of international regulators was to prevent instability. Evidence was presented indicating that these regulators saw intense competition, narrowing spreads and declining profit margins as important contributors to instability. The Concordat and capital agreement were effective responses to these problems given existing institutional capacity and the constraints imposed on regulators by their roles.

These points help to establish a causal link between the intensification of atomistic competition and regime formation. As discussed above, purposive behaviour is an important element of causation in human affairs. I have not needed to resort to some mysterious notion of deep structure nor to functional imperatives operating "behind the backs" of human agents to explain why regulators constructed a regime.

STRUCTURATIONIST CONNECTIONS: SECURITIES

Perceptions

As noted in Chapter 4, IOSCO's stated goal is to cooperate on the regulation of markets through information sharing, standard setting and enforcement. The current structure of the Technical Committee's four working parties indicate IOSCO's more specific priorities: (1) regulation of secondary markets; (2) regulation of market intermediaries primarily through capital adequacy standards; (3) information sharing and cooperation on enforcement primarily through the MOUs; and (4) multinational disclosure and accounting, with a key focus on the facilitation of multinational offerings, of which the MJDS is a key example. Additional goals include encouraging the creation and professionalization of equity markets in the developing countries, to which the various working parties of the Development Committee are committed, as well as developing standards for the ethics of intermediaries.

To what extent can these goals be seen as responding to the indicators of atomistic competition, or to the problems likely to be associated with the absence or decay of a private regime? In contrast with the Basle Committee's work, the work of IOSCO involves more varied goals that are less directly related to reducing competition. A closer look at these goals in the light of the private regime discussed in Chapter 4 is revealing.

First, with the exception of capital standards, IOSCO's goals are far less focused on regulating the main firms involved in the Eurosecurities markets than are the goals of the Basle Committee. The primary focus in the regulation of secondary markets is to consider the impact of derivative markets and off-market trading. Both are sources of instability in the market and represent new challenges to regulators because they are not carried on in the traditional institutional setting of the stock exchanges. The major competitive threat these new activities represent is to the organized exchanges, not to the Eurosecurities firms which have generally carried on their work outside traditional channels of regulation.

Similarly, information sharing and enforcement, as developed in the MOUs, are primarily aimed at preventing cross-border fraud. While such fraud, like money laundering for banking, can be considered a form of unacceptable competition, these enforcement measures are not aimed at protecting the major firms involved in the Eurosecurities markets. These Eurosecurities firms, as noted in Chapter 4, have managed to prevent damaging fraudulent activities through the control exercised by their private regime. The primary purpose of the MOUs, as with the regulation of secondary markets, is to prevent threats to domestic securities markets. The rules for ethics for intermediaries play a very similar role.

To the extent that IOSCO initiatives on enforcement and ethics have promoted the US model of securities regulation in which insider trading is considered a crime, it is possible to say that competitive pressures on US securities firms are being reduced. Insider trading has been considered acceptable in other countries and by advocates of the free market. Pressures to prohibit insider trading, by forcing other countries to adopt the US system, impose costs of regulatory convergence on countries other than the US. Yet, as noted above, this type of struggle does not primarily involve the practices of the main firms involved in the Eurosecurities markets, but rather involves competing national markets.

IOSCO's work on multinational disclosure and accounting is primarily oriented towards multinational offerings of equity rather than debt. As noted in Chapter 4, equity offerings are relatively new in international markets. While the interest in this issue on the part of regulators may superficially appear to correspond to the interest of bank supervisors in the new financial instruments, the impact of the new developments on the core firms is quite different. In the case of the new financial instruments, the major concern of regulators was the failure of banks to adequately account for the risks involved under intense competitive pressures. Much of this competitive pressure stemmed from the compatibility of these new instruments with the traditional bank competitors – that is securities firms. In contrast, there is no indication that multinational offerings represent threats to the viability of international securities firms. Indeed, these firms appear to be major beneficiaries of the expansion of the Euroequity market. Like clearance and settlement, the work on multinational offerings appears designed to facilitate expansion of this activity.

The work of IOSCO's Development Committee also differs from the role that the Offshore Group plays in the banking regime. At first glance one might expect them to play similar roles because both incorporate expanding markets from outside the Group of Ten industrialized countries. Instead their goals are contrary. IOSCO's Development Committee's main goal is to encourage the growth of emerging markets. While this involves ensuring that these markets are adequately regulated and supervised, the purpose of this regulation and supervision is primarily to ensure that these markets are able to attract investors and to grow. This goal has been incorporated into IOSCO's work from the beginning: the organization was founded in 1974 at the initiative of the World Bank and the Organization of American States in order to assist in the development of securities markets in Latin America.[7] There has been a greater effort to incorporate developing markets into the decision-making process than is the case with the Offshore Group, as indicated by the presence at various times of such countries as Hong Kong, Mexico, Brazil, Ecuador, Chile, Nigeria, Poland, Turkey and India on the Executive Committee of IOSCO. Indeed the expansion of the Executive Committee by five members in 1991 was designed to enhance the representation of countries not adequately represented on the Committee.

In contrast, the jurisdictions involved in the Offshore Group are ones that had already grown rapidly at the time of the Group's formation, and were challenging traditional banking centres. The primary purpose of incorporating the banking centres represented in the Offshore Group into the regime was to restrain their ability to drain banking away from the traditional centres by offering less regulated environments. Despite claims that there is a two-way learning process between the Basle Committee and the Offshore Group, the most important function of the latter has been to accept initiatives, such as the Concordat and the capital agreement, developed in the Basle Committee. There is no representation from developing markets in the Basle Committee itself.

In contrast to IOSCO's work discussed above, its work on capital adequacy standards for securities firms resembles more closely the main work of the Basle Committee. There are, however, two key differences. First, the capital negotiations have been less successful. Second, they are being driven by different developments: by banking regulators seeking to reduce the competitive threat from securities firms for banks, and by the EC seeking to harmonize regulations in order to be able to increase cross-border transactions. Thus on capital standards as well, there is much less interest displayed by securities regulators in disciplining and stabilizing the core international firms than is the case in banking.

Looking at the above analysis of international securities regulators' perceptions and motivations as a whole, it is clear that their goals differed significantly from those of international banking regulators. While banking regulators were primarily concerned with preventing instability in or the collapse of the largest banks at the centre of the international banking market, securities regulators were much more concerned with the negative impact on domestic markets of successful international securities markets, or with removing impediments in domestic markets to more rapid expansion of international securities markets. The autonomy of the private regime in international securities markets is evident in the relative lack of concern expressed by securities regulators for improving the performance of the top firms involved in the private regime.

At the same time, securities regulators were not entirely unconcerned about problems that can be linked to the weakening of the private securities regime, which was described in Chapter 4. Both the ability of international securities markets to threaten the operation of domestic markets, as with the increase in cross-border fraud, and the need to formally modify domestic regulations in order to facilitate international transactions, as in efforts to coordinate standards for multi-national offerings, indicate that international securities markets have begun to outgrow the private regime. Where previously the Eurobond market could be left to its own devices, with firms devising ad hoc solutions to barriers to internationalization, now the state is increasingly stepping in to shape the institutions that facilitate the operation of the market.

Tools

If, as is argued in the previous section, the securities regime is driven more by concerns about the impact of globalization and of the competitive abilities of securities firms on traditional national markets and on banks, as well as with altering domestic barriers in order to speed up globalization, than by concerns about the health and survival of the largest firms in the industry, then it is useful to ask whether the characteristics of the securities regime are appropriate given alternative processes.

Four characteristics in particular were symptomatic of the securities regime's weaknesses. First was a lack of commitment to IOSCO agreements, as evident for example in the numbers of regulators that had not signed the 1986 and 1989 agreements on cooperation. Second was a lack of specificity in IOSCO agreements. Third was an eclecticism and lack of focus in IOSCO's agenda, an indication of a lack of learning. Fourth was a greater reliance on policies and implementation developed outside the multilateral process of the securities regime than was the case with the Basle Committee. The role of the US in driving the MOU and MJDS policies, the role of bilateral agreements in implementing the MOU and MJDS policies, and the role of the Basle Committee and the EC in driving the capital negotiations, are examples.

Can these weaknesses be connected to the goals of regulators as discussed in the previous section? Are there reasons why regulators would not have chosen alternative institutional arrangements, such as multilateral treaties for carrying out IOSCO policies, or a more integrated agenda? There are two reasons for answering these questions in the affirmative. First, the lack of urgency with regard to the performance of the largest international securities firms is likely to have led to an unwillingness to commit the types of institutional resources needed to construct a stronger regime. Second, the greater focus on national-level problems than was the case in the Basle Committee is likely to have contributed to eclecticism and a preference for more decentralized implementation of IOSCO policies. Haas (1990) has argued that aside from demise, the alternative to learning for organizations is adaption. Adaption involves turbulence, ad hoc agendas and lack of focus as national concerns prevail over consensual knowledge.

Roles

While the mandate of securities regulators bears some similarities to banking regulators in its concern with stability, an important difference is the acceptability of secrecy in the practice of the two roles. Banking regulators have successfully argued that secrecy is a legitimate tool because if regulators were to reveal suspicions about a bank, depositors would rush to withdraw funds, exacerbating a real problem, or perhaps even creating a problem where none had really existed. In contrast, securities regulation has been based on the disclosure of information with the aim of providing investors with sufficient information to take appropriate responses to risk.[8]

IOSCO's greater preference for publicity, as evident in the greater release of information about its operations compared with the Basle Committee, is likely to be related to this difference in the role of securities and bank regulators. The Basle Committee's strength has been greatly enhanced by its control over information. In addition to its greater release of information, IOSCO has also felt the need to incorporate a greater range of participants into its organizational structure, including regulators from outside the Group of Ten and self-regulatory organizations that are not formally part of the states involved.

Perceptions, Tools and Roles of Securities Regulators: Summary

The above discussion has filled in the gaps between the structure of the industry and the strength of the regulatory regime. In particular, it has shown that regulators' perceptions of the problems differed from those of banking regulators. National-level issues, such as the impact of cross-border fraud on domestic markets, rather than the health of the largest international securities firms were most important. These differences, as well as securities regulators' lack of urgency and preference for arrangements outside the multilateral process, can be seen as the purposive connection between conditions in the industry and the strength of the regime. Compared with the banking industry, the private regime in the securities industry has coped quite well with issues central to the performance of top firms. The regime process chosed by securities regulators is understandable given the more eclectic and nationally specific nature of the remaining issues.

CAUSATION AND CORRELATION: CONCLUSION

The above discussion of regulators' perceptions, tools and roles has argued that the relationship between industry structure and regime strength, which was analyzed in Chapters 3 and 4, can be seen as involving causation. The model of causation employed was derived from structuration theory, which emphasizes the purposive actions of knowledgable agents as constrained by institutional capacity and the need to call upon roles as a source of power. An examination of differences and similarities of banking and securities regulators' perceptions, tools and roles has aimed to support the view that the character of the interstate regime can be said to have been caused by the structure of the industry.

This model of causation is interpretative. It establishes causation by linking an observed relationship to aspects of social systems that are assumed to be fundamental drivers of change for the system as a whole. There are alternative plausible interpretations of causation to the structurationist model adopted here. For instance a world-systems perspective would look to the evolutionary imperatives of the capitalist world economy, while rational choice models might stress the belief that agents always seek to maximize individual wealth and power. Ultimately models of causation, like other aspects of metatheory involving untested assumptions, are rooted in alternative paradigms. An explanation such as the one developed in this book cannot be dismissed simply by calling upon an alternative model of causation rooted in a different paradigm. However comparison of explanations provided by alternative paradigms is useful in providing additional evidence with which to evaluate the merit of each. It is to such a comparison that I now turn.

ALTERNATIVE EXPLANATIONS FOR THE BANKING AND SECURITIES REGIMES

In this section the major explanatory generalizations that have been developed within the regime approach – hegemonic stability theory, the transactions cost approach and the epistemic communities approach – are looked at for their contributions to explaining the banking and securities regimes.

Hegemonic Stability Theory

Hegemonic stability theory (HST) predicts that regime creation and the preeminence of a single hegemonic power are correlated. Variants that emphasize the coercive nature of the hegemon attribute the success of regimes under hegemony to the enforcement capabilities of the hegemon. Variants that emphasize the benign nature of the hegemon argue that public goods will be provided only when a single power's benefits from these goods are greater than the costs of unilaterally providing the goods.

These predictions of HST rest on the more general realist view that outcomes can be predicted from the distribution of capabilities.[9] The most consistently realist position, which stresses military power as most important and as fungible, and thus tries to predict regime formation in all issue areas from the distribution of military capabilities, is of little use in analyzing the banking and securities regimes. The US predominates militarily and yet trends in US capabilities do not match trends in the strengthening of these regimes. Because there is no evidence that US power increased sharply during this period this theory cannot explain why these regimes were created and strengthened. Furthermore there is no evidence that US military capabilities influenced either regime. Finally, by not disaggregating power by issue area it is impossible for such theories to explain the differences between the banking and securities regimes.

Some analysts (for example Keohane, 1984) have brought liberal notions of power into HST in arguing that power is fragmented by issue area, and that one should therefore look at the distribution of capabilities by issue area. There are two problems with this approach. First, based on an analysis of distribution of market shares, Japan rather than the US should be considered the hegemon in the issue areas of global banking and securities markets. There is no evidence, however, that the Japanese have played a leading role in the construction of these two regimes. This corresponds to the lack of leadership provided by Japan in other financial areas (Murphy, 1989:74; Strange, 1990). Second, even if we consider the US to still be hegemonic in these issue areas by invoking such non-realist factors as ideology, learning or national cultural traditions, changes in US power do not correspond to changes in banking and securities regimes. The securities regime is weaker than the banking regime despite the fact that the US share of international securities markets is greater than its share of international banking markets.[10] Thus contrary to what one would expect based on hegemonic stability theory, the US dominance is less in banking, which has a strong interstate regime, than in securities, which has a weak interstate regime. Furthermore the US share of both these markets was declining over the period in which the interstate regimes were being strengthened.[11] A related issue is that the weaker regime (securities) was the regime in which US power was most visibly and directly applied. If the role of a single power was critical to regime formation, then one would expect regimes in which such a role is most evident to be strongest.[12]

The one contribution that realism does make to our understanding of these regimes is not in analyzing why the regimes emerged and were strengthened, but rather in analyzing the way in which states tried to shape the content of the agreements. The efforts of the US to restrict its major competitor, Japan, in the Basle accord, and to impose such idiosyncratic modes of regulation as insider trading rules on other countries through the securities regime, are examples. These realist insights provide the sharpest contrast with the approach developed in the present book, in which little attention has been paid to specific conflicting national interests. There has been no effort, for instance, to trace the wording of specific provisions of the Basle accord to trade-offs among national regulators seeking to maximize their power. Instead of focusing on interstate relationships, the relationship between states and industries has been central.

While making use of realism in this way appears to offer certain insights, on closer examination these insights are quite limited because such an approach provides no way to put content into the national interest. Why should the US have become interested in a capital accord at this point in time? Why would more energy have been devoted by the great powers to a banking regime than to a securities regime? These are fundamental questions for which realism has only ad hoc answers. References to globalization are brought in without any theory to connect the evolution of globalization with specific changes in regimes. References to the role of US regulators are made without an adequate method of assessing the power they bring to negotiations, and without explaining how the choice of policies are connected to this power. If, in contrast, their choice of policy is connected to developments at the industry level, then references to the relative power of regulators are of secondary importance.

In sum, realism in general and HST specifically is of limited value in analyzing the international banking and securities regimes. If we abandon HST and rely on realism's more modest insights regarding state actions then we do get some important insights into the impact of diverging national interests on the character of the regimes. Realism fails, however, to provide us with answers to some of the most important questions regarding regime formation. Let us now turn to a more sophisticated rational-actor approach, transactions costs theory, to see if it fares better.

Transactions Costs Theory

Transactions costs are used both to explain why rational actors are *motivated* to create and comply with regimes, and to explain why it is possible for these actors to successfully *negotiate* regime creation.[13] In the study of international relations the focus has been on transactions costs between *states*.

Actors are motivated to support regimes because these actors anticipate that the regimes will reduce various transactions costs. Regimes can provide economies of scale in negotiation; they can reduce the costs of enforcing contracts by making side-payments, issue linkage, and "iterated plays" possible; and they can provide information that is trusted by participants in the regime more efficiently than can an individual state, which may be partisan.

Actors are able to overcome the collective action problem in establishing regimes if the transactions costs involved in the necessary negotiations are reduced. Such reductions can result if technological change reduces the costs of enforcing compliance; if the regime is nested in a broader extant regime, the institutional resources of which it can draw upon; and if negotiations involve a small number of participants among which trust and compliance can be encouraged by face-to-face interactions.

In the case of the interstate regimes for banking and securities, insights from transactions costs analysis are of limited value in explaining differing *motivations* of participants over time and between industries. While both regimes might theoretically be expected to provide economies of scale in negotiation, it is difficult to see why such economies would have increased at particular points in time, or why they would have differed between the two regimes without bringing in factors exogenous to the approach. It is difficult to assess whether the reliance of the securities regime on a set of bilateral agreements indicates a diseconomy of scale in multilateral negotiations, or simply a delay in regime creation due to other factors. Similarly, it is difficult to see why the issue areas would vary over time on the degree to which regime creation could reduce enforcement costs. The significance of the two regimes' ability to provide information is also ambiguous. The sharing of information between supervisors is a key aspect of both regimes, but it is difficult to explain variations in the strength of the two regimes with respect to variations in the value of information-sharing. Regulation of the securities industry has traditionally involved greater public disclosure of information than has regulation of the banking industry. One might therefore expect that the value to participants of a regime's information-producing capacity would be less in the case of the securities regime. On the other hand, more ongoing disclosure of information independent of the regime would make negotiations over the securities regime easier.

The transactions costs approach is more useful in its assessment of the transactions costs involved in setting up the two regimes. In the case of the banking regime, the transactions costs involved in the creation of the Basle Supervisors' Committee were reduced by the prior existence of two institutions designed to facilitate cooperation between central bankers on other matters: the Bank for International Settlements, which provides the Committee's secretariat, and the Group of Ten, of which the Committee is a part. The BIS, which has been described as a "service organization for central banks from the world's 25 richest countries" (Fairlamb, 1991:30), has provided a forum for cooperation related to international monetary stability (Howell, 1989), as well as providing information and functioning as a secretariat for international projects of central bankers before the Basle Committee was set up. The Group of Ten Central Bank Governors had gathered considerable experience in working together in its role in the General Arrangements to Borrow during the 1960s. Since bank regulation, because of its relationship to monetary policy, has generally been the responsibility of central banks, the creation of an international regulatory body concerned with bank regulation could draw on prior institutionalized cooperation to facilitate its creation. In contrast, there was no comparable cooperative precedent for securities regulators. Furthermore, banking regulation has traditionally been more centralized in domestic markets than has securities regulation. In some markets it has been difficult even to identify the competent authority for securities regulation (Kuebler, 1987:118). In some markets self-regulatory organizations play a key role, making international negotiations more difficult because of the variety of actors involved. Thus this variable is useful in explaining the different strengths of the two regimes relative to each other. It is not useful, however, in explaining why the regimes emerged at a particular historical moment. The impact of technological change on the costs of enforcement, in contrast, does not appear to be a useful explanatory factor. The impact of technological change on regulation and supervision appears to be greater in the securities industry than in the banking industry, although it is not clear whether this change has helped or hindered regulation and supervision. In both industries technological change has made it more difficult to assess systemic risks. In the banking industry international electronic funds transfer and assessment of the risks involved in new financial instruments are examples of developments that have made prudential regulation more difficult (Group of Ten, 1986; BIS, 1990). In the securities industry the shift to electronic marketplaces, the linking of exchanges, and the use of computer trading have increased volatility and the incidence of cross-border fraud, making enforcement more difficult. On the other hand, the computerization of trading has assisted regulators by facilitating the creation of "audit trails" and the identification of irregular patterns of trading that may indicate the use of inside information (Saunders and White, 1986; see also Langevoort, 1985; OECD *Financial Market Trends*, 1990:28). The computerization of clearance and settlement mechanisms in the securities industry reduces systemic risks, as it eliminates the back-office chaos that has existed in the past (Group of Thirty, 1989; United States Congress, Office of Technology Assessment, 1990). Thus it appears that the net impact of technology on reducing transactions costs in securities enforcement may be greater than in banking, although the ambiguity involved in this effect is too great to make this variable very useful.

In sum, the transactions costs approach is most useful in its identification of the importance of nesting new regimes in existing institutional arrangements. However this insight by itself is inadequate for explaining why the two interstate regimes emerged when they did.

Epistemic Communities Approaches

Some theorists (for example Haas, 1989; 1992) have argued that epistemic (knowledge-producing) communities can contribute to cooperation between states by creating new "consensual" knowledge (Haas, 1990) which transforms states' perceptions of their national interest. At first glance the banking and securities regimes would seem to be ideal candidates for the application of an epistemic communities approach. In both regimes the knowledge involved is highly technical, state and non-state knowledge-producers work closely together,[14] and mechanisms exist to produce new knowledge that is then fed quickly into the policy process. All of these features of the issue areas should contribute to the ability of epistemic communities to shape the regime.

Kapstein's (1992) assessment of the value of the epistemic communities approach to international bank regulation in an *International Organization* volume on epistemic communities illustrates some of the weaknesses of the approach. Kapstein himself sees national power rather than an epistemic community as critical for this issue area. More important than his rejection of the epistemic communities approach, however, is the arbitrariness of that rejection. Determining the influence of an epistemic community rests on carefully tracing the evolution of ideas to determine their impact on policy-making. Yet Kapstein diminishes the importance of the work of the Basle Committee that preceded the US–UK bilateral agreement. If he had given this early work the attention it has received in the present book, his conclusion regarding the existence of an epistemic community may have been reversed. That such differences of interpretation could so easily lead to contrary evaluations of the existence of the central theoretical entity in the approach is disturbing. In the approach developed in this book, in contrast, qualitative analysis was supplemented with quantitative measures.

The problem cited in the previous paragraph is symptomatic of more general problems associated with the attenuation of an approach that focuses so heavily on ideas. Tracing the evolution of ideas does not explain why these particular ideas emerged. For instance, why did consensus emerge around a risk-based capital adequacy approach to international bank regulation? The present book has argued that this particular technique was an appropriate response from the point of view of regulators given changes at the industry level, given existing institutional capacity in terms of alternative regulatory tools and given the roles of regulators. In an epistemic communities approach the link to changes at the industry level and to the institutional capacity of regulators to alter markets is missing. Instead the focus is on the institutional mechanisms by which knowledge is produced and transmitted.

Despite these problems the epistemic communities approach does bring insights into the features of institutional learning. The role of consensual knowledge in supporting cooperation and the importance of integrated analytical frameworks in enhancing the effectiveness of organizational actions are examples. However, while these concepts capture particular features of successful organizations they do not adequately explain why these features are present. In the approach developed in this book learning was used as an indicator of regime strength, the dependent variable, rather than as an independent variable that could be used to explain regime strength. The examples of learning in the Basle Committee and IOSCO were useful in measuring strength, but it is difficult to see how they can provide a useful explanation of strength. For instance, to point to the ability of Committee to correct the mistakes of the 1975 Concordat with the 1983 revised Concordat is not to explain why they did so. In the present book this explanation involved connecting organizational outcomes to changes in the industry through the perceptions of regulators. Thus learning was integrated more thoroughly into a broader framework than is the case in the epistemic communities approach.

In sum, the careful tracing of the evolution of ideas and the impact of knowledge-producing institutions on policy formation is an important area of research for regime analysis to which the epistemic communities approach has made a major contribution. At the same time it is far from adequate as an explanation of the formation and strengthening of the banking and securities regimes. Without connecting knowledge more closely to patterns external to the knowledge-producing community itself, the approach retains an element of arbitrariness and has difficulty in accounting for the specific types of knowledge around which consensus develops.

Comparing Explanations: Conclusion

The purpose of examining the above three alternative approaches to explaining regimes was to provide an additional criterion on which to judge the approach developed in this book and to see whether these alternative approaches can provide additional insights.

All three of the above approaches display serious weaknesses in explaining variations in the two regimes' strength over time and with respect to each other. Hegemonic stability theory is most deficient. Even after relaxing substantially the theory's core assumptions, it is able to provide little insight into why the regimes were constructed and strengthened when they were, and why the banking regime was stronger than the securities regime. Only a more modest realist claim – that states seek to shape interstate regimes in order to promote their interests – is useful in understanding the content of international agreements. Realism in general and hegemonic stability theory in particular is of limited value because it does not allow us to explain how or why the perceptions of the great powers of their national interests were determined.

The transactions costs approach also is weak in its ability to explain variations in strength. Its neglect of changes at the industry level forces the approach to rely too heavily on transactions costs between states. If these remain relatively constant, as was the case with important transactions costs in the banking and securities regime, then there is no way to explain regime change. On the other hand, when they vary they can be an additional source of explanation. One example is the way in which the transactions costs approach draws our attention to the importance of nesting for reducing transactions costs in establishing regimes. The historical traditions of central bank cooperation have been important for the speed with which the banking regime emerged. For instance the prior history of the Group of Ten assisted it in acting quickly in establishing the Basle Committee in response to the banking crises of 1974. Similarly, the Basle Committee was able to call upon the BIS to supply its secretariat and provide a source of information on international banking. While the approach developed in this book referred to such factors to a certain degree by stressing institutional capacity and regulators' roles, as for instance in the highlighting of secrecy as a legitimate and powerful tool of bank regulators, the transactions costs approach provides a different and more direct way of appraising these interstate institutional differences.

The epistemic communities approach similarly fails to provide a basis upon which to explain the emergence of particular ideas at particular times. By limiting itself too strictly to the internal dynamics of knowledge production, this approach has difficulty in addressing the link between the object of the community's study and the substance of the knowledge produced. By incorporating the concept of learning into the measures of regime strength the present book was able to draw on some of the insights of the epistemic communities approach while also analyzing the additional relationship to which that approach is blind.

Overall therefore, the approach developed in the present book does provide us with new facts and relationships that alternative approaches do not. However, the present approach does not displace alternative approaches entirely, but rather provides insights into an important but neglected dimension of regime formation and strength. I conclude this book, therefore, with a brief consideration of the significance for international relations theory in general of the relationship between industry structure and the strengthening of interstate regimes that has been established for banking and securities.

CONCLUSION: INDUSTRY AND REGIME

The book has confirmed the value of bringing industry structure into the analysis of international regulatory regimes. Despite the emphasis on the relationship between industry structure and regulatory arrangements at the domestic level, as for instance in the economic literature on domestic regulation and in the corporatism literature, attempts to establish such links have been minimal at the international level. As noted previously, markets are treated as resources wielded by states or as natural forces that are part of the state's external environment, but not as sets of social institutions that can provide alternative mechanisms for carrying out some of the important functions usually associated with the state. In the present book neither the state nor the market is taken as "ontologically primitive," to use Wendt's (1987) term. Rather than assigning particular functions by assumption to the state and to markets respectively, how functions are distributed between state and non-state social institutions is taken as a question to be asked.

The concept of a private regime has proved useful in answering this question because it highlights the similarities between sets of non-state social institutions and the interstate regimes upon which international relations theorists traditionally focus. In the present book, not only was such a regime discovered in international securities markets, but its presence was associated with a weaker interstate regime than was the case with banking. Thus the concept of a private regime is not only intrinsically interesting as another form of global cooperation, but is also a potentially important factor in the degree to which interstate regimes are constructed and strengthened.

There are two paths for further inquiry that are suggested by the findings of this book. The first is to determine whether a similar relationship between industry structure and the strength of interstate regimes is present in other industries. Although there are certain characteristics specific to financial industries, such as the importance of the payments system to the economy as a whole and the long tradition of strong domestic regulation, these do not preclude the possibility that similar relationships exist in other industries. While the unique qualities of financial industries should be taken into account, they should not be overstated. For instance telecommunications, railroads, agriculture and a variety of other industries have at different times been subject to strong regulations domestically and have been seen as key industries for the economy as a whole. The central role of commercial banks in the payments system is rapidly eroding as new forms of making payments proliferate (Podolski, 1986:vii–viii). In short, there are many lessons to be learned by analyzing the relationship between industry structure and interstate regimes in other industries.

The second path for further inquiry is to understand better the relationship between varieties of institutions at the international level. By looking for private regimes this book has highlighted a type of international institution that is often overlooked. Too often institutions such as states, multinational corporations and international organizations are taken as unitary actors with discrete boundaries marking off internal hierarchies and external environments. This book has begun to highlight the problematic nature of these boundaries by pointing to the impact of private regimes, which rely upon, but involve more than, the corporate hierarchies traditionally associated with the multinational enterprise. There is much to be done to understand better the relationship between the great variety of institutional arrangements that structure the interactions among firms and states.

In sum, the relationship between industry structure and interstate regimes does matter. This book has demonstrated that the banking and securities regimes were strengthened in response to particular features of the two industries they sought to regulate: increasing pressures of atomistic competition and the absence or weakening of private regimes. As the search continues for the sources of order and regularity in the international political economy it will be important to continue to move beyond a focus on the interactions of states to look at the great multiplicity of institutional arrangements that exist within industries.

Notes and References

1 Introduction: Theory, International Institution and Global Finance

1. Because of the blurring of the distinction between the activities of banks and securities firms it is increasingly difficult to distinguish clearly between the two industries. There are four main types of international financial transactions (Resnick, 1989:35): (1) Eurocurrency markets (involving banks that seek deposits and make loans in foreign currencies), (2) the foreign exchange market, (3) the international bond market and (4) the international market for equities. Commercial banks are primarily involved in the first two, and securities firms in the second two markets. Recent innovations have created a large number of derivative and hybrid instruments, many of which do not fit easily into these categories. Because of domestic regulations in some countries that require the two types of firms to be separated, and because of traditions of specialization, the two types of firms can still be distinguished.

2. IOSCO was created in 1974 under its original name, the Inter-American Association of Securities Commissions and Similar Organizations. Initially all of its members were from the Americas. The decision to create a genuinely global organization, and to adopt the present name, was taken in 1984 (interview with Jean-Pierre Cristel, Assistant to the Secretary General, IOSCO, 16 October 1991; telephone interview with Paul Guy, Secretary General, IOSCO, 12 May 1992; Kuebler, 1987:117; Securities and Exchange Commission, 1987:VII-75).

3. The Group of Ten originally included Belgium, Canada, France, Germany, Italy, Japan, the Netherlands, Sweden, the US and the UK. The name was retained after Switzerland became the eleventh member.

4. In the literature on bank regulation there is a distinction between "regulation," which involves use of more formal rules, and "supervision," which involves ongoing monitoring of firms. In practice these functions often overlap. In this study these terms will be used interchangeably.

5. Membership as of 26 September 1991 (International Organization of Securities Commissions, 1991b). Regular members must be securities commissions or similar government agencies, but other regulatory bodies and international organizations can join as associate or affiliate members. Private-sector representatives can attend annual meetings as observers. The membership and structure of IOSCO are discussed in Chapter 4.

6. The figures on signatories are current as of 20 October 1991, as provided by IOSCO to the author. More detail on the work of IOSCO is given in Chapter 4.

7. There are some exceptions for the Basle Committee on Banking Supervision. In the fields of international relations, international political

economy and international law there are several very useful studies. Kapstein (1989, 1992) and Tobin (1991) have both analyzed the Committee making use of international relations theory. Both have focused on interactions at the state level rather than the relationship of the Committee to changes at the industry level. Although he does not make use of the international relations literature, Dale (1984) has produced an excellent account of the work of the Committee up to the 1983 revised Concordat. Strange (1986) makes reference to the Committee but tends to underestimate its effectiveness, as is evident from her failure to mention it in a 1990 article on the regulation of international finance. Norton (1989a, 1989b) provides a very useful analysis of the Committee from the perspective of international and domestic law. Spero (1980) provides an excellent case study of one of the crises that stimulated the institutionalization of international bank supervision. IOSCO has received even less attention. Tobin's (1991) unpublished thesis provides the only analysis of IOSCO within the international relations literature, and there are only a few dated and/or superficial analyses in the international legal literature.

8. See for instance Kaplan (1989:47–8) who during this period was involved in both historical comparisons of alternative states systems and more quantitative analysis: "The historical studies that were being carried out in my workshops were, in my opinion, more valuable than the computer project.... Unfortunately, the profession did not recognize the study of the past in the 1960s unless done quantitatively.... I was not prepared to encourage my students to carry out projects that I thought would be superficial or to carry out good projects that would blight their careers."

2 Rethinking Regimes: Industry and Institution

1. The first two labels are Mitnick's (1980). Moran (1986) distinguishes four approaches to regulation: teleological and instrumental, which correspond to Mitnick's two, as well as cultural approaches (like Gerschenkron,1966, which stress historico-cultural differences) and administrative theories, which stress the difficulty of matching organizational tools with problems. Insights compatible with the cultural and instrumental approaches are dealt with in the discussion of the new comparative political economy below.

2. Philippe Schmitter has been the leading proponent of the corporatist approach. See Peter J. Williamson, 1989:14.

3. "Community" refers to the social organization that results from mutual understanding developed from long-term mutually rewarding relationships. Ouchi (1980) refers to this as "clan." There has been considerable criticism of Williamson for ignoring this category. See for instance the contributions in Francis, Turk and Willman, 1983.

4. An exception is recent analysis of corporatism at the European Community level by Streeck and Schmitter (1991). Interestingly, a book edited by Willetts (1982) entitled *Pressure Groups in the Global System* has no chapter on transnational business organizations.

5. One can attempt to resolve this contradiction while preserving the notion of markets as natural by arguing that the legal rules that sustain markets are also natural. Distinguishing in any rigorous way between "natural" social contracts and bodies of common law, and politically constructed state institutions seems impossible, however. See Rubin, 1988:1263.

6. There is a large literature on the demise of the Bretton Woods system. See for instance Gowa, 1983 and Odell, 1982. I discuss the institutional nature of money and finance more extensively elsewhere (Porter, 1991).

7. The application of the new institutional economics to banking is extensive. See for instance the essays on financial intermediation in Bhattacharya and Constantinides, 1989. The impact of deposit insurance on bank behaviour, the impact of the difficulty of assessing creditworthiness of customers on the way in which banks allocate credit, and the need for a bank regulation to offset the inability of bank customers to assess bank soundness are some examples where imperfect information and institutional structure have been seen as relevant. See for instance Goodhart, 1988.

8. Differential tax treatment of debt and equity was subsequently incorporated into this model as an explanatory variable.

9. Mayer (1990) usefully distinguishes between transaction costs theories information theories, and control theories as alternative approaches to analyzing the institutional factors that shape the debt/equity choice. These address the difficulty of negotiating contracts, the problems of imperfect information and the problems of enforcement of contracts respectively. Williamson (1988a) distinguishes between agency costs and transactions costs approaches. All these approaches overlap, and here they are treated as variations within the NIE.

This new economic literature can be seen as a belated recognition of the importance of the longstanding debate over the question of who controls the corporation. Sociologists, especially Marxists, have been far more likely than economists to see this as a relevant research question. The points made in this paragraph, and others in this section, could have been written in a Marxist "idiom." However this idiom is better suited to macrostructures, and is not as flexible in its ability to analyze the relationship between micro and macrostructures. On this sociological and Marxist literature, see Herman, 1981; Kotz, 1978; Stokman, Ziegler and Scott, 1985; Zeitlin, 1989.

10. Both the stock markets and currency markets are sometimes cited as paradigmatic examples of free markets.

11. The role of global social institutions in constituting states as egoistic actors, while important, is not dealt with here. See Keohane, 1988; Krasner, 1988; Porter, 1991; Thomas, Meyer, Ramirez and Boli, 1987; Wendt, 1990.

12. Neoinstitutionalism in comparative politics bears some similarity to Allison's (1971) analysis of bureaucratic politics, the usefulness of which has long been recognized by many international relations scholars. Keohane and Nye's (1977) concept of transgovernmental relations, where common interests develop between lower level bureaucrats and their opposite numbers in other states, is also similar. Both of these

approaches, while sensitive to the impact of bureaucracy, do not attribute as independent a role to social institutions as do neoinstitutionalist comparativists.

13. For example, as noted previously Willetts' *Pressure Groups in the Global System* (1982) includes no chapter on international business associations.

14. See for instance Hexner, 1946; Mason, 1946; Mayall, 1951.

15. The role of strategic partnerships in protecting firms against competitive pressures when costly investments in new technology are required (Mytelka, 1991) fits with this pattern noted by Magee.

16. Analysing these markets is complex since research, production and marketing are separable phases of a production process, each of which may be characterized by differing stages of technological maturity.

    Attempting to develop transhistorical generalizations about the relationship of forms of supra-firm governance structures, such as direct colonialism, cartels, strategic alliances and state-led strategic trade policies to industry cycles would be very interesting. Efforts to synthesize political and economic long cycles (Goldstein, 1988) are suggestive. Pursuing such speculation with any seriousness goes far beyond what is possible in this book.

17. An alternative approach that has been used is to attempt to identify each of the elements in Krasner's definition of a regime, and to treat missing elements or incoherence between these elements as evidence of regime weakness (Kratochwil and Ruggie, 1986:770). There are a number of problems with this, however. First is the difficulty of clearly differentiating between principles, norms, rules and decision-making procedures. Second is the assumption of a hierarchy of importance; for instance, that norm change, not rule change, is evidence of regime change. As Kratochwil (1984:687) points out, a change in the scope of rules (for example extending the scope of taxes) can also involve regime change. Third is the assumption that coherence is a measure of strength. There are cases where incoherence can contribute to regime persistence. Kratochwil and Ruggie (1986:771) point to the US Constitution as a robust but incoherent institution. Overall, this approach to measuring regimes tends to reify them, treating them as real objects that can be known by their attributes rather than as theoretical constructs.

18. The use of the concept of institutionalization by comparativists in the study of state formation is illustrative of its strengths and weaknesses. A key puzzle for comparativists in the early 1960s was why new states exhibited signs of chronic instability. Earlier theories had suggested that the development of Western political institutions would follow fairly automatically from a unilinear process of economic and social development (Lipset, 1959; Rostow, 1960). It had subsequently become clear, however, that economic, ethnic, and violent political conflicts were persisting. Two major analytical shifts emerged in response to this anomaly. The first, dependency theory, traced the problem to continuing exploitation of the third world by the first (Blomström and Hettne, 1984). The second, political development theory, attempted to identify the institutional factors contributing to the construction of strong states (Apter, 1987; Binder, 1986; Higgott, 1983; Weiner and Huntington,

1987). For Samuel Huntington (1968), the principal advocate of the second approach, institutionalization was a key concept.

Initially the second approach came under heavy criticism for its extremely conservative bias towards preserving the status quo, which was seen as reinforcing military dictatorships and justifying repression of popular movements. More recently, however, there has been an attempt to integrate some of the insights from this earlier institutionalism with the insights from dependency theory regarding economic conflict. Indeed, this integration is a key aspect of the neoinstitutionalist agenda in comparative politics. In this more recent view, neither breaking exploitative economic links nor the creation of stronger states by themselves will lead to desired outcomes. The dependency advocacy of economic autonomy needs to be supplemented with a concrete analysis of the institutional conditions for effective state intervention. Political development theory's emphasis on strong states and stability, without sensitivity to class conflict and global economic inequality, will only lead to greater repression.

The theoretical trajectory of the study of international institutions echoes that of political development theory. Initial optimism that democratic international organizations would emerge automatically in conjunction with a unilinear process of economic development has disappeared as economic, ethnic and violent political conflicts among nation-states have persisted. Given the parallels, it seems useful to look again at the concept of institutionalization as it was developed by Huntington in the context of state formation.

19. My use of Huntington here, as with Parsons (1954) earlier, in no way indicates agreement with what I would overall consider the disastrous and highly conservative use that has been made of their work. Many of these problems stem from functionalism and a denial of the relevance of class. Giddens (1984), to some extent, develops many of Parsons' themes while avoiding these problems.

20. The primary reason that regimes are of interest to international relations theorists is that they may be able to modify the practices of the actors involved. Of these four measures compliance measures this most directly. Specificity less directly measures the modification of practices, but is closely related to compliance since compliance with vague regime injunctions is less meaningful than compliance with specific injunctions. Learning and autonomy are less directly linked to the effect of the regime on the actors involved, but rather are based on theoretical assumptions about the characteristics of institutions that are able to have such effects.

21. Analysis of this correlation in international finance is even less developed than for domestic finance. The literature for international banking is discussed by Bourke (1990). A brief analysis of the Eurobond market is presented by Smith and Walter (1990:601–3).

22. Herfindhal's index is the sum of the squares of each firm's share of the market. For a discussion of the properties of the index see Jacquemin, 1987:51.

23. This is because to be effective constancy ratios must be calculated with each year in a historical series as a base period that is then compared with

several ensuing years. Without doing this the use of a single idiosyncratic base year could provide a misleading ratio.

24. For an interesting discussion of this phenomenon see Teece, 1987.
25. See Blaug, 1980:137. Lakatos (1970:129) distinguishes between interpretative theory "which provides the 'hard' facts" and explanatory theory "which 'tentatively' explains them."
26. These sets of mutual expectations, which have been called "roles" by sociologists, can be seen to constitute and empower individuals. Giddens (1984) has developed this approach to structure, while avoiding the negative consequences of the functionalism of earlier sociologists such as Talcott Parsons.
27. Further analysis of why supervisors would pursue policies designed to restrict competition would also be useful. Public choice and capture theory suggest that regulators pursue the interests of the regulatees because the regulatees are better positioned to lobby than are the consumers of the regulated services. For such an argument as applied to banking, see Macey, 1989. By itself such an argument has difficulty explaining the major transformation in the mode of regulating banking which the use of capital adequacy ratios represents, however.

3 The Regime for Bank Regulation

1. This summary draws on Bryant (1987), supplemented with OECD and BIS data.
2. There is a large literature on international banking. See for instance Khoury, 1990; Meerschwam, 1991; Pecchioli, 1983, 1987; Smith and Walter, 1990. The reasons for globalization presented below are commonly cited in this literature.
3. Although many other international institutions have played a role in organizing global finance the Basle Committee is unique because it is the only interstate institution that aims to develop generalized principles, norms and rules for the ongoing conduct of banks, applicable throughout the world. While the regime for regulating banking is centred in the Basle Committee rather than the Group of Ten, the latter group plays an important part in the regime since it initiated the committee and has endorsed its major initiatives. The Group of Ten was created in 1961 as a way for its ten member-states to exercise control over the new resources they were called upon to provide to the IMF (Strange, 1976:113). Switzerland joined soon afterward because of the importance of its currency. The Group of Ten saw a need to deal with international banking problems as an extension of its responsibility for international monetary stability that had evolved over the 1960s. However, although the Basle Committee is formally responsible to the Group of Ten Central Bank Governors, in practice it is the Basle Committee rather than the Group of Ten that has initiated and implemented developments in international banking supervision. See for instance Cooke, 1990:314–15, on the genesis of the capital accord.
4. Liquidity can be defined as the availability of funds to meet claims, while solvency can be defined as a condition in which liabilities exceed assets

(Bannock and Manser, 1989). A bank can be solvent, but have a problem with liquidity if, for example, it has assets (such as loans) that are adequate to cover depositors' claims over the long run, but which cannot be converted into cash quickly in the event of a bank-run by depositors.

5. As *Institutional Investor* (Makin, 1991:94) comments: "Funded by Arab capital, BCCI had an unregulated parent holding company in Luxembourg, conducted the bulk of its business through banks incorporated in Luxembourg and the Cayman Islands and was run from London by expatriate Pakistanis."

6. Cooke (1990:314) notes that "by the late 1970s, virtually all the G10 countries had reviewed or refined their own national approaches for monitoring banks' capital adequacy."

7. Domestically central banks have also made use of secrecy and of other organizational barriers to reduce the ability of political pressures to influence monetary policy. Thus the central bank representatives to the Committee bring a culture of secrecy to Basle.

8. Based on hegemonic stability theory (HST) one might predict that Japan, which was quickly coming to dominate listings of the world's largest banks at the time of the capital negotiations, would have played a leading role in the provision of a regime. There is no evidence of this.

9. Peter Cooke, who was the Committee chair during this period, has noted that by the end of the 1970s,

> [a]s to the method of relating capital to the size of business, the Committee was roughly divided into two camps. Most of the European countries – France, Germany, Switzerland, Belgium, the Netherlands, Sweden and the United Kingdom – favoured an approach which weighted assets according to the degree of risk as providing the best measure of the adequacy of a bank's capital. However, Italy and Luxembourg, as well as Canada, Japan, and the United States, still used systems based on a gearing ratio approach which related capital funds to the unweighted total of the balance sheet (1990:314).

10. See for instance, Federal Reserve regulator Taylor's comments, "A Panel of Federal Regulators," 1987:267.

11. J. Andrew Spindler (1988:16–17), a Federal Reserve regulator who was involved in the Basle negotiations, notes that "In the United States, the effort to develop a risk-based capital measure began intensively in the summer of 1985. This effort was undertaken primarily in response to the tremendous growth and change in the nature of risks to which banking organizations had become exposed in the early 1980s, and also as an attempt to move US capital standards more closely in line with those used in many other industrial countries."

12. Subsequently the Japanese stock market crashed. For comments noting the accord's negative impact on US banks, see the following articles from the *Wall Street Journal* and *New York Times*: Bryan, 1987:32; Melloan, 1988a, 1988b; Sesit, 1988b; Nash, 1988b, 1988d. Norman (1987b:10) quotes a senior officer at a major New York bank as saying of the December 1987 version: "It's apparent to me that the Federal Reserve was out-negotiated."

13. As Gordon (1991:508) notes: "Trade groups argued against the limit on loan loss reserve inclusion in supplementary capital, as well as its exclusion from core capital.... These groups claimed that such reserves were no different from common equity because they are permanent, subordinate, and available to absorb potential losses on an ongoing basis."

14. On the origins of the new US regulations in the Basle process, see the statements of regulators before the US Senate Committee on Banking, Housing and Urban Affairs (1990:7–18).

15. For information on these institutions, see BSC, *Report on International Developments in Bank Supervision*, various years.

16. A BIS series which categorizes international activities by the nationality of the parent bank is available for years beginning with 1983. Centralization by nationality of ownership is likely to enhance the formation of private regimes independently of territorial centralization because the development of common sets of norms and rules is facilitated by shared national traditions. However, because the trend within this series is quite similar to that for territorial centralization, and because of lack of data for the years before 1983, this series is not displayed here. The difference is that London was much better at retaining its territorial dominance at around 30 per cent while British banks were only able to retain between 5 and 10 per cent of market share. The relative importance of territory and nationality of ownership is reversed for Japan. The cultural factor connected to concentration by nationality of ownership is therefore likely to have been even more disruptive for traditional private social institutions than was locational dispersion since the Japanese rise and British decline is more dramatic.

17. The Group of Ten Study Group defines a NIF as "a medium-term legally binding commitment under which a borrower can issue short-term paper in its own name, but where underwriting banks are committed either to purchase any notes which the borrower is unable to sell, or to provide standby credit" (Group of Ten, 1986:19).

18. *Bank of England Quarterly Bulletin*, May 1991:254, citing data from the International Swap Dealers Association. In the second half of 1989 currency and interest swaps with a value (notional principle) of $500 million were transacted.

19. As a *Banker* article (Nisse, 1988:7–10) notes, "during the 1980s the balance of power between commercial banks and their corporate clients was irrevocably tipped in the clients' favour.... Corporates are bringing much financial experience in-house as they lose faith in their bankers. Says Chloride's [treasurer Kent] Price, 'Most corporations used to turn to a bank for general information because bankers are smarter than them. But it's unusual now to find a reasonably large corporation that doesn't have a finance department with people at least as good as the banks.'"

20. Cooper credits Morton Lane of the Discount Corporation of New York for this term.

21. A third approach to analyzing social institutions is to try to assess the degree to which transactions within the banking industry are channelled through bank corporate hierarchies as opposed to more atomised

interbank markets. Corporate hierarchies involve sets of social institutions which could support a private regime. Though difficult to measure precisely, interbank markets grew substantially in importance over the 1970s (Pecchioli, 1983:29). As the Group of Thirty has noted, "reliance on interbank funding tends to be higher for smaller banks and newcomers in the international market" (1982:16). Thus corporate hierarchies were undermined. One effect of the capital accord of 1988 was to severely restrict the expansion of interbank markets (Hakim, 1984:S36; IMF, 1984a:21, 1991b:2; the Bank for International Settlements, *International Banking Developments*, July 1987). This general pattern corresponds to the trends discussed in this chapter. Due to lack of data a fuller analysis of these patterns is not yet possible. BIS data on intrabank and interbank lending, while very useful, was only started in 1983 and is therefore of limited use for the time frame of this chapter.

22. The *Euromoney Annual Financing Report* noted in March 1989 (p.30) that "the top houses are toying with the idea," and in March 1990 that belief in this solution was "growing" (p. 26).

23. In the first half of 1991 there were no Japanese banks among the top twenty arrangers of syndicated loans, while there were five Japanese banks among the top twenty providers (Darbyshire, 1991:34).

24. This drop in Japanese participation can also be interpreted as an indication that the growing power of Japanese banks is characterized by the preference of these banks for traditional interconnections with other Japanese banks rather than for providing leadership to banks from other countries through syndicates. I am indebted to Lynn Mytelka for this point.

25. Phone call to IIF staff member, 11 October 1991.

26. While other private international banking institutions play a role in organizing international banking activity, they too are not sufficiently developed to impose discipline on the industry. These institutions include clearing houses, information vendors and netting systems (Sarver, 1988:210; Smedresman and Lowenfeld, 1989; Bank of International Settlements, 1990:22).

4 The Regime for Securities Regulation

1. As noted previously, the only treatment of the securities regime in the international relations literature is a chapter of Tobin's (1991) unpublished dissertation.

2. Gordon S. Macklin, President of NASD Inc., statement in US Senate Committee on Banking, Housing and Urban Affairs, 1986:37.

3. Sudweeks notes that equity and bond markets have mobilized more funds for development through new issues than have World Bank loan disbursements. The World Bank is strongly advocating the development of equity markets as a solution to the financial problems encountered by LDCs (see International Bank for Reconstruction and Development, 1989; Gill, 1986:39–53).

4. SEC calculations, reported in Chuppe *et al.*, 1989:37.
5. A Salomon Brothers publication (Salomon Brothers International Limited, 1991:47) comments that "there are already signs that the multinational is a dinosaur."
6. The European Community and the NASAA are limited as they are both regional organizations. IOSCO's other competitors are limited by their narrow focus or lack of institutionalization. The Group of Thirty, which includes representatives from regulatory agencies as well as the private sector, has a narrow focus on clearance and settlement problems (Group of Thirty, 1989). The Wilton Park Group, sponsored by the United Kingdom Department of Trade and Industry, also has a narrow focus on exchange of information and practical enforcement problems and is limited to informal annual discussions among 14 regulatory agencies (interview with anonymous regulator, 13 May 1992). The International Society of Securities Administrators, based in Switzerland, has had little impact on international regulation. As is the case with banking, the GATT has not been a major forum. The SEC only began to get involved with the GATT in 1990 ("Mann Notes New SEC Involvement", 1990:590).
7. IOSCO's previous name was the "Inter-American Association of Securities Commissions and Similar Organizations" (Kuebler, 1987:117; SEC 1987:VII-75). IOSCO was initiated by the World Bank and the Organization of American States in 1974 in order to assist in the development of securities markets in Latin America. In its first decade IOSCO's activities were limited to annual meetings (telephone interview with Paul Guy, Secretary General, IOSCO, 12 May 1992).
8. The figures on signatories are current as of 20 October 1991, as provided by IOSCO to the author.
9. For the full text of the resolution see SEC, 1987:VII-77-8.
10. On the MOU process see, in addition to the sources cited in the text, Bartos, 1988; Deal, 1987:21; Goelzer, Mills, Gresham and Sullivan, 1988; Jimenez, 1990; Warren, 1990.
11. The figures on signatories are current as of 20 October 1991, as provided by IOSCO to the author.
12. Work on the 1988 accord between US and French regulators was begun in 1985 ("US, French to Sign Accord," 1988:1552).
13. Goelzer, Mills, Gresham and Sullivan, 1988:631; Winters, 1989:E1.
14. The critical response is evident in academic journals, as well as in the letters received by the SEC in response to the release. Examples of those who sent critical letters include the West German ambassador, an official at the Ontario Securities Commission, the Chair of the New York Stock Exchange's Advisory Committee on International Capital Markets, and the Chair of Merrill Lynch International, Inc. See Greenstein, 1987:317-9.
15. For instance detecting insider trading involves monitoring the access of traders to information.
16. See comments of Michael Mann, one of the SEC's principle MOU negotiators ("SEC has Sought Enforcement Help," 1988:1294). See also Jiminez, 1990:295-306; Levine and Callcott, 1989:125-6.
17. On the 1986 SEC proposals at IOSCO, see comments by Bevis Longstreth in US House of Representatives, Committee on Energy and Commerce,

1987:111; SEC *Annual Report*, 1986. On the European reaction, see Hawes, 1987:258.

18. On the Rio Declaration, see comments of Acting SEC Chair Charles Cox before the US House of Representatives Committee on Energy and Commerce, 1987:60. On the resolution on cooperation, see comments of SEC Commissioner Charles Cox ("IOSCO Technical Committee Considers," 1989:427). According to this report the technical committee agreed to circulate Cox's resolution among its members for their approval.

19. The Swiss, New Zealand and UK regulators expressed criticisms of the SEC proposals. For details, including the points in the SEC proposal, see "Regulators Agree to Move," 1988:1861. See also Reuter, 1988a:36, 1988b:B6.

20. The International Securities Enforcement Cooperation Act. See Jiminez, 1990. Then SEC Chair David Ruder stated in 1989 that the Freedom of Information Act was frustrating MOU negotiations ("Global Securities Accords," 1989:447). Modification of the Freedom of Information Act was needed before the US–French agreement of December 1989 could go into effect. Such legislation was signed into law on 15 November 1990 ("SEC, French Agency," 1991:172).

21. For details on British domestic regulatory modifications related to the MOUs, see Rider, 1990:210. On Swiss modifications, see Harari and Hirsch, 1987. In Canada a court case challenged the constitutionality of the 1988 Canada–US MOU on the grounds that a province did not have the authority to enter into such an agreement, and that if the OSC abided by the MOU a number of provisions of the Charter of Rights and Freedoms would be violated ("Constitutional Attack Mounted," 1988:1337). While ultimately unsuccessful, the case demonstrates the potential controversy regarding sovereignty that the MOUs can create.

22. Karmel (1989), a professor of law, lawyer and former SEC Commissioner, claims that the MJDS "developed out of IOSCO meetings." Jean-Pierre Cristel, IOSCO's Assistant to the Secretary General also claims that IOSCO played a role in the MDJS (interview with Jean-Pierre Cristel, Assistant to the Secretary General, IOSCO, 16 October 1991). Other sources of information on the MJDS include interviews with Cally Jordan, who was involved for the Ontario Securities Commission (OSC) as a lawyer in the negotiations, 16 October 1991; with a regulator at the OSC, 7 August 1991; as well as Claxton, Foulkes and Ottenbreit, 1989:11–14; Connelly, 1987; Critchley, 1991; Cushing, 1987; Gira, 1988; Jordan and Gibson, 1990:18; Karmel, 1990; Reguly, 1991. A speech by Ketchum (1986), who was Director of the Division of Market Regulation at the SEC, presents an SEC view.

23. See also comments by Acting SEC Chair Cox (US House of Representatives Committee on Energy and Commerce, 1987:58) indicating that the initiative came from the US: "we took the two systems that are the closest to the US system."

24. On this claim, see "Breeden Says Several Nations," 1989:1847. The SEC and Japanese officials have also stated that they have taken the first steps towards developing a MJDS ("Breeden, Japanese Officials," 1991:42).

25. The UK was dropped both because the UK was focused on reform of its domestic system and on the EC, and because the difficulty of the undertaking became clearer (interview with Cally Jordan, a lawyer involved in the negotiations, 16 October 1991).
26. On Japan see "Breeden, Japanese," 1991:42. On the UK, interview with Cally Jordan, a lawyer involved in the negotiations, 16 October 1991.
27. The report, *Comparative Analysis of Disclosure Regimes*, was issued at the 1991 Annual Conference (IOSCO, 1991g).
28. Interview with a regulator at the Ontario Securities Commission, 8 August 1991.
29. Then SEC Chair David Ruder and OSC Chair Stanley Beck, cited in "Canada, US Seen Moving," 1988:1629.
30. On these negotiations see Corrigan and Preston, 1992; Lee, 1992; Preston and Corrigan, 1992; Waters, 1992a, 1992b.
31. The Executive Committee had eleven members until the 1991 annual meeting, at which five new members were added. See Table 4.6.
32. Phone interview with Paul Guy, Secretary General, IOSCO, 12 May 1992.
33. I am indebted to Mahoney (1990:305) for pointing out the second quote from the Policy Statement. He makes a number of points regarding the SEC's continuing intolerance of alternative systems. The Policy Statement is Release No. 6807, 1988, and is reprinted in IOSCO, 1988b.
34. See for instance the comments by Richard Breeden, Chair of the SEC, ("Administrative Conference of the United States," 1991:352–3) on the MOU process in which no mention is made of IOSCO: "These agreements have been spreading. We very strongly support that process. I think as we go down the road, ultimately we may see multilateral arrangements, perhaps ripening at some point into multilateral treaty obligations, to provide the kind of assistance in investigations that will make effective enforcement possible around the world." Breeden did refer to IOSCO with reference to capital standards, disclosure and accounting later in this speech.
35. Interview with regulator at the Ontario Securities Commission, 8 August 1991.
36. The figures are from *Business Week*, 30 October 1989, and are cited in Arthur R. Pinto, 1990:55–88, 62. Foreign issues registered in the United States as a percentage of total registrations in the US declined from 13 per cent in 1977 to 3 per cent in 1986 (Karmel, 1990:16).
37. The authors note that "Since the operation of the MOUs is not generally a matter of public record, few details of cooperation are available for discussion in this article."
38. The SEC noted, in response to a request for information on the top securities firms in the world from Congress, that "We have determined that, with the information currently available, we cannot formulate a listing of the ten largest securities firms." Two reasons for this are (1) that the securities business is frequently included in the much larger activities of banks and other financial firms, and (2) many securities firms are closely held (US House of Representative, Committee on Energy and Commerce, 1987:81).
39. The process by which a new bond is launched is called issuance.

40. Although there is some indication that barriers between currency segments are eroding, as firms cross over into markets in which they had not previously operated, this erosion is slow. The impact of this erosion on concentration is also offset by the relative decline of the US dollar segment in relationship to other currencies since the intensity of competition in this segment had always been greater than was the case in other currency segments (Frank, 1988a).

41. Securities firms have become sufficiently international that one would expect long-term differences in profitability between US domestic markets and international markets to be reduced by a process of arbitrage as firms shifted resources to the most profitable markets.

42. Cross-border mergers and acquisitions rose from $71 billion in 1987, to $110 billion in 1988, $118 billion in 1989, and an estimated $100 billion in 1990 (Salomon Brothers International Limited, 1990:8).

43. The article goes on to quote Peter Anderson, head of equity primary markets at Swiss Bank Corporation in London, as saying, "The houses who are already established in Euro-equities have such a head start that it would be very difficult to enter now."

44. The general shift from floor-based trading systems in stock exchanges to screen-based trading systems as well as the expansion of information vendors such as Reuters are examples (IMF, 1990a:8. See also Ziegler, 1990:6). Resistance to screen-based trading in the Eurobond market has been fierce (Evans, 1988; Keller, 1989:12). *Euromoney* notes that "there are few traders who do not loathe the idea. They stand to lose their jobs, as street-smart, highly-paid traders are replaced by run-of-the-mill price updaters" (Evans, 1988:56).

45. See *Euromoney Annual Financing Report*, March 1989:34. A 1972 OECD report concluded that reliance on the criterion of "good standing" in the Eurobond market was comparable to "the most closely supervised domestic markets" (cited in Rich, 1980:542).

46. This latter practice was altered with various sovereign immunity acts (Rich, 1980:517).

47. The consortia were Bondtrade AG, Eurotrading, Western American Bank and Orion Bank (Kerr, 1984:85).

48. This shift was accompanied by the formation of a Eurobond syndicate club by Sheldon Prentice of Salomon Brothers in the late 1970s, criticized by smaller securities firms as a cartel (Kerr, 1984:109).

49. Punishment can be meted out by excluding cheaters from future syndicates. According to *Global Finance* (Munroe, 1990:20), "The front among Eurobond dealers is so united, in fact, that resistance to the new style has been pushed back into the corners of the market, among smaller dealers, and even underground."

50. See also Munroe, 1991:22, who cites the accusation of Peter Crane, syndicate head at Mitsubishi, that major dealers have set up a cartel to keep smaller firms out.

51. Two other important international private self-regulatory securities associations are the Fédération Internationale des Bourses de Valeurs (FIBV) and the International Council of Securities Associations (ICSA). The FIBV is the major international institution of the stock exchanges and

addresses many of the same issues as IOSCO, but seeks to minimize state involvement in regulation (FIBV, 1990:14, 22). While not a serious competitor to IOSCO, FIBV's existence underlines the greater reliance of securities markets on private institutions.

The International Councils of Securities Dealers and Self-Regulatory Associations was established in 1988. Set up at the initiative of the Japanese, it originally also included representatives from Canada, the US and the UK. Subsequently associations from Australia, France and Korea, as well as the International Securities Markets Association (formerly the AIBD), have joined. The original members were all affiliate members of IOSCO dissatisfied with the lack of attention they received in that organization. Current foci are (1) the regulation of screen trading; (2) responding to IOSCO's capital rules as they are negotiated; and (3) a study group on issues such as the mutual recognition of licencing courses. The organization meets twice a year: one annual meeting and one additional meeting that coincides with IOSCO meetings. Although FIBV representatives have attended ICSA meetings, the two have distinct agendas. In addition, some tension between the members of the two organizations reduce interactions. Although the ICSA has displayed significant growth since its formation in 1988, it remains limited in its influence. Defining its role and priorities have been problems for its members. To date none of its discussions have had a discernable effect on international securities markets (telephone interview with a senior executive of an ICSA member-agency, 13 May 1992; Ellwand, 1988:21; Reed, 1989; "Stock trading plan", 1990:B8).

5 Conclusion: Industry and Regime

1. Metatheory is theory about theory. Epistemology (which establishes criteria for legitimate knowledge), ontology (which specifies what entities should be taken as real), axiology (which addresses values) and methodology are all examples of metatheoretical concerns.
2. The term is used by Ibn Hassan (1987:193) in another context.
3. On structuration theory see Giddens, 1984, Held and Thompson, 1989, Hollis and Smith, 1991, 1992; Wendt, 1987, 1991, 1992.
4. There is some empirical evidence that the higher capital ratios that have occurred as a result of the Basle Accord have increased the value of bank equity to shareholders, indicating that the market had failed to maximize bank value (Shome, Smith and Heggestad, 1987).
5. Informal moral suasion is only likely to work with a private regime. Moran (1984) for instance, describes the way in which the financial community in London used to be run as an informal club. Once disrupted by competitive forces a more formalized and bureaucratic form of regulation was adopted.
6. There is a large literature arguing this point. See for instance Haraf and Kushmeider, 1988.
7. Telephone interview with Paul Guy, Secretary General, IOSCO, 12 May 1992.
8. See Garten, 1986, 1988, for a discussion of disclosure and bank regulation.

9. I do not consider treating outcomes instead of market share as a measure of capability (as suggested by Susan Strange to the author, 1 April 1992) because such an approach vitiates the uniqueness of realism and introduces the danger of tautology (that is, a regime was created because the power of a single state was preeminent. We know that this state was preeminent because it succeeded in creating a regime).

10. See for instance the figures on the nationality of the top ten banks and securities firms in Chapter 4, which further indicate that the US has been far more successful in retaining a major share of the Eurobond market than it has in retaining its share of spots among the top ten banks.

11. For instance the US share of world foreign assets of deposit banks declined from 17 per cent in 1982 to 12 per cent in 1988. The US share of world securities market capitalisation declined from 55 per cent in 1982 to 31 per cent in 1989 (IMF *International Financial Statistics*; *Business Week*, 30 October 1989, cited in Pinto, 1990:62).

12. A second problem is that US conduct, including an aversion to multilateralism at key points and a heavy reliance on techniques developed elsewhere, is not what one would expect of the hegemon painted by HST.

13. See Keohane, 1984 for a development of this approach to regimes.

14. The use of academics by the BIS and the OECD are examples, as is the Group of Thirty which combines experts from government and industry, and which has played an important role in analyzing the debt crisis in banking, and clearance and settlement of securities markets.

Bibliography

Note: This bibliography is separated into two sections: (1) books and periodicals and (2) documents with institutions as authors. Documents authored by individuals are included in the first section. In addition to these sources thirteen interviews, the majority by phone, were conducted with individuals involved with the institutions and agreements discussed in this book. In most cases these sources are anonymous. Where material from interviews has been relied upon this has been indicated in the text.

Books and Periodicals

Acworth, William (1992) "IIF to take a Stronger Role in International Regulatory Affairs", *International Banking Regulator*, 21 Sept., p. 6.

Adler, Patricia A. and Peter Adler (1984) *The Social Dynamics of Financial Markets* (Greenwich and London: Jai Press).

"Administrative Conference of the United States Colloquy: Globalization of Securities and Financial Market Regulations in the 1990s" (1991) *Annual Review of Banking Law*, pp. 345–77.

Alexander, James (1990) "A Question of Semantics", *The Banker*, Dec., pp. 14–18 (on the US interpretation of the Basle capital agreement).

Allison, Graham T. (1971) *Essence of Decision* (Boston: Little, Brown and Company).

Aoki, Masahiko, Bo Gustafsson and Oliver Williamson (eds) (1990) *The Firm as a Nexus of Treaties* (London: Sage).

"A Panel of Federal Regulators on the Challenges of Increased Regulatory Supervision" (1987) *Annual Review of Banking Law*, pp. 257–70.

Apter, David E. (1987) *Rethinking Development: Modernization, Dependency Theory, and Postmodern Politics* (Newbury: Sage).

"A Risky Business" (1988) (swaps and options), *Economist*, 28 May, pp. 81–2.

Aronson, Jonathan David (1977) *Money and Power: Banks and the World Monetary System* (Beverly Hills and London: Sage).

Austin, Robert P. (1987) "Regulatory Principles and the Internationalization of Securities Markets", *Law and Contemporary Problems*, vol. 50(3), pp. 221–50.

Bain, Andrew (1987) "Where the New Instruments Will Take Banking", in Ian Cooper, Andrew Bain, John Donaldson and Lionel Price, *New Financial Instruments* (London: The Chartered Institute of Bankers) pp. 30–44.

Ballarin, Eduard (1986) *Commercial Banks Amid the Financial Revolution* (Cambridge: Ballinger).

Banks, Michael (1985) "The Inter-Paradigm Debate", in Margot Light and A. J. R. Groom (eds) *International Relations* (London: Pinter) pp. 7–26.

Bannock, Graham and William Manser (1989) *International Dictionary of Finance* (London: The Economist and Hutchinson Business Books).

Banting, Keith (Research Coordinator) (1986), *The State and Economic Interests*, volume 32 of the Report of the Royal Commission on the Economic Union and Development Prospects for Canada (University of Toronto Press).

Bardos, Jeffrey (1987–8) "The Risk-based Capital Agreement: A Further Step Towards Policy Convergence", *Federal Reserve Bank of New York Quarterly Review* (Winter) pp. 26–34.

Barnea, Amir, Robert A. Haugen and Lemma W. Senbet (1985) *Agency Problems and Financial Contracting* (London: Prentice-Hall).

Bartos, James (1988) "London Stock Exchange-SEC agreement on market making", *International Financial Law Review*, Jan., pp. 32–4.

"Basel 'Loophole' to Allow US Banks to Raise Capital, Boost Lending" (1991) *International Banking Regulator*, 11 Oct., pp. 1–2.

"Basel Proposals on Forex Risks May Be Delayed by Key Regulators" (1991) *International Banking Regulator*, 27 Sept., pp. 1–2.

Baumol, William J., John C. Panzar and Robert D. Willig (1982) *Contestable Markets and the Theory of Industry Structure* (Harcourt: New York).

Begin, Brad (1986) "A Proposed Blueprint for Achieving Cooperation in Policing Transborder Securities Fraud", *Virginia Journal of International Law*, vol. 27(1), pp. 65–96.

Bennett, A. LeRoy (1991) *International Organizations* (Englewood Cliffs: Prentice Hall).

Benzie, Richard (1992) *The Development of the International Bond Market* (Basle: Bank for International Settlements).

Bhattacharya, Sudipto and George M. Constantinides (eds) (1989) *Financial Markets and Incomplete Information: Frontiers of Modern Financial Theory* (Totowa: Rowman and Littlefield Publishers).

Binder, Leonard (1986) "The Natural History of Development Theory", *Comparative Studies in Society and History*, vol. 28 pp. 3–33.

"BIS Proposals for the Inclusion of General Provisions and Loan Loss Reserves in Capital" (1991) *World of Banking* (March–April) pp. 30–1.

Blaug, Mark (1980) "Kuhn Versus Lakatos, or Paradigms Versus Research Programmes in the History of Economics", in Garry Gutting (ed) *Paradigms and Revolutions* (Notre Dame: University of Notre Dame Press) pp. 137–59.

Blomström, Magnus and Bjorn Hettne (1984) *Development Theory in Transition* (London: Zed).

Bourke, Phil (1990) "International Bank Profitability: Theory and Evidence", in Edward P. M. Gardener (ed) *The Future of Financial Systems and Services: Essays in Honour of Jack Revell* (London: Macmillan), pp. 143–69.

Brady, Simon (1990a) "Dressing up without a killing", *Euromoney* (April) pp. 77–80.

Brady, Simon (1990b) "Euro-equity? Nein Danke!", *Euromoney* (May) pp. 68–74.

Breeden, Richard C. (1986) "Reforming Regulation of Financial Services in the United States: Issues and Opportunities", *International Lawyer* vol. 20(3), pp. 775–83.

"Breeden, Japanese Officials Reveal Plans to Expand Enforcement Accord" (1991) *Securities Regulation and Law Report*, vol. 23, p. 42.

"Breeden Says Several Nations Interested in Facilitating Cross-Border Offerings" (1989) *Securities Regulation and Law Report*, vol. 21, pp. 1847–8.

Breyer, Stephen (1982) *Regulation and Its Reform* (Cambridge, Massachusetts and London: Harvard University Press).

Bröker, G. (1989) *Competition in Banking* (Paris, OECD).

Brozen, Yale (1982) *Concentration, Mergers, and Public Policy* (New York: Macmillan).

Bryan, Lowell L. (1987) "Capital Guidelines Could Weaken Banks", *Wall Street Journal*, 23 April, p. 32.

Bryant, Ralph C. (1987) *International Financial Intermediation* (Washington: Brookings Institution).

"Canada, U.S. Seen Moving Toward Reciprocal Registration Procedures" (1988) *Securities Regulation and Law Report*, vol. 20, pp. 1628–9.

"Capital Adequacy: Bringing out the tin helmets" (1990), *The Economist*, 13 October, pp. 88–9

Casey, Robert W. (1990a) "Banks Make a Slow Start Into Underwriting", *Global Finance* (June) pp. 60–5.

Casey, Robert W. (1990b) "Is the World Overbanked?", *Global Finance* (Jan.), pp. 38–44.

Cawson, Alan (ed) (1985) *Organized Interests and the State: Studies in Meso-Corporatism* (London: Sage).

Cerny, Philip G. (1991) "The Reregulation of Financial Markets in a More Open World", paper prepared for the annual conference of the Political Studies Association of the UK, University of Lancaster, 15–17 April.

Chessen, James (1987) "Capital Comes to the Fore", *Issues in Bank Regulation* (Spring) pp. 3–15.

Cho, Kang Rae (1985) *Multinational Banks: Their Identities and Determinants* (Ann Arbor: UMI Research Press).

Chu, Franklin J. (1988) "The Myth of Global Investment Banking", *The Bankers Magazine* (Jan.–Feb.) pp. 58–61.

Chuppe, Terry M., Hugh R. Haworth and Marvin G. Watkins (1989) *The Securities Market in the 1980s: A Global Perspective* (Washington: SEC).

Clarke, Robert L. (Comptroller of the Currency) (1987) "The Limits of Bank Regulation", *Annual Review of Banking Law 1987*.

Claxton, Edward B., Hilary S. Foulkes and Kenneth G. Ottenbreit (1989) "Multi-jurisdictional Disclosure: a practitioners' view", *International Financial Law Review* (Oct.) pp. 11–14.

Cohen, Benjamin J. (1983) "Balance of Payments Financing: Evolution of a Regime", in Stephen D. Krasner, *International Regimes* (Ithaca and London: Cornell University Press) pp. 315–36.

Cohen, Benjamin J. (1986) *In Whose Interest?: International Banking and American Foreign Policy* (New Haven and London: Yale University Press).

Cohen, Kalman J. *et. al.* (1986) *The Microstructure of Securities Markets* (Englewood Cliffs, New Jersey: Prentice-Hall).

Coleman, William D. (1988) *Business and Politics in Canada: A Study of Collective Action* (Kingston and Montreal: McGill-Queen's University Press).

"Common Capital Standards Accord Emerging for Securities Industry" (1991) *International Banking Regulator*, Oct. pp. 1–2

Connelly, Mark Q. (1987) "Mulitinational Offerings: A Canadian Perspective", *Law「ard Contemporary Problems*, vol. 50(3) pp. 251–71.

"Constitutional Attack Mounted on Recent SEC Memorandum, Ontario Act" (1988) *Securities Regulation and Law Report*, vol. 20, p. 1337.

Cooke, Stephanie (1990) "A Break in the Battle of the Clearers", *Institutional Investor* (May) pp. 98–100.

Cooke, W. P. (1979) "The Central Bank's Regulatory Role", paper presented at the Conference on the Role of Central Banks in the Economic Decisionmaking Process, Jerusalem, 18–20 Nov.

Cooke, W. P. (1981) "Banking Regulation, Profits, and Capital Generation", *The Banker* (Aug.) pp. 21–3.

Cooke, W. P. (1984a) "The Basle 'Concordat' on the Supervision of Banks' Foreign Establishments", *Aussenwirtschaft*, vol. 39, pp. 151–65.

Cooke, W. P. (1984b) "The Basle Supervisors' Committee", *Issues in Bank Regulation* (Summer) pp. 7–10.

Cooke, W. P. (1988) "Comments on Expanding Bank Powers: An International Perspective", in *Merging Commercial and Investment Banking*, proceedings of a conference on Bank Structure and Competition (Chicago: Federal Reserve Bank of Chicago) pp. 62–9.

Cooke, W. P. (1990) "International Convergence of Capital Adequacy Measurement and Standards", in Edward P. M. Gardener (ed), *The Future of Financial Systems and Services: Essays in Honour of Jack Revell* (London: Macmillan) pp. 310–35.

Cooper, Allan R. (Canadian Banker's Association) (n.d.) "Capital Adequacy Guidelines: Possible Global Competitive Imbalances", notes for a speech.

Cooper, Ian (1986) "Innovations: New Market Instruments", *Oxford Review of Economic Policy*, vol. 2(4) (Winter) pp. 1–17.

Cooper, Ian (1987) "New Instruments: An Overview", in Ian Cooper, Andrew Bain, John Donaldson and Lionel Price, *New Financial Instruments* (London: The Chartered Institute of Bankers) pp. x–29.

Cooper, Ian, Andrew Bain, John Donaldson and Lionel Price (1987) *New Financial Instruments* (London: The Chartered Institute of Bankers).

Corrigan, Tracy (1991) "Basle Warms to Swaps Change", *Financial Times* (London), 27 Sept., p. 24.

Corrigan, Tracy (1992) "Hopes Dwindle for New Agreement on Capital Requirements", *Financial Times* (London), 28 Oct., p. 24.

Corrigan, Tracy and Robert Preston (1992) "IOSCO Setback over Common Capital Requirements", *Financial Times* (London), 27 Oct., p. 28.

Cox, Charles C. (1987) "Internationalization of the Capital Markets: The Experience of the Securities and Exchange Commission", *Maryland Journal of International Law and Trade*, vol. 11(2) (Summer) pp. 201–21.

Cox, Robert W. (1983) "Gramsci, Hegemony and International Relations: An Essay in Method", *Millennium*, pp. 162–75.

Cox, Robert W. (1987) *Production, Power and World Order* (New York: Columbia University Press).

Crane, Dwight B. and Samuel L. Hayes III (1983) "The Evolution of International Banking Competition and its Implications for Regulation", *Journal of Bank Research*, pp. 39–58.

Critchley, Barry (1991) "New Rules Open up Cross-Border Financings", *Financial Post*, 23 Sept.

Crum, M. Colyer and David M. Meerschwam (1986) "From Relationship to Price Banking: The Loss of Regulatory Control", in Thomas K. McCraw (ed), *America versus Japan* (Boston: Harvard Business School Press) pp. 261–97.

Cushing, Paul M. (1987) "Barriers to the International Flow of Capital: The Facilitation of Multinational Securities Offerings", *Vanderbilt Journal of Transnational Law*, vol. 20(8), pp. 81–122.

Dale, Richard (1984) *The Regulation of International Banking* (Cambridge: Woodhead-Faulkner).

Darbyshire, Christopher (1991) "Syndicated Loans: That Sinking Feeling", *Euromoney* (Aug.) pp. 33–8.

Deal, Jill B. (1987) "Policing securities and commodities markets", *International Financial Law Review* (Jan.) pp. 21–3.

"Delayed Harmony" (1992) [on EC financial services legislation] *Economist*, 4 July, pp. 68–70.

Der Derian, James and Michael Shapiro (eds) (1989) *International/Intertextual Relations* (Lexington: Lexington Books).

Dessler, David (1991) "Beyond Correlations: Toward a Causal Theory of War", *International Studies Quarterly*, vol. 35(3) (Sep.) pp. 337–55.

"Developments in Banking Law: 1988, Risk-Based Capital Plan" (1989) *Annual Review of Banking Law*, pp. 65–7.

"Developments in Banking Law: 1989, Capital Requirements" (1990) *Annual Review of Banking Law*, pp. 54–61.

"Developments in Banking Law: 1990, Capital Standards" (1991) *Annual Review of Banking Law*, pp. 118–25.

Diamond, Douglas W. (1984) "Financial Intermediation and Delegated Monitoring", *Review of Economic Studies*, pp. 393–414.

"Dingell Introduces Bill to Encourage International Enforcement Cooperation" (1988) *Securities Regulation and Law Report*, vol. 20, pp. 1065–6.

Dunning, John H. (1988) *Explaining International Production* (London: Unwin Hyman).

Dupont-Jubien, André (1987) "The Cooperation in Matters of Surveillance and Repression of Infractions", in International Organization of Securities Commissions, *12th Annual Conference of IOSCO*, 1–4 Sept., Rio de Janeiro, documents tabled at the conference, document no. 5, 15 pages.

Dyson, Kenneth (1983) "The Cultural, Ideological and Structural Context", in Kenneth Dyson and Stephen Wilks (eds) *Industrial Crisis: A Comparative Study of the State and Industry* (Oxford: Martin Robertson) pp. 245–72.

Dyson, Kenneth and Stephen Wilks (eds) (1983) *Industrial Crisis: A Comparative Study of the State and Industry* (Oxford: Martin Robertson).

Economist, "Banks in Trouble" (1990a) editor's introduction to article by Norman Macrae, 8 Sept. p. 21.

Eden, Lorraine and Fen Osler Hampson (1990) "Clubs are Trump: Towards a Taxonomy of International Regimes", working paper, Centre for International Trade and Investment Policy Studies, Carleton University.

Edwards, Franklin R. (1986) "Concentration in Banking: Problem or Solution?", in George F. Kaufman and Roger C. Kormendi (eds) *Deregulating Financial Services* (Cambridge Mass: Ballinger) pp. 145–59.

Edwards, Franklin R. (1988) "The Future Financial Structure: Fears and Policies", in William S. Haraf and Rose Marie Kushmeider (eds) *Restructuring Banking and Financial Services in America*, (Washington: American Enterprise Institute for Public Policy Research) pp. 113–55.

Edwards, Jeremy (1987) "Recent Developments in the Theory of Corporate Finance", *Oxford Review of Economic Policy*, vol. 3(4) (Winter) pp. 1–12.

Einzig, P. (1949) *Primitive Money* (London: Eyre and Spottiswoode).

Ellwand, Geoff (1988) "Securities Firms Form International Council", *Financial Post* 8 Dec. p. 21.

Emmott, Bill (1991) "Gamblers, Masters, and Slaves", *Economist*, 27 April, pp. S5–46.

Euromoney Annual Financing Report (various issues).

Evans, Gary (1988) "How to Stop the Eurobond Market Committing Suicide", *Euromoney* (May) pp. 45–58.

Evans, Gary (1989) "Euroequities: Riches in Store", *Euromoney* (Sep.) pp. 71–4.

Evans, John J. (1986) "The Globalization of Operations", *The Bankers Magazine* (May–June) pp. 7–20.

Evans, Peter B., Dietrich Rueschemeyer and Theda Skocpol (eds) (1985) *Bringing the State Back In* (Cambridge University Press).

Evans, Peter and John D. Stephens (1988) "Studying Development Since the Sixties: The Emergence of a New Comparative Political Economy", *Theory and Society*, vol. 17; pp. 713–45.

Fairlamb, David (1991) "How the Capital Quest is Reshaping Banking", *Institutional Investor*, International Edition (March) pp. 27–30.

Fennema, Meindert and Kees van der Pijl (1987) "International Bank Capital and the New Liberalism", in Mark S. Mizruchi and Michael Scwhartz (eds), (1987) *Intercorporate Relations* (New York: Cambridge University Press) pp. 298–317.

"'Fighting' Corrigan from NY Fed New Chairman of Cooke Committee", (1991) *International Banking Regulator*, 19 July, pp. 1–2.

Fisher, Frederick G. III (1984) *International Bonds* (London: Euromoney Publications).

Foucault, Michel (1982) "Afterword: The Subject and Power", in Hubert L. Dreyfus and Paul Rabinow, *Michel Foucault: Beyond Structuralism and Hermeneutics* (University of Chicago Press) pp. 208–26.

Foucault, Michel (1984) *The Foucault Reader* (New York: Pantheon).

Francis, Arthur, Jeremy Turk and Paul Willman (eds) (1983) *Power, Efficiency, and Institutions* (London: Heinemann).

Frank, David (1988a) "Games without Frontiers?", *The Banker* (May) pp. 16–21.

Frank, David (1988b) "Win a Few, Lose a Few", *The Banker* (April) pp. 26–7.

Frank, David (1990) "A Growing Appetite for Foreign Equities", *Global Finance* (Aug.) pp. 63–5.

Frankel, S. Herbert (1977) *Money: Two Philosophies* (Oxford: Basil Blackwell).

Frieden, Jeffrey A. (1987) *Banking on the World: The Politics of American International Finance* (New York: Harper and Row).

Friedman, Benjamin M. (1986) *Financing Corporate Capital Formation* (Chicago and London: University of Chicago Press).

Gardener, Edward P.M. (ed) (1990) *The Future of Financial Systems and Services: Essays in Honour of Jack Revell* (London: Macmillan).

Garten, Helen A. (1986) "Banking on the Market: Relying on Depositors to Control Bank Risks", *Yale Journal on Regulation*, pp. 129–72.

Garten, Helen A. (1988) "Still Banking on the Market: A Comment on the Failure of Market Discipline", *Yale Journal on Regulation*, pp. 241–51.

Garten, Helen A. (1989) "Regulatory Growing Pains: A Perspective on Bank Regulation in a Deregulatory Age", *Fordham Law Review*, vol. LVII(4), pp. 502–77.

George, Susan (1989) *A Fate Worse than Debt* (London: Penguin).

Gerschenkron, Alexander (1966) *Economic Backwardness in Historical Perspective* (Cambridge: Belknap Press).

Giddens, Anthony (1984) *The Constitution of Society* (Cambridge: Polity Press).

Giddens, Anthony (1987) *The Nation-State and Violence* (Berkeley: University of California Press).

Giddens, Anthony (1989) "A Reply to my Critics", in Held and Thompson, *Social Theory of Modern Societies: Anthony Giddens and his Critics* (Cambridge University Press) pp. 249–301.

Gill, David B. (1986) "The Emerging Global Equity Market", *Boston University International Law Journal*, vol. 4., pp. 39–53.

Gill, Stephen P. and David Law (1989) "Global Hegemony and the Structural Power of Capital", *International Studies Quarterly*, vol. 33, pp. 475–99.

Gilpin, Robert (1987) *The Political Economy of International Relations* (Princeton University Press).

Gira, Thomas R. (1988) "Toward a Global Capital Market: The Emergence of Simultaneous Multinational Securities Offerings", in Marc I. Steinberg (ed) *Contemporary Issues in Securities Regulation* (Butterworth Legal Publishers) pp. 195–219.

"Global Securities Accords Held Up Over FOIA Exemption Issue, SEC Says" (1989) *Securities Regulation and Law Report*, vol. 21, pp. 447–8.

Goelzer, Daniel L., Robert Mills, Katharine Gresham and Anne H. Sullivan (1988) "The Role of the U.S. Securities and Exchange Commission in Transnational Acquisitions", *International Lawyer*, vol. 22(3), pp. 615–41.

Goelzer, Daniel L., Jacob H. Stillman, Elisse B. Walter, Anne H. Sullivan and Douglas C. Michael (1985) "The Draft Revised Restatement: A Critique from a Securities Perspective", *International Lawyer*, vol. 19(2), pp. 431–85.

Goelzer, Daniel L., Anne Sullivan and Robert Mills (1988) "Securities Regulation in the International Market Place: Bilateral and Multilateral Agreements", *Symposium: Internationalization of the Securities Markets, Michigan Yearbook of International Legal Studies*, pp. 53–90.

Gold, Joseph (1984) *Legal and Institutional Aspects of the International Monetary System* (Washington: IMF).

Goldstein, Joshua (1988) *Long Cycles* (New Haven: Yale University Press).

Goodhart, Charles (1986) "Financial Innovation and Monetary Control", *Oxford Review of Economic Policy*, vol. 2(4) (Winter) pp. 79–99.

Goodhart, Charles (1988) "Information Inadequacy Leading to the Emergence of 'Clubs'", in Gianni Toniolo (ed), *Central Banks' Independence in Historical Perspective* (Berlin and New York: Walter de Gruyter) pp. 57–76.

Goodman, John B. and Louis W. Pauly (1990) "The New Politics of International Capital Mobility", paper prepared for the University of Pennsylvania–Rutgers University Colloquium on European Integration, 15–16 Nov.

Gordon, Kenneth J. (1991) "Risk-Based Capital Requirements: The Proper Approach to Safe and Sound Banking?", *Annual Review of Banking Law 1991*, pp. 491–519.

Gowa, Joanne (1983) *Closing the Gold Window: Domestic Politics and the End of the Bretton Woods System* (Ithaca and London: Cornell University Press).

Green, Christopher (1990) *Canadian Industrial Organization and Policy*, 3rd edn (Toronto: McGraw-Hill Ryerson Limited).

Greenstein, Laura S. (1987) "The Future of Global Securities Transactions: Blocking the Success of Market Links", *Maryland Journal of International Law and Trade*, vol. 11(2) (Summer) pp. 283–328.

Guttentag, Jack M. and Richard Herring (1987) "Emergency Liquidity Assistance for International Banks", in Richard Portes and Alexander Swoboda (eds), *Threats to International Financial Stability* (Cambridge University Press), pp. 150–85.

Gutting, Gary (ed.) (1980) *Paradigms and Revolutions* (Notre Dame: University of Notre Dame Press).

Haas, Peter M. (1989) "Do Regimes Matter? Epistemic communities and Mediterranean pollution control", *International Organization*, vol. 43(3) (Summer) pp. 377–403.

Haas, Ernst (1990) *When Knowledge is Power: Three Models of Change in International Organizations* (Berkeley: University of California Press).

Haas, Peter (1992) "Introduction: epistemic communities and international policy coordination", in *Knowledge, Power and International Policy Coordination*, a special issue of *International Organization*, vol. 46(1) (Winter) pp. 1–35.

Haggard, Stephan and Beth A. Simmons (1987) "Theories of International Regimes", *International Organization* vol. 41(3) (Summer) pp. 491–517.

Hakim, Jonathan (1984) "A New Awakening", *The Economist*, International Banking Survey, 24 March, pp. 5–78.

Hall, Peter,(1986) *Governing the Economy* (New York: Oxford University Press)

Haraf, William S. and Rose Marie Kushmeider (eds) (1988) *Restructuring Banking and Financial Services in America* (Washington: American Enterprise Institute).

Harari, Maurice and Alain Hirsch (1987) "The Swiss Perspective on International Judicial Assistance", *University of Pennsylvania Journal of International Business Law*, vol. 9, pp. 519–37.

Hassan, Ibn (1987) *The Postmodern Turn* (Ohio State University Press).

Hawes, Douglas W. (1987) "Internationalization Spreads to Securities Regulators", *University of Pennsylvania Journal of International Business Law*, pp. 257–63.

Hawley, James P. (1984) "Protecting Capital From Itself: US Attempts to Regulate the Eurocurrency System", *International Organization* vol. 38(1) (Winter) pp. 131–65.

Hayes, Samuel L. III, A. Michael Spence and David Van Praag Marks (1983) *Competition in the Investment Banking Industry* (Cambridge: Harvard University Press).

Hayward, Peter C. (1990) "Prospects for International Cooperation by Bank Supervisors", *International Lawyer*, vol. 24(3) (Fall) pp. 787–801.

Hayward, Peter C. (1991) "The Basle Committee's Current Concerns", remarks by the Secretary of the Basle Committee on Banking Supervision at the Financial Times Conference, London, 13 Feb.

Hayward, Peter C. (1992) "Future Direction of the Basle Committee", remarks by the Secretary of the Basle Committee on Banking Supervision at the Annual Washington Conference of the Institute of International Bankers, 9 March.

Heggestad, Arnold A. and John J. Mingo (1976) "Prices, Non-Prices, and Concentration in Commercial Banking", *Journal of Money, Credit and Banking*, vol. VIII(1) (Feb) pp. 107–17.

Held, David and John B. Thompson (eds) (1989) *Social Theory of Modern Societies: Anthony Giddens and His Critics* (Cambridge University Press).

Helleiner, Eric (1989) "Money and Influence: Japanese Power in the International Monetary and Financial System", *Millennium*, vol. 18(3), pp. 343–58.

Herman, Edward S. (1981) *Corporate Control, Corporate Power* (Cambridge University Press).

Hexner, Ervin (1946) *International Cartels* (London: Pitman).

Higgott, Richard A. (1983) *Political Development Theory* (London: Croom Helm).

Hirsch, Fred (1976) *Social Limits to Growth* (Cambridge: Harvard University Press).

Hobson, Dominic (1990) "Playing by New Rules", *Global Finance* (April) pp. 70–4.

Hodgson, Geoffrey M. (1988) *Economics and Institutions* (Cambridge: Basil Blackwell).

Holland, David S. (1986) "Foreign Bank Capital and the United States Federal Reserve Board", *International Lawyer*, vol. 20(3), pp. 785–818.

Hollingsworth, J. Rogers and Leon N. Lindberg (1985) "The Governance of the American Economy: The Role of Markets, Clans, Hierarchies, and Associative Behaviour", in in Wolfgang Streeck and Philippe C. Schmitter (eds) *Private Interest Government: Beyond Market and State* (London: Sage), pp. 221–54.

Hollis, Martin and Steve Smith (1991) "Beware of Gurus: Structure and Action in International Relations", *Review of International Studies*, vol. 17(4) (Oct.) pp. 393–410.

Hollis, Martin and Steve Smith (1992) "Structure and Action: Further Comment", *Review of International Studies*, 18(2) (April) pp. 187–8.

Howell, Kristin K. (1989) "Central Bank Cooperation and the Role of the Bank for International Settlements in International Monetary Stability", unpublished PhD dissertation, University of Kentucky, Lexington, Kentucky.

Hubbard, R. Glen (ed) (1990) *Asymmetric Information, Corporate Finance, and Investment* (University of Chicago Press).

Humphrey, David B. (1986) "Payments Finality and Risk of Settlement Failure", in Saunders and White (eds) *Technology and the Regulation of Financial Markets* (Lexington: Lexington Books) pp. 97–120.

Humphrey, Stacie F. and David B. Humphrey (1988) "How Risk-Based Capital Will Affect Bank Operations", *The Bankers Magazine* (March–April) pp. 22–7.

Huntington, Samuel P. (1968) *Political Order in Changing Societies* (New Haven and London: Yale University Press).

Ikenberry, G. John (1988) "Conclusion: an Institutional Approach to American Foreign Policy", *International Organization*, vol. 42(1) (Winter) pp. 219–43.

Ikenberry, G. John, David A. Lake and Michael Mastanduno (1988) "Introduction: Approaches to Explaining American Foreign Economic Policy", *International Organization*, vol. 42(1) (Winter) pp. 1–14.

"International Banking Takes its Toll" (1984) *The Banker*, June, pp. 107–8.

"IOSCO Drops Overview of Crash Studies, Looks Ahead to Working Group Findings", (1988) *Securities Regulation and Law Report*, vol. 20, p. 1585.

"IOSCO Technical Committee Considers Enforcement Proposal", (1989) *Securities Regulation and Law Report*, vol. 21, p. 427.

Jacquemin, Alexis (1987) *The New Industrial Organization* (Cambridge, Massachusetts: MIT Press).

Jensen, Michael C. and William H. Meckling (1976) "Theory of the Firm: Managerial Behaviour, Agency Costs and Ownership Structure", *Journal of Financial Economics*, vol. 3, pp. 305–60.

Jewett, Walter G., Bertrand G. Shelton, Jean-Louis Lelogeais and Lieng-Seng Wee (1989) "Restructuring under New Capital Regulations: Asking the Right Questions", *The Bankers Magazine* (March–April) pp. 9–14.

Jiminez, Pamela (1990) "International Securities Enforcement Cooperation Act and Memoranda of Understanding", *Harvard International Law Journal*, vol. 31(1), (Winter) pp. 295–311.

Jordan, Cally and Pamela Gibson (1990) "Easing Cross-border Securities Offerings", *Financial Post*, 7 Dec., p. 18.

Jordan, William A. (1972) "Producer Protection, Prior Market Structure and the Effects of Government Regulation", *Journal of Law and Economics*, vol. 15, pp. 151–76.

Kaplan, Morton A. (1989) "A Poor Boy's Journey", in Joseph Kruzel and James N. Rosenau (eds) *Journeys through World Politics* (Lexington and Toronto: Lexington Books) pp. 41–52.

Kapstein, Ethan B. (1989) "Resolving the Regulator's Dilemma: international coordination of banking regulations", *International Organization*, vol. 43(2) (Spring) pp. 323–47.

Kapstein, Ethan B. (1992) "Between Power and Purpose: Central Bankers and the Politics of Regulatory Convergence", in Peter M. Haas (ed) *Knowledge, Power and International Policy Coordination*, a special issue of *International Organization*, vol. 46(1) (Winter) pp. 256–88.

Kareken, John (1984) "Bank Capital Adequacy in an International Setting", *Issues In Bank Regulation* (Summer) pp. 43–6.

Karmel, Roberta S. (1989) "The IOSCO Venice Conference", *New York Law Journal* 19 Oct., pp. 3–4.

Karmel, Roberta S. (1990) "SEC Regulation of Multijurisdictional Offerings", *Brooklyn Journal of International Law*, vol. XVI, pp. 3–17.

Keller, Paul (1989) "Coming Soon at the AIBD: Fireworks", *Euromoney* (Dec.) p. 12.

Keohane, Robert O. (1980) "The Theory of Hegemonic Stability and Changes in International Regimes, 1967–1977", in Ole Holsti (ed) *Change in the International System* (Boulder: Westview Press).

Keohane, Robert O. (1984) *After Hegemony* (Princeton University Press).

Keohane, Robert O. (1988) "International Institutions: Two Approaches", *International Studies Quarterly*, vol. 32 (Dec.) pp. 379–96.

Keohane, Robert O. (1989) *International Institutions and State Power* (Boulder: Westview Press).

Keohane, Robert O. and Joseph Nye Jr (1977) *Power and Interdependence* (Boston: Little, Brown).

Keohane, Robert and Joseph Nye Jr (1987) *"Power and Interdependence* Revisited", *International Organization*, vol. 41(4) (Autumn) pp. 725–53.

Kerr, Ian M. (1984) *A History of the Eurobond Market: The First 21 Years*, (London: Euromoney Publications).

Ketchum, Richard G. (1986) "The Role of the Securities and Exchange Commission in Regulating International Securities Trading: Looking to the Future", *Boston University International Law Journal*, vol. 4, pp. 33–8.

Key, Sydney J. and Hal S. Scott (1991) *International Trade in Banking Services: A Conceptual Framework*, Occasional Paper 35 (Washington: Group of Thirty).

Khoury, Sarkis J. (1980) *Transnational Mergers and Acquisitions in the United States* (Lexington: Lexington Books).

Khoury, Sarkis J. (1990) *The Deregulation of the World Financial Markets* (London: Quorum).

Kitschelt, Herbert (1991) "Industrial Governance Structures, Innovation Strategies, and the Case of Japan: Sectoral or Cross-National Comparative Analysis?", *International Organization*, vol. 45(4) (Autumn) pp. 453–93.

Klock, Mark S. (1987) "A Comparative Analysis of Recent Accords which Facilitate Transnational SEC Investigations of Insider Trading", *Maryland Journal of International Law and Trade*, vol. 11(2), (Summer) pp. 243–82.

Kotz, David M. (1978) *Bank Control of Large Corporations in the United States* (Berkeley: University of California Press).

Krasner, Stephen D. (ed.) (1983) *International Regimes* (Ithaca and London: Cornell University Press).

Krasner, Stephen D. (1988) "Sovereignty: An Institutional Perspective", *Comparative Political Studies*, vol. 21(1) (April) pp. 66–94.

Kratochwil, Friedrich (1984) "The Force of Prescriptions", *International Organization*, vol. 38(4) (Autumn) pp. 685–708

Kratochwil, F. and Ruggie J.G. (1986) "International Organization: A State of the Art on an Art of the State", in *International Organization*, vol. 40(4) (Autumn) pp. 753–76.

Kuebler, Friedrich (1987) "Regulatory Problems in Internationalizing Trading Markets", *University of Pennsylvania Journal of International Business Law*, vol. 9(1), pp. 107–20.

Kuhn, Thomas S. (1970) *The Structure of Scientific Revolutions* (University of Chicago Press).

Lakatos, Imre (1970) "Falsification and the Methodology of Scientific Research Programs", in Imre Lakatos and Alan Musgrave (eds) *Criticism and the Growth of Knowledge* (Cambridge University Press).

Langevoort, Donald C. (1985) "Information Technology and the Structure of Securities Regulation", *Harvard Law Review*, vol. 98, pp. 747–804.

Lapid, Yosef (1989) "The Third Debate: On the Prospects of International Theory in a Post-Positivist Era", *International Studies Quarterly*, vol. 33, pp. 235–79.

Lee, Peter (1992) "Securities Houses Face Capital Clampdown", *Euromoney* (April) pp. 32–43.

Levine, Theodore A. and W. Hardy Callcott (1989) "The SEC and Foreign Policy: The International Securities Enforcement Act of 1988", *Securities Regulation Law Journal*, vol. 17, pp. 115–50.

Light, Margot and A. J. R. Groom (eds) (1985) *International Relations* (London: Pinter).

Lipset, Seymour M. (1959) "Some Social Requisites of Democracy: Economic Development and Political Legitimacy", *American Political Science Review*, vol. LIII(1) (March) pp. 69–105.

Longstreth, Bevis (1988) "Global Securities Markets and the SEC", *University of Pennsylvania Journal of International Business Law*, vol. 10(2), pp. 183–93.

Lovett, William A. (1989) "Moral Hazard, Bank Supervision, and Risk-Based Capital Requirements", *Ohio State Law Journal*, vol. 49, pp. 1364–95.

Lowi, Theodore J. (1979) *The End of Liberalism* (Norton: New York).

Macey, Jonathan R. (1989) "The Political Science of Regulating Bank Risk", *Ohio State Law Journal*, vol. 49, pp. 1277–98.

Macey, Jonathan R. and Elizabeth H. Garrett (1988) "Market Discipline by Depositors: A Summary of the Theoretical and Empirical Arguments", *Yale Journal on Regulation*, vol. 5, pp. 215–39.

Magee, Stephen P. (1977) "Multinational Corporations, the Industry Technology Cycle and Development", *Journal of World Trade Law*, vol. 11(2) (July/Aug.) pp. 291–321.

Mahoney, Paul G. (1990) "Securities Regulation by Enforcement: An International Perspective", *Yale Journal on Regulation*, vol. 7, pp. 305–20.

Makin, Claire (1991) "Regulation: Learning from BCCI", *Institutional Investor* (Nov.) pp. 93–7.

"Mann Notes New SEC Involvement in International Trade Negotiations", (1990) *Securities Regulation and Law Report*, vol. 22, p. 590.

March, James G. and Johan P. Olsen (1984) "The New Institutionalism: Organizational Factors in Political Life", *American Political Science Review*, vol. 78(3) (Sept.) pp. 734–49.

March, James G. and Johan P. Olsen (1989) *Rediscovering Institutions: The Organizational Basis of Politics* (New York: Free Press).

Mason, Edward S. (1946) *Controlling World Trade: Cartels and Commodity Agreements* (New York: McGraw-Hill).

Masulis, Ronald W. (1988) *The Debt/Equity Choice* (Cambridge: Ballinger).

Mayall, Kenneth L. (1951) *International Cartels* (Rutland and Tokyo, Charles E. Tuttle Company).

Mayer, Colin, (1986) "The Assessment: Financial Innovation: Curse or Blessing", *Oxford Review of Economic Policy*, vol. 2(4) (Winter) pp. i–xix.

Mayer, Colin (1987) "The Assessment: Financial Systems and Corporate Investment", *Oxford Review of Economic Policy*, vol. 3(4) (Winter) pp. i–xvi.

Mayer, Colin (1990) "Financial Systems, Corporate Finance, and Economic Development", in R. Glenn Hubbard, *Asymmetric Information, Corporate Finance, and Investment* (Chicago and London: University of Chicago Press) pp. 307–32.

McCormick, James M. (1988) "Off-Balance Sheet Banking after Risk-Based Capital" (interview), *The Bankers Magazine* (Nov.–Dec.) pp. 5–9.

Meerschwam, David (1989) "International Capital Imbalances: The Demise of Local Financial Boundaries", in Richard O'Brien and Tapan Datta (eds) *International Economics and Financial Markets*, The AMEX Bank Review Prize Essays (Oxford University Press) pp. 289–307.

Meerschwam, David M. (1991) *Breaking Financial Boundaries* (Boston: Harvard Business School).

Melloan, George (1988a) "Global Bank Regulation Fans a New Debate", *Wall Street Journal*, 15 March, p. 35.

Melloan, George (1988b) "New Risk Rules Could Redirect Bank Lending", *Wall Street Journal*, 22 March, p. 35.

Millar, Anita (1990) "The Multinational Banking Industry: An Analysis", unpublished paper, 16 April.

Miller, William (1990) "Europeans in Battle over Stock Market", *Globe and Mail*, 4 June, p. B10.

Mills, Joslin Landell (1986) *The Fund's International Banking Statistics* (Washington: International Monetary Fund).

Mills, Rodney H. with the assistance of Cynthia Hart (1986) "Foreign Lending by Banks: A Guide to International and U.S. Statistics", *Federal Reserve Bulletin* (Oct.) pp. 683–94.

Milner, Brian (1991) "Banks Bolstering their Capital", *Globe and Mail*, 13 March.

Mitnick, Barry M. (1980) *The Political Economy of Regulation* (New York: Columbia).

Mitrany, David (1975[1943]) "A Working Peace System", in David Mitrany, *The Functional Theory of Politics* (London: Martin Robertson).

Modigliani, F. and M.H. Miller (1958) "The Cost of Capital, Corporation Finance, and the Theory of Investment", *American Economic Review*, vol. 48 (June) pp. 261–7.

Moran, Michael (1984) *The Politics of Banking: The Strange Case of Competition and Credit Control* (London: Macmillan).

Moran, Michael (1986) "Theories of Regulation and Changes in Regulation: the Case of Financial Markets", *Political Studies*, vol. XXXIV, pp. 185–201.

Muehring, Kevin (1989) "A New Deal for the Eurobond Market", *Institutional Investor* (International Edition) (Dec.) pp. 79–83.

Muller, H.J. (1988) "Address", in International Conference of Banking Supervisors, (1988), *5th International Conference of Banking Supervisors*, Tokyo, 12–13 Oct., report on conference.

Muller, H.J. (1990) "A Supervisor's View of Risk Management", *World of Banking* (Nov.–Dec.) pp. 22–4.

Munroe, Ann (1990) "Euromarket Warms to Fixed-Price Syndication", *Global Finance* (Nov.) pp. 17–22.

Munroe, Ann (1991) "Canada Eyes US Rules – Skeptically", *Global Finance* (Aug.) pp. 3–16.

Murphy, R. Taggart (1989) "Power without Purpose: The Crisis of Japan's Global Financial Dominance", *Harvard Business Review*, vol. 89(2) (March–April) pp. 71–83.

Mussa, Michael (1981) *The Role of Official Intervention*, occasional paper No. 6 (New York: Group of Thirty).

Mytelka, Lynn Krieger (1991) *Strategic Partnerships: States, Firms and International Competition* (London: Pinter).

Nash, Nathaniel (1988a) "Agreement on Banks' Capital Set", *New York Times*, 12 July, p. IV1:6.

Nash, Nathaniel (1988b) "Capital Plan Feared as a Burden on Banks", *New York Times*, 15 July, p. IV1:3.

Nash, Nathaniel (1988c) "Fed Approves Rules Requiring More Capital At All Banks", *New York Times*, 4 Aug., p. IV2:1.

Nash, Nathaniel (1988d) "Plan Could Stall Banking Mergers", *New York Times*, 1 Feb., p. D1, D8.

Nisse, Jason (1988) "Anything you can do, we can do better", *The Banker* (Jan.) pp. 7–10.

Nordlinger, Eric A. (1986) *On the Autonomy of the Democratic State* (Cambridge: Harvard University Press).

Norman, Peter (1987a) "Seventeen Industrial Nations Draft Pact on Big Banks' Capital Adequacy Needs", *Wall Street Journal*, 23 Oct., p. 23.

Norman, Peter (1987b) "Ways to Boost Global Banking Stability Proposed by 12 Industrialized Nations", *Wall Street Journal*, 11 Dec., p. 10.

Norman, Peter (1988) "Capital Ratio is Set by Banks of 12 Nations", *Wall Street Journal*, 12 July, pp. 3, 17.

North, Douglass C. and Robert P. Thomas (1973) *The Rise of the Western World* (Cambridge University Press),

North, Douglass C. (1981) *Structure and Change in Economic History* (New York: Norton).

Norton, J. J. (1989a) "The Work of the Basle Supervisors Committee on Bank Capital Adequacy and the July 1988 Report on 'International Convergence of Capital Measurement and Capital Standards' ", *International Lawyer*, vol. 23(1) (Spring).

Norton, J. J. (1989b) "Capital Adequacy Standards: A Legitimate Regulatory Concern for Prudential Supervision of Banking Activities?", *Ohio State Law Journal*, vol. 49, pp. 1299–363.

Nye, Joseph, S. (1988) "Neorealism and Neoliberalism", *World Politics*, vol. XL(2) (Jan.) pp. 235–51.

Odell, John S. (1982) *U.S. International Monetary Policy: Markets, Power and Ideas as Sources of Change* (Princeton University Press).

Oliver, Peter and Jean-Pierre Bache (1989) "Free Movement of Capital between the Member States: Recent Developments", *Common Market Law Review*, vol. 26, pp. 61–81.

"On the World Agenda: The Capital Crunch" (1991) *World Link*, including articles by Michael Williams, *World Link* Senior Editor; Alexandre Lamfalussy, General Manager of the Bank for International Settlements;

Helmut Schlesinger, Deputy Governor of the Deutsche Bundesbank; Jacob A. Frenkel, Economic Counselor and Director of Research, IMF; David Suratgar, Group Director, Morgan Grenfell & Co.; and Keikichi Honda, Member, Board of Directors, Bank of Tokyo, May/June.

Orgler, Yair E., and Benjamin Wolkowitz (1976) *Bank Capital* (New York: Van Nostrand Reinhold Company).

Osborn, Neil and Evans, Garry (1988) "Cooke's Medicine: Kill or Cure?", *Euromoney* (July) pp. 34–54.

Ouchi, William G. (1980) "Markets, Bureaucracies, and Clans", *Administrative Science Quarterly*, vol. 25, pp. 129–41.

Parsons, Talcott (1954[1945]) *Essays in Sociological Theory* (New York: Free Press).

Pauly, Louis W. (1988) *Opening Financial Markets* (Ithaca: Cornell).

Pecchioli, R. M. (1983) *The Internationalisation of Banking: The Policy Issues* (Paris, Author).

Pecchioli, R. M. (1987) *Prudential Supervision in Banking* (Paris, Author).

Pinto, Arthur R. (1990) "The Internationalization of the Hostile Takeover Market: Its Implications for Choice of Law in Corporate and Securities Law", *Brooklyn Journal of International Law*, vol. XVI:1, pp. 55–88.

"Plan to 'Fine-Tune' Basle Capital Ratios Strongly Rejected by Bank of England" (1991) *International Banking Regulator*, 29 Nov., p. 6.

Podolski, T. M. (1986) *Financial Innovation and the Money Supply* (Oxford: Basil Blackwell).

Polanyi, Karl (1944) *The Great Transformation* (New York: Rinehart and Company).

Porter, Michael E. (1985) *Competitive Advantage: Creating and Sustaining Creative Performance* (New York: Free Press).

Porter, Tony (1990) "Post-Modern Political Realism and International Theory's Third Debate", paper presented at the Canadian Political Science Association Annual Meeting, Victoria, British Columbia, 27 May.

Porter, Tony (1991) "The Practice of Sovereignty and the Globalization of Finance", paper presented at the International Studies Association Annual Meeting, Vancouver, British Columbia, 22 March.

Porter, Tony (1992) "International Financial Collaboration under Stress: The Basle Capital Adequacy Accord", paper presented at the Canadian Political Science Association Annual Meeting, Charlottetown, 2 June.

Portes, Richard and Alexander K. Swoboda (eds) (1987) *Threats to International Financial Stability* (New York: Cambridge University Press).

Poster, Mark (1990) *The Mode of Information: Poststructuralism and Social Context* (University of Chicago Press).

Powell, G. C. (1984) "Offshore Group of Banking Supervisors", *Issues in Bank Regulation* (Summer) pp. 11–5.

Powell, G. C. (1991) Head of the Offshore Group of Banking Supervisors, letter to author, 22 May.

Preston, Robert and Tracy Corrigan (1992) "Breeden Opposes IOSCO Capital Standard", *Financial Times* (London) 28 Oct., p. 1.

Price, Lionel (1987) "Regulation of the Markets", in Ian Cooper, Andrew Bain, John Donaldson and Lionel Price, *New Financial Instruments* (London: The Chartered Institute of Bankers) pp. 64–89.

Price Waterhouse (1991) *Bank Capital Adequacy and Capital Convergence* (London: Author).

"Proposals of Central Banks May Boost Market for Euro-Floating Rate Notes" (1987) *Wall Street Journal*, 14 Dec., p. 37.

"Proposal to Create International GAAP Must Overcome SEC Staff's Reservations" (1989) *Securities Regulation and Law Report*, vol. 21, pp. 860–2.

Reed, Deborah (1989) "Rush to Global Markets Slows", in special report on Stock Exchanges, *Financial Post*, 20 March.

Reed, Howard Curtis (1983) "Appraising Corporate Investment Policy: A Financial Center Theory of Foreign Direct Investment", in Charles P. Kindleberger and David B. Audretsch (eds) *The Multinational Corporation in the 1980s* (Cambridge and London: MIT Press) pp. 219–44.

"Regulators Agree to Move Cautiously on Enforcement, Information Exchanges" (1988) *Securities Regulation and Law Report*, vol. 20, p. 1861.

"Regulators Propose Minimum Capital Rules for Securities Industry" (1992) *International Banking Regulator*, 10 Feb., pp. 1–2

"Regulatory Strategies to Meet the Challenges of the Nineties" (1990), a panel including John D. Hawke, Jr (Moderator) and Thomas A. Brooks, Paul Nelson, Aulana L. Peters, Richard F. Syron and William Taylor (panelists), *Annual Review of Banking Law*, pp. 399–408.

Reguly, Eric (1991) "Now ... Free Trade in Stock Markets", *Financial Post*, 31 May, p. 1.

Reich, Robert B. (1991) *The Work of Nations* (New York: Knopf).

Resnick, Bruce G. (1989) "The Globalization of World Financial Markets", *Business Horizons* (Nov.–Dec.) pp. 34–41.

Reuter (1988a) "Global Securities Regulators Talking Tough", *Financial Post*, 21 Nov., p. 36.

Reuter (1988b) "Regulators Join Forces to Halt Market Abuses", *Globe and Mail*, 19 Nov., B6.

Reuter (1989) "New World Securities Rules Worked Out", *Globe and Mail*, 16 Aug., p. B7.

Rhoades, Stephen A. (1977) "Structure–Performance Studies in Banking: A Summary and Evaluation", Federal Reserve research paper.

Rich, Frederic C. (1980) "Eurobond Practice: Sources of Law and the Threat of Unilateral National Regulation", *Virginia Journal of International Law*, vol. 20(2), pp. 505–45.

Rider, Barry A.K. (1990) "Policing the International Financial Markets: An English Perspective", *Brooklyn Journal of International Law*, vol. XVI, pp. 179–221.

"Risk-based Capital Picks Up Steam" (1988) *ABA Banking Journal* (May) pp. 8–13.

Rohlwink, Anthony (1987) "Is this the Age of the Universal Bank?", *The Banker* (Jan.) pp. 23–9.

Rosenau, James N. (ed.) (1976) *In Search of Global Patterns* (New York: Free Press).

Rosenau, James N. and Ernst-Otto Czempiel (eds) (1992) *Governance without Government: Order and Change in World Politics* (Cambridge University Press).

Rostow, W. W. (1960) *The Stages of Economic Growth: A Non-Communist Manifesto* (Cambridge University Press).

Rubin, Edward L. (1988) "Deregulation, Reregulation and the Myth of the Market", *Washington and Lee Law Review*, vol. 45(4) (Fall) pp. 1249–74.

Ruder, David S. (1989) "Cooperative International Securities Regulation", in International Organization of Securities Commissions, *14th Annual Conference of IOSCO*, 18–21 Sept., Venice, documents tabled at the conference, document no. 5.

"Ruder Says Unreleased IOSCO Report could be Blueprint for Global Offerings" (1989) *Securities Regulation and Law Report*, vol. 21, p. 1438.

Ruggie, John Gerard (1972) "Collective Goods and Future International Collaboration", *American Political Science Review*, vol. 66, pp. 874–93.

Ruggie, John Gerard (1983) "International Regimes, Transactions, and Change: Embedded Liberalism in the Postwar Economic Order", in Stephen Krasner (ed) *International Regimes* (Ithaca and London: Cornell University Press) pp. 195–232.

Rugman, Alan (1981) *Inside the Multinationals: The Economics of Internal Markets* (New York: Columbia University Press).

Rugman, Alan and S. J. Kamath, (1986) *International Diversification and Multinational Banking*, Dalhousie Discussion Papers in International Business (Dalhousie University).

Salomon Brothers International Limited (1990) *International Equity Flows: 1990 Edition, New Investors, New Risks, and New Products* (London: Salomon Brothers).

Salomon Brothers International Limited (1991) *International Equity Flows: 1991 Edition, Games without Frontiers* (London: Salomon Brothers).

Samuel, Margaret Maureen (1988–9) "International Financial Markets and Regulation of Trading of International Equities", *California Western International Law Journal*, vol. 19(2), pp. 327–82.

Sarver, Eugene (1988) *The Eurocurrency Market Handbook* (New York: New York Institute of Finance, Prentice Hall).

Saunders, Anthony (1987) "The Inter-Bank Market, Contagion Effects, and International Financial Crises", in Richard Portes and Alexander K. Swoboda (eds) *Threats to International Financial Stability* (New York: Cambridge University Press).

Saunders, Anthony (1988) "Bank Holding Companies: Structure, Performance and Reform", in William S. Haraf and Rose Marie Kushmeider (eds) *Restructuring Banking and Financial Services in America* (Washington: American Enterprise Institute), pp. 156–202.

Saunders, Anthony and Lawrence J. White (eds) (1986) *Technology and the Regulation of Financial Markets* (Lexington: Lexington Books).

Schwartz, Robert A. (1988) *Equity Markets: Structure, Trading and Performance* (New York: Harper & Row).

"SEC, French Agency Exchange Letters to Bring Assistance Accord into Force" (1991) *Securities Regulation and Law Report*, vol. 23, p. 172.

"SEC has Sought Enforcement Help under Swiss Treaty, Attorney Says" (1988) *Securities Regulation and Law Report*, vol. 20, pp. 1294–5.

Sesit, Michael (1988a) "Rules for New Bank Capital Standards Move into Spotlight as Conference Opens", *Wall Street Journal*, 6 June, p. 6.

Sesit, Michael B. (1988b) "Banks' New Minimum Capital Rules Add to International Bankers Worries", *Wall Street Journal*, 12 July, p. 17.

Shapiro, Alan C. (1988) *International Corporate Finance*, 2nd edn (Cambridge: Ballinger).

Shaw, Karen (1988) "Regulating the Regulators", *The Bankers Magazine* (July–Aug.) pp. 60–3.

Shearer, Ronald A., John F. Chant and David E. Bond (1984), *The Economics of the Canadian Financial System*, 2nd edn (Scarborough: Prentice-Hall).

Shome, Dikip K., Stephen D. Smith and Arnold A. Heggestad (1987) "Do Banks have Adequate Capital?", *The Bankers Magazine* (July–Aug.), pp. 21–3.

Skocpol, Theda (1976) "France, Russia, China: A Structural Analysis of Social Revolutions", *Comparative Studies in Society and History*, vol. 18(2), pp. 175–210.

Skocpol, Theda (1979) *States and Social Revolutions* (Cambridge University Press)

Skocpol, Theda (1980) "Political Response to Capitalist Crisis: Neo-Marxist Theories of the State and the Case of the New Deal", *Politics and Society*, vol. 10(2), pp. 155–201.

Smedresman, Peter S. and Andreas F. Lowenfeld (1989) "Eurodollars, Multinational Banks, and National Laws", *New York University Law Review*, vol. 64(4), (Oct.) pp. 733–804.

Smith, Roger K. (1989) "Institutionalisation as a Measure of Regime Stability: Insights for International Regime Analysis from the Study of Domestic Politics", *Millennium*, vol. 18(2) (Summer) pp. 227–244.

Smith, Roy C. and Ingo Walter (1990) *Global Financial Services* (New York: Harper Business).

Snidal, Duncan (1985) "The Limits of Hegemonic Stability Theory", *International Organization*, vol. 39(4) (Autumn) pp. 579–614.

Spero, Joan E. (1980) *The Failure of the Franklin National Bank* (New York, Columbia University Press).

Spero, Joan E. (1988/9) "Guiding Global Finance", *Foreign Policy*, vol. 73 (Winter) pp. 114–34.

Spindler, J. Andrew (1988) "Comments", in Brooklyn Law School, *Proceedings of the Symposium on Risk-Based Capital Adequacy Guidelines* (Brooklyn, New York).

Stigler, George (1975) *The Citizen and the State: Essays on Regulation* (Chicago and London: University of Chicago Press).

"Stock Trading Fix-it Plan gets International Backing" (1990) *Globe and Mail*, 16 April, p. B8.

Stokman, Frans N., Rolf Ziegler and John Scott (1985) *Networks of Corporate Power* (Cambridge: Polity).

Story, Christopher (1986) "The Globalization of Financial Markets: Central Banks Warn of Grave, Unnecessary Risks", *International Currency Review* (April–May) pp. 6–11.

Strange, Susan (1976) *International Monetary Relations*, vol. 2 of Andrew Shonfield (ed.) *International Economic Relations of the Western World 1959–71* (London: Oxford University Press).

Strange, Susan (1983) "*Cave! Hic Dragones:* A Critique of Regime Analysis", in Stephen D. Krasner (ed.) *International Regimes* (Ithaca and London: Cornell University Press) pp. 337–54.

Strange, Susan (1986) *Casino Capitalism* (Oxford: Basil Blackwell).

Strange, Susan (1990) "Finance, Information and Power", *Review of International Studies*, vol. 16, pp. 259–74.

Strange, Susan and Roger Tooze (1981) *The International Politics of Surplus Capacity* (London: George Allen and Unwin).

Streeck, Wolfgang and Philippe C. Schmitter (1985) "Community, Market, State – and Associations? The Prospective Contribution of Interest Governance to Social Order", in Wolfgang Streeck and Philippe C. Schmitter (eds) *Private Interest Government: Beyond Market and State* (London: Sage) pp. 1–29.

Streeck, Wolfgang and Philippe C. Schmitter (eds) (1985) *Private Interest Government: Beyond Market and State* (London: Sage).

Streeck, Wolfgang and Philippe C. Schmitter (1991) "From National Corporatism to Transnational Pluralism: Organized Interests in the Single European Market", in *Politics and Society*, vol. 19(2), pp. 133–64.

Sudweeks, Bryan Lorin (1989) *Equity Market Development in Developing Countries* (New York, Praegar).

Taylor, William (Federal Reserve) (1987) "Comments", in "A Panel of Federal Regulators on the Challenges of Increased Regulatory Supervision", *Annual Review of Banking Law 1987*, pp. 257–69.

Taylor, William (Federal Reserve) (1990) "Comments", in *Annual Review of Banking Law* (1990) "Regulatory Strategies to Meet the Challenges of the Nineties".

Teece, David J. (ed.) (1987) *The Competitive Challenge* (Cambridge: Ballinger).

Thomas, George M., John W. Meyer, Francisco O. Ramirez and John Boli (eds.) (1987) *Institutional Structure: Constituting State, Society, and the Individual* (Newbury Park: Sage).

"Thoroughly Modern Safety Net" (1991) ("Banks in the 1990s are doing less lending and more trading. International regulators are just starting to catch up"), *Economist*, 26 Oct., pp. 95–6.

Tobin, Glenn Patrick (1991) *Global Money Rules: The Political Economy of International Regulatory Cooperation* (Harvard University: unpublished PhD dissertation).

Underhill, Geoffrey R. D. (1991) "The Politics of Expanding Global Markets: The Uruguay Round and Trade in Financial Services", paper presented to the International Studies Association Annual Conference, Vancouver, 19–23 March.

"U.S., French to Sign Accord Aimed at Reducing Secrecy Obstacles" (1988) *Securities Regulation and Law Report*, vol. 20, pp. 1552–3.

Vernon, Raymond (1971) *Sovereignty at Bay* (New York: Basic Books).

Wall, John T. (1989) "Formal Links among Exchanges", in Henry C. Lucas and Robert A. Scwartz (eds) *The Challenge of Information Technology for the Securities Market: Liquidity, Volatility and Global Trading* (Homewood: Dow Jones-Irwin) pp. 253–62.

Waltz, Kenneth (1979) *Theory of International Politics* (Reading: Addison-Wesley).

Warren, Manning Gilbert III (1990) "Global Harmonization of Securities Laws: The Achievements of the European Communities", 31(1) (Winter) pp. 185–232.

Waters, Richard (1991) "IOSCO Gives Glimpse of Standard", *Financial Times* (London), 27 Sept., p. 24.

Waters, Richard (1992a) "An Emotive Topic for International Regulators", *Financial Times* (London), 31 Jan., p. 24.

Waters, Richard (1992b) "Search for Security", *Financial Times* (London), 23 Oct., p. 20.

Weiner, Myron and Samuel P. Huntington (eds) (1987) *Understanding Political Development* (Boston and Toronto: Little, Brown and Co.).

Wendt, Alexander (1987) "The Agent Structure Problem in International Relations Theory", *International Organization*, vol. 41(3) (Summer) pp. 335–70.

Wendt, Alexander (1990) "Sovereignty and the Social Construction of Power Politics", unpublished paper, May.

Wendt, Alexander (1991) "Bridging the Theory/Metatheory Gap in International Relations", *Review of International Studies*, vol. 17(4) (Oct.) pp. 383–91.

Wendt, Alexander (1992) "Levels of Analysis vs. Agents and Structures, Part III", *Review of International Studies*, vol. 18(2) (April) pp. 181–5.

Wendt A. and R. Duvall (1989) "Institutions and International Order," in E. O. Czempiel and J. Rosenau (eds) *Global Changes and Theoretical Challenges* (Lexington: Lexington Books), pp. 51–74.

Wessel, David and Michael R. Sesit (1988) "Leading Nations Set Capital Ratio of 8% for Big Global Banks", *Wall Street Journal*, 12 July, pp. 3, 17.

Willetts, Peter (ed.) (1982) *Pressure Groups in the Global System* (London: Frances Pinter).

Willetts, Peter (1990) "Transactions, Networks and Systems", in A. J. R. Groom and Paul Taylor (eds) *Frameworks for International Co-operation* (London: Pinter), pp. 255–84.

Williamson, Oliver E. (1975) *Markets and Hierarchies: Analysis and Antitrust Implications* (New York: The Free Press).

Williamson, Oliver E. (1985) *The Economic Institutions of Capitalism* (New York: Free Press).

Williamson, Oliver E. (1986) *Economic Organization* (New York University Press).

Williamson, Oliver E. (1988a) "Corporate Finance and Corporate Governance", *The Journal of Finance*, vol. XLIII(3) (July) pp. 567–91.

Williamson, Oliver E. (1988b) "The Economics and Sociology of Organization: Promoting a Dialogue", in George Farkas and Paula England (eds) *Industries, Firms and Jobs* (New York: Plenum), pp. 159–83.

Williamson, Oliver E. (1990) "The Firm as a Nexus of Treaties: An Introduction", in Aoki, Gustaffson and Williamson (1990), pp. 1–25.

Williamson, Peter J. (1989) *Corporatism in Perspective* (Sage: London).

Williamson, Stephen (1986) "Costly Monitoring, Financial Intermediation, and Equilibrium Credit Rationing", *Journal of Monetary Economics*, vol. 18, pp. 159–79.

Winters, Robert (1989) "New Havens of Secrecy Popping Up: British regulator," *Montreal Gazette*, 14 Sept., p. E1.

Young, Harrison (1986) "Bank Capital Adequacy in the United States", *Issues in Bank Regulation* (Spring) pp. 3–10.

Young, Oran R. (1986) "International Regimes: Toward a New Theory of Institutions", in *World Politics*, vol. 39(1), pp. 104–22.

Young, Oran R. (1989) *International Cooperation* (Ithaca and London: Cornell University Press).

Zeitlin, Maurice (1989) *The Large Corporation and Contemporary Classes* (Cambridge: Polity).

Ziegler, Dominic (1990) "Stormy Past, Stormy Future: Capital Markets Survey", *Economist*, 21 July.

Zysman, John (1983) *Governments, Markets and Growth: Financial Systems and the Politics of Industrial Change* (Ithaca and London: Cornell University Press).

Documents

Note: All documents issued by the Basle Committee on Banking Supervision, even under its previous name (Committee on Banking Regulations and Supervisory Practices), have been listed under "Basle Supervisors' Committee."

Bank for International Settlements (BIS), *International Banking and Financial Market Developments* (various issues) (Basle: Author).

Bank for International Settlements, *International Banking Developments* (various issues) (Basle: BIS).

Bank for International Settlements, *Annual Report*, (various years) (Basle: Author).

Bank for International Settlements (1984) *The BIS and the Basle Meetings* (Basle: Author).

Bank for International Settlements (1985) *The Nationality Structure of the International Banking Market and the Role of Interbank Operations* (Basle: Author).

Bank for International Settlements (1989) *Report on Netting Schemes* (Basle: BIS, Feb.).

Bank for International Settlements (1990) *Report on the Committee on Interbank Nettings Schemes of the Central Banks of the Group of Ten Countries* (Basle: BIS, Nov.).

Bank for International Settlements (1991) "The International and Domestic Bond Markets", *International Banking and Financial Market Developments* (Basle: Author, June).

Bank of England (1987) "Convergence of capital adequacy in the UK and US: Notice Issued by the Bank's Banking Supervision Division 9 January 1987", *Bank of England Quarterly Bulletin*, (Feb.) pp. 85–223.

Bank of England (1991) "Is There a 'Credit Crunch'?", *Bank of England Quarterly Bulletin* (May) pp. 256–9.

Basle Supervisors' Committee (BSC) (1982) *Report on International Developments in Banking Supervision 1981* (Basle: Author, July).

Basle Supervisors' Committee (1983a) "Principles for the Supervision of Banks' Foreign Establishments", typed manuscript, 9 pages (Basle: Author).

Basle Supervisors' Committee (1983b) *Report on International Developments in Banking Supervision 1982* (Basle: Author, March).

Basle Supervisors' Committee (1985) *Report on International Developments in Banking Supervision, 1984* (Basle: Author, April).

Basle Supervisors' Committee (1986) *Report on International Developments in Banking Supervision* (Basle, Author, Sept.).

Basle Supervisors' Committee (1988a) "International Convergence of Capital Measurements and Capital Standards", typed manuscript, 32 pages including 4 annexes.

Basle Supervisors' Committee (1988b) *Report on International Developments in Banking Supervision*, no. 6 (Basle: Author, Sept.).

Basle Supervisors' Committee (1990) *Report on International Developments in Banking Supervision*, no. 7 (Basle: Author, Sept.).

Basle Supervisors' Committee (1991) "Measuring and Controlling Large Credit Exposures", *World of Banking* (March/April) pp. 9–12, 29.

Basle Supervisors' Committee (1992) *Report on International Developments in Banking Supervision* (Basle: Author, Sept.).

Federal Reserve Board (1987) "Capital Maintenance; Revision to Capital Adequacy Guidelines", *Federal Register*, vol. 52(33) 19 Feb. pp. 5119–39.

Fédération Internationale des Bourses de Valeurs (FIBV) (1990) *Rapport Annuel* (Paris, FIBV).

Group of Ten (1986) *Recent Innovations in International Banking* (Basle: BIS).

Group of Ten (1988) "Press Statement by the Chairman of the Governors of the Group of Ten", 11 July (on the capital accord).

Group of Thirty (1982) *Risks in International Bank Lending* (New York: Author).

Group of Thirty (1989) *Clearance and Settlement Systems in the World's Securities Markets* (New York and London: Author).

International Auditing Practices Committee of the International Federation of Accountants in association with the Committee on Banking Regulations and Supervisory Practices (1989) "The Relationship between Bank Supervisors and External Auditors", International Statement on Auditing, July.

International Auditing Practices Committee of the International Federation of Accountants (1990) *The Audit of International Commercial Banks*, International Statement on Auditing, issued after consultation with the Basle Committee on Banking Supervision.

International Bank for Reconstruction and Development (IBRD) (1989) *World Development Report 1989* (London: Oxford University Press).

International Conference of Banking Supervisors (1988) *5th International Conference of Banking Supervisors*, Tokyo, 12–13 Oct., report on conference.

International Conference of Banking Supervisors (1990) "Press Release: Sixth Annual Conference of Banking Supervisors", 11 Oct.

International Monetary Fund (IMF) (1981) *International Capital Markets: Developments and Prospects* (Washington: Author).

International Monetary Fund (1982) *International Capital Markets: Developments and Prospects* (Washington: Author).

International Monetary Fund (1983) *International Capital Markets: Developments and Prospects* (Washington: Author).

International Monetary Fund (1984a) *International Capital Markets: Developments and Prospects* (Washington: Author).

International Monetary Fund (1984b) *International Financial Statistics: Supplement on Output Statistics* (Washington: Author).

International Monetary Fund (1986) *International Capital Markets: Developments and Prospects* (Washington: Author).

International Monetary Fund (1988a) "Bank Capital Levels and Measurement", *IMF Survey*, 25 Jan., pp. 25–7.

International Monetary Fund (1988b) *International Capital Markets: Developments and Prospects* (Washington: Author).

International Monetary Fund (1988c) *International Financial Statistics: Supplement on Trade Statistics* (Washington: Author).

International Monetary Fund (1989) *International Capital Markets: Developments and Prospects* (Washington: Author).

International Monetary Fund (1990a) *International Capital Markets: Developments and Prospects* (Washington: Author).

International Monetary Fund (1990b) *International Financial Statistics* (Washington: Author).

International Monetary Fund (1991a) *Determinants and Systematic Consequences of International Capital Flows*, occasional paper no. 77 (Washington: Author).

International Monetary Fund (1991b) *International Capital Markets: Developments and Prospects* (Washington: Author).

International Organization of Securities Commissions (IOSCO) (1987) *12th Annual Conference of IOSCO*, 1–4 Sept., Rio de Janeiro, documents tabled at the conference.

International Organization of Securities Commissions (1988a) *Annual Report 1988* (Montreal: IOSCO).

International Organization of Securities Commissions (1988b) *13th Annual Conference of IOSCO*, 13–17 Nov., Melbourne, documents tabled at the conference.

International Organization of Securities Commissions (1989a) *Annual Report, 1989* (Montreal: IOSCO).

International Organization of Securities Commissions (1989b) *14th Annual Conference of IOSCO*, 18–21 Sept., Venice, Documents tabled at the conference.

International Organization of Securities Commissions (1990a) *Annual Report 1990* (Montreal: IOSCO).

International Organization of Securities Commissions (1990b) *15th Annual Conference of IOSCO*, 11–15 Nov., Santiago, Chile, documents tabled at the conference.

International Organization of Securities Commissions (1991a) *Annual Report* (Montreal, IOSCO).

International Organization of Securities Commissions (1991b) "Final Communique of the XVI Conference of the International Organization of Securities Commissions (IOSCO)", unpublished.

International Organization of Securities Commissions (1991c) "Index of Memoranda of Understanding and Similar Agreements", 20 Aug., unpublished list.

International Organization of Securities Commissions (1991d) *IOSCO News* (May).

International Organization of Securities Commissions (1991e) "Liste des organismes qui ont signe la resolution concernant l'assistance reciproque", unpublished list.

International Organization of Securities Commissions (1991f) "Resolution sur la cooperation: liste des signataires", unpublished list.

International Organization of Securities Commissions (1991g) *XVI Annual Conference Documents*, vols 1 and 2 (Washington DC, 23–26 Sept.).

Organization for Economic Cooperation and Development (OECD) *Financial Market Trends* (various issues) (Paris: Author).

Organization for Economic Cooperation and Development (1979) *Financial Statistics*, vol. 13(1), pp. 814–15.

Organization for Economic Cooperation and Development (1987) *Trade in Services: Securities* (Paris: Author)

Organization for Economic Cooperation and Development (1988) "Special Feature: Arrangements for the Regulation and Supervision of Securities Markets in OECD Countries", *Financial Market Trends*, vol. 41 (Nov.).

Organization for Economic Cooperation and Development (1989) *Competition in Banking*, by G. Bröker (Paris: OECD).

Organization for Economic Cooperation and Development (1990) "Special Feature: Recent Trends in the Organization and Regulation of Securities Markets", *Financial Market Trends*, vol. 46 (May).

Securities and Exchange Commission (SEC) *Annual Report* (various issues) (Washington, Author).

Securities and Exchange Commission (1984) "Request for Comments Concerning a Concept to Improve the Commission's Ability to Investigate and Prosecute Persons Who Purchase or Sell Securities in the U.S. Markets from Other Countries", Exchange Act Release no. 21186, 30 July 1984, in *Federal Securities Law Reports Transfer Binder*, pp. 86976–92.

Securities and Exchange Commission (1987) *Internationalization of the Securities Markets*, report of the staff of the US Securities and Exchange Commission to the Senate Committee on Banking, Housing and Urban Affairs and the House Committee on Energy and Commerce, 27 July (Washington: Author)

Securities and Exchange Commission (1988) *The October 1987 Market Break*, a report by the Division of Market Regulation, U.S. Securities and Exchange Commission, Feb. (Washington: Author).

United Nations (1990) *National Accounts Statistics: Analysis of Main Aggregates, 1987* (New York: United Nations).

United States Congress, Office of Technology Assessment (1990) *Trading Around the Clock: Global Securities Markets and Information Technology*, background paper, July (Washington: Author).

United States, General Accounting Office (1986) *International Banking: International Coordination of Bank Supervision: The Record to Date*, report to the Chairmen, House Committee on Banking, Finance, and Urban

Affairs, and Senate Committee on Banking, Housing, and Urban Affairs, Feb. (Washington: US Government Printing Office).

United States House of Representatives, Committee on Banking, Finance and Urban Affairs (1987) *Risk-Based Capital Requirements for Banks and Bank Holding Companies*, 30 April (Washington: US Government Printing Office).

United States House of Representatives, Committee on Energy and Commerce (1987) *Globalization of Securities Markets*, 5 Aug. (Washington, US Government Printing Office).

United States Senate Committee on Banking, Housing and Urban Affairs (1986) *The Internationalization of Capital Markets* Feb 26, 27 (Washington: US Government Printing Office).

United States Senate Committee on Banking, Housing and Urban Affairs (1988) *Financial Modernization Act of 1988*, report to accompany S. 1886 together with additional views, 22 March (Washington: US Government Printing Office).

United States Senate Committee on Banking, Housing and Urban Affairs (1990) *Banking Regulators' Report on Capital Standards*, 10 Sept. (Washington: US Government Printing Office).

Index